RALPH McGILL

Ralph McGill:
A Biography

Barbara Barksdale Clowse

Mercer University Press
Macon, Georgia

ISBN 0-86554-612-6   MUP/H461

The paper used in this publication meets the minimum requirements
of American National Standard for Information Sciences—Permanence
of Paper for Printed Library Materials, ANSI Z39.48-1984.

Library of Congress Cataloging-in-Publication Data

Clowse, Barbara Barksdale,
    Ralph McGill: A Biography /Barbara Barksdale Clowse
        ix + 332 pp.   6" x 9" (15 x 22 cm.)
    Includes bibliographical references and index.
    ISBN 0-86554-612-6 (alk. paper)
1. Ralph McGill, 18981968. 2. Southern states—Race relations. 3. Afro-Americans—Civil rights—Southern States. 4. Journalists—United States—Biography. I. Title.
PN4874.M37C58 1998
070.92—dc21
[B]
                                                        98-41987
                                                        CIP

For

Steve and Martin

who made the difference

CONTENTS

LIST OF PHOTOGRAPHS

Photographs appear after page 165.

INTRODUCTION

RALPH EMERSON MCGILL (1898-1969) WAS IN NEWSPAPER WORK for half a century. He received every honor that could come to a journalist, from a Pulitzer Prize in 1959 to the Presidential Medal of Freedom in 1964. He counseled four presidents and touched millions of Americans through articles, books, syndicated columns and personal appearances. During the civil rights movement McGill was called "the conscience of the South." Some scholars group him with the modern South's liberal journalists and analyze closely his writings about race relations.

Preparing McGill's biography, I came to know a complex man often at odds with these cachets that only apply to his final dozen years. He never questioned the South's racial mores until the late 1940s. For the next few years he agonized in full view of a wide readership as he evolved from a patronizing segregationist to an advocate of racial justice. His job as editor and columnist at the *Atlanta Constitution* required making pressured daily commentary on events that were traumatic for white readers. Often he admitted being as confused as they about racial change.

However, as many in the southern press turned against the civil rights movement, McGill began to assume his role as conscience of the South. In 1954 he was one of the few to support editorially the *Brown* decision on school integration. He opposed the region's "massive resistance" to desegregation and defended President Eisenhower's use of federal coercion in the 1957 Little Rock school crisis.

That same year the *Constitution* replaced McGill's hostile segregationist boss with his best friend and protector. At the very time when "the entire South fell silent" he could speak out more freely.[1] Also his column was syndicated in newspapers everywhere. For the next dozen years he commanded a growing national audience. He urged southerners to accept desegregation and forsake violent resistance. He confronted all Americans with the realities of prejudice and intolerance.

What brings an individual to such a niche in history? One can become a human rights advocate in various ways. Abstract ideas or ideology persuade those of intellectual bent. Others are compelled by the law or religious dogma. For many, it turns on a simple but strong sense of human decency and justice. McGill was such a person. He had the temperament, background, and personal experiences that enabled him eventually to confront whites with what blacks as fellow human beings endured under segregation.

Like all southerners born at the turn of the century, McGill entered a segregated world of white supremacy but one far different from that of the Deep South. His East Tennessee kinfolks were staunch Republicans, proud of having fought for the Union and "old Abe." Abraham Lincoln became his lifelong idol. His birthday, February 5, was a week before the celebration of Lincoln's. The coincidence inspired him from childhood to discover all he could about the Civil War president and to pattern his work after Lincoln.

One of McGill's proudest moments came in February 1960 when he spoke at the Cooper Union on the centennial occasion of Lincoln's address there. Like Lincoln, McGill that day pleaded for moderation and a national dialogue on critical issues like race relations. Throughout his editorial career he saw himself as a mediator rather than a crusader. Asking readers to consider all sides of the race question exposed him to unending attacks. Blacks and liberal whites called him an apologist for the status quo and a "Jim Crow liberal." White supremacists persecuted him as a traitor to the South.

The strong Presbyterian faith of his parents, pastor, and schoolmasters also shaped McGill and imparted the Calvinist conviction that he had a calling to fulfill. This came in April 1938 on what he always said was "the most important day of my life." Hitler was in Vienna exulting over the addition of Austria to his Third Reich. McGill, sports editor of the *Atlanta Constitution*, was there as well. For several months he had been on sabbatical in Europe as the unlikely recipient of a Rosenwald Fellowship. He had already witnessed a Berlin rally and speech by the Nazi leader.

What he saw and heard in Vienna was, he told Bible belt readers, "a Damascus road experience." He vowed to fight hatred, intolerance, and especially racial prejudice for the rest of his days.

Across the ocean in Atlanta an opportunity opened for him to fulfill this vow. The executive editor of the *Constitution* died, and its owners chose McGill as successor. His long, riveting European dispatches about the coming war had gained a transfer from sports to the editorial desk. When word of his promotion reached Europe, McGill knew he might fulfill his calling. However, he was forty years old and unschooled in economics, political science, and history.

Sports defined his first four decades. He went from being a football star at the McCallie Preparatory School in Chattanooga to Vanderbilt University where the campus newspaper called him "one of the scrappiest linemen that ever wore the Gold and Black." Beginning in 1921, he covered sports for the *Nashville Banner*. Throughout a golden age of sports McGill fraternized with its heroes and regaled a growing regional audience with tales of their feats. All the while he burned with ambition to be a serious writer. In 1929 he transferred to the *Atlanta Constitution*, only to endure another long frustrating decade on the sports beat. Then came the Rosenwald and his Damascus road experience.

McGill regretted spending one-third of his career in sports and sometimes took pains to conceal it. Yet the experience served him well and made his work unique. His better editorials and columns had the same driving force that brought fame as a sportswriter. He had also learned to "mix his pitches," varying tone and content more than other columnists. Second, he bonded with fans who were his readers, and he delighted in responding to their reactions. This dialogue became a hallmark of McGill's career. It is not possible to prove a columnist's influence, but in reader polls McGill was always the best liked, least liked, and best read *Constitution* writer. National syndication in 1957 brought mail from across the US.

Third, an old-fashioned sports ethos shaped his early writing about race relations. Both as an athlete and sportswriter, McGill prized the ideals of fairness and decency. He hated cheating and poor sportsmanship. Initially he would attack segregation in the idiom of a sportsman: give all a fair chance, level the playing field, obey the rules—i.e., separate and equal must actually be equal. He was comfortable with this approach and hoped that readers and his bosses would find it less objectionable than didactics.

To say that the *Constitution*'s new editor in 1938 learned on the job would be an understatement. With his writing talent, capacity to absorb information, and compulsion about traveling to observe events firsthand, McGill gradually made a name for himself. Since adolescence, he had been an intense competitor who knew how to win. His personal ambition to be a national commentator fused with Atlanta's intention to become a national city. Yet for two more decades his efforts were hindered by management problems at the paper and his own personal troubles.

Meanwhile McGill traveled the globe, doing "foreign correspondence" that had an authority lacking in his columns about race relations. He cultivated news sources everywhere and sold his articles about World War II and the postwar world. If he had published nothing but these "traveler" pieces, he would have been a significant journalist. When the civil rights movement began, these trips gave him unique perspective on the South's problems. Nazism became his framework for interpreting the civil rights era whereas other southern leaders used the Reconstruction paradigm. Also he argued forcefully against segregation as a detriment in waging Cold War long before he decided how to resolve state-federal conflicts.

Gradually, however, McGill envisioned a new gestalt in American race relations: blacks must be protected from violence to pursue education, jobs, and decent housing; both races must enjoy the same economic opportunities as well as legal rights; public opinion leaders must stop lying to both races and confront their common humanity. McGill knew this vision would be harder to realize than dismantling the South's Jim Crow system, and he was right. Moreover, he insisted that in spite of segregation in the South, racism transcended his region. This assertion confused local readers and angered neoabolitionists in the North.Some scholars assert that moderates like McGill waged a futile effort, but his vision is the crux of racial dilemmas a generation after his death and must somehow be realized[2]

This book follows McGill's life story as it unfolded for him. To portray him as inevitably successful would, I believe, belittle his struggles. At several junctures he was almost undone by family tragedy, intransigent bosses, and disastrous behavior patterns. Somehow he chose not to give up or go under—efforts that are the very heart of biography.

PART I:

1898-1937

1

REPUBLICAN FROM EAST "TENN-O-SEE": 1898-1917

RALPH WALDO EMERSON MCGILL CAME INTO THE WORLD ON A farm but grew up in a city. He was a transitional southerner, feet planted in urban milieus but often facing back to country ways. Ben McGill and his wife, Mary Lou, were joyful that she had safely delivered a boy on February 5, 1898. Ben chose his new son's name, a decision that did not set well with family and neighbors who preferred a biblical namesake to that of a freethinking New Englander. As usual, however, Ben McGill stuck to his guns. They guarded their hopes for this child. The year before a baby boy had died within hours of his birth, grieving the young mother sorely. Mary Lou Skillern and Ben McGill grew up on adjoining East Tennessee farms.[1]

Ralph was a sickly baby with digestive problems. To be near a physician, his anxious parents moved ten miles from the farm into the town of Soddy. A third son lived just fifteen months despite good care. At three years of age, frail little Ralph was their only surviving child. Ben's father, David McGill, had also died, leaving the six hundred acre farm to his wife and their seven children. Dividing the land was out of the question. Ben sold his share to others who would try to make a living at the homeplace for their families. Ben well knew how hard that would be. Crop failures had already forced him to try working in nearby Soddy coal mines during winters. He tried again.[2]

Ralph remembered the brief period his father worked as a miner. Ben McGill came into the house every night, his hands and face blackened with coal dust. Ralph also sensed his mother's anxiety. The family needed money. Yet in Soddy, like countless other grimy little mining towns that dotted the Cumberland

Plateau of East Tennessee, the "pay was scant and the danger ever-present." When a miner was injured, he received no compensation. Survivors of those who died in the frequent accidents "had no recourse to law." Mary Lou McGill decided she could do without funds but not her strong husband. Ben soon quit the mines.[3]

He began looking for work in Chattanooga, only twenty miles away but far down the road to modern life. His education consisted of a few years at a one-room rural school. Yet a small heating and roofing company hired him to do clerical work and then sales. He commuted from Soddy to Chattanooga every day on the train. He thus joined thousands of southerners who found new opportunities in the cities. Chattanooga's population more than doubled between 1880 and 1900. With rich deposits of coal and some iron nearby plus water and rail transportation, boosters envisioned "the Pittsburgh of the South." Instead Birmingham dominated southern steel production. Chattanoogans developed a varied economic base. By the early 1900s new citizens poured in to work for small manufacturing concerns, railroad shops, textile mills, or iron and steel works. Ben McGill was luckier than most leaving farms for the New South of industry and commerce. He had a white collar job that led eventually to his becoming an officer of the firm.[4]

Mary Lou yearned for the time when the entire family could move to the city of thirty thousand. In 1904, when Ralph was six and a half, his mother's dream came true. He listened excitedly to the moving plans. Two farm wagons would bear their household goods. He would travel with his parents and baby sister by train. Exploring the little frame house to which they came from Soddy, the boy found a bathroom on the back porch rather than out in the yard. His father caught the electric trolley to work half a block from home. The McGills had indeed moved to town![5]

The McGills remained close to their kinfolk. Some now lived in Chattanooga. Others came and went between the city and the valley farm upriver. Rather than taking the train to Soddy then horse and buggy to the farm, they sometimes traveled by steamboat. Up from their landing stretched pasture and fields of the McGill farm. For three quarters of a century they had grown corn, some wheat but no cotton on the land. Ralph was six years old before he ever saw a black person and later felt this set him apart from Deep South people. Yet like most southerners of his generation, he was steeped in the lore of rural life. His feelings probably were so fond because he never depended on agriculture for livelihood. Also he never suffered from rural isolation but enjoyed contact with a broadening world.[6]

Ralph learned all he could about his ancestors, whose choice to settle in the east valley of the Tennessee River rather than to travel farther across the mountains, had shaped his existence. There was no end of kinfolk to answer his questions. His McGill forefather was born in 1753 during passage from Northern Ireland to Pennsylvania. After the Revolution the family moved with countless other settlers down the Appalachian valleys to the Tennessee frontier.

The fertile bottom lands that his family worked lay halfway between the towns of Soddy and Daisy. To the west of this valley rose the Cumberland Escarpment, known locally as Walden's Ridge. To the east were the Smoky Mountains. Ralph learned that his mother's people, the Clifts, came from Wales to extract great quantities of the bituminous coal found at the foot of Walden's Ridge. Besides opening the mine in Soddy, they developed large grants of land and built a mill in the 1820s. During the Civil War some fought for the Union like so many other East Tennessee families.[7]

What impressed Ralph about his father's family was their commitment to Presbyterianism and strong reliance on the Book. Along with the river, the Bible was a powerful determinant of the boy's imagination. He heard passages read aloud at home every evening before family prayers. Of the handful of books at the old McGill homestead, most either were Bibles or collections of sermons. The family was also scrupulous about keeping the Sabbath.[8]

In a tiny Presbyterian church Ralph listened to scriptures expounded upon in long and, he thought, unnecessarily stern fashion. "I must have been twelve years old before I had my first laugh about Presbyterians," he recalled. An older cousin had confided, "They sin, but they never enjoy it." It became easy to reject this part of his background that seemed to him so "grim and unrelenting."[9]

However, the seventeenth century idiom and cadences of King James' Bible bore into the deepest grooves of his mind. Its tracings appeared in the pace and tone of his writings as prominently as did images of river life. Once "an old fellow whose clothes smelled of wood smoke and mothballs" wandered into McGill's *Constitution* office and observed, "'You must read the Bible a right smart.'" McGill allowed that he did. Even when he disdained the church, he wrote and spoke in the lingua franca of the Bible Belt.[10]

Both his parents were devout. Ben McGill seemed to Ralph "pretty much the Calvinist Puritan" who never smoked, drank, or swore. Ben clearly communicated to his children his conviction that the way whites usually treated blacks was wrong. From the 1890s southerners relied on the laws and customs of segregation (Jim Crow) as well as violence to deny African Americans their civil rights, keep them in the worst jobs and out of most public facilities. Mary Lou McGill agreed with her husband, often reminding the four young McGills that "We are all God's children." She taught them "not to be afraid and not to hate or fear or dislike other persons," including blacks. From childhood they "regarded a Negro as a person," and Ralph remembered that even as a boy his "Calvinist conscience was stirred by some of the race prejudice I saw."[11]

His fondest remembrances focused on his mother. Mary Lou McGill favored her only surviving son, and Ralph delighted in all her ways. As he grew, he came to understand as well as to love this spirited woman. Her father, Anderson Skillern, took her mother, Nancy Clift, from Tennessee to Texas, where he expected to further his career as a journalist. The Clifts of Soddy were skeptical of Skillern's plans. Sure enough, Ralph's grandfather vanished. His wife, son, and daughter waited for word until eventually the Clifts reclaimed them. Back home in Soddy, her mother died young and

Mary Lou Skillern grew up sensitive about Clift charity. It meant everything having a place all her own.[12]

Life in the Chattanooga neighborhood of white clapboard houses was drastically different from grimy Soddy or the riverside farm. The struggle to make ends meet continued nonetheless. Eventually with three daughters besides Ralph to feed and clothe, Mary Lou McGill had to manage carefully. All the children remembered ways their mother stretched meager means. Her work load was heavy, but she was buoyed by her faith. Through the years she and Ralph had a favorite exchange when he came into the house. "Mam," he would ask, "are we still poor?" Mary Lou laughed and answered, "Yes, we are. And we always will be."[13]

The girls—Sarah, Lucille, and Bessie—often teased their mother about ways she favored their brother. He was surprised at how well his sisters tolerated the favoritism of "Mama's-son-Ralph." Continued fears for his health may have prompted Mary Lou to give him special attention. His sensitive nature and strong capacity for love was a big factor. Mary Lou often remarked, "I've never had to whip that boy. God made him good the day he was born." He never received a spanking from his father though, looking back, he thought such punishment was deserved.[14]

Hoping that country air would benefit Ralph, the doctor regularly sent him to the McGill farm, sometimes for entire summers. The boy found everything about the McGill farm to be meaningful and carried a strong attachment to the place through-out life. His grandmother, whom he called "Mammy," gave Ralph the run of the place. Often he stayed close to her, especially when she sat at her loom weaving.[15]

Mammy and Ralph took the buggy into Soddy at least once a week. As the horse stepped along, she recalled her own childhood. Ralph learned about early days in Hamilton County and especially about Mammy's mother who "had the Gaelic." In Soddy they shopped and collected whatever family mail had arrived by train from Chattanooga. The railroad station was a focal point of the town. They shipped out large quantities of the coal mined nearby. Some they converted into coke for use in metallurgy manufacturing shops that dotted the area. Ovens for coking Soddy coal were just by the tracks. Ralph linked their "gassy smell" and "red flare" with images of hell he learned in church. Seeing the flaming coke ovens against darkening mountains of Walden's Ridge, he thought, "How awful it would be to be thrust into flame much hotter than that which burned with such a red-and-white heat." He decided that he would be very good.[16]

In his case the damnation motif was played against a cycle of serious illnesses that seemed unending. He overheard family remarks about his bad health. Twin fears of dying and damnation became particularly acute when an attack of fever came on at night. In a recurring nightmare he saw a whirling whiteness that might sweep him away from loved ones. He was terrified, unable to feel his limbs. He wondered if this harbinger of death would dump him in hell. Fire and brimstone preaching frightened many a youngster and helped drive this one away from the church. When he reclaimed Christianity's ancient truths in 1953, the South was beginning its racial revolution, and he sometimes scourged readers like an Old Testament prophet.[17]

As Ralph grew stronger, he did farm chores with the men. He learned to pitch hay and bundle wheat. He took hold of a double-shovel plow and went into large corn fields. Valley farmers grew the same variety cultivated by local Indians whose prehistoric mounds he explored. To the end of his days he loved thinking about "the mystery of being lost in the long rows of corn, the stalks taller than I." Tennessee farmers had always prided themselves on the strain of mules developed in the area. "Plowing around the corn," behind his uncles' mules, McGill also developed a lifelong admiration for the sturdy animals. Later he often said that unlike horses, mules practiced the art of the possible.[18]

After a long summer on his grandmother's farm, eight year old Ralph went to the Fourth District School. The city's public schools, begun in 1873, were a point of pride with Chattanoogans. In fact most white students got only a fair dose of the three Rs; many blacks far less. Young McGill never took to "rithmetic," but his enthusiasm for the other two Rs was boundless. Besides school books, he found a treasure trove of reading material at a substantial Carnegie Library. Nothing like the Carnegie existed in towns such as Soddy. It became Ralph's favorite haunt. Neighbors who lived along the two mile route between his house and the library grew accustomed to seeing the boy almost daily bicycling along with some borrowed books.

Like the biblical tracings in his prose style, the Victorian values of his early reading shaped the future editor's interpretation of the day's events. He struck many colleagues as "being from an earlier time" perhaps because this boyhood reading opened vistas onto a world already lost in terms of values—if indeed it ever existed in industrializing America. The novels of Robert Louis Stevenson, the poetry of Rudyard Kipling, the stories of George Henty and H. Rider Haggard stirred the child to think in terms of bravery. Their heroes were willing to fight for "the right" and for those they loved. The adventures of the hero usually climaxed in a triumph of good over evil.[19]

Certain realities about the work of these nineteenth century writers were lost on the impressionable boy. The struggles were romanticized. The adventures were exotic. The denouement was far fetched. In a few years Ralph devoured an entire body of literature that conditioned him to prize loyalty, to personalize forces of good and evil, and to respond emotionally rather than intellectually to movements and ideas. By his own admission and according to the testimony of all who knew him, his was a very sentimental nature. Decades later, grappling with social realities instead of literary fantasies, feelings still outweighed analysis.

He learned America's two favorite sports, baseball and football, launching four decades of identity with athletics. Football games became popular in Chattanooga before the turn of the century. College teams and players from the athletic associations of neighboring towns drew big crowds at the University of Chattanooga's Chamberlain Field. The city also had a professional baseball club that played in the South Atlantic League. The entire McGill family regularly rode the trolley downtown to watch the Lookouts play at Chamberlain Field.[20]

When Ralph was eleven, the Lookouts won the league championship and went on to beat Atlanta, the Southern Association champions. His hero that summer was the Lookout's catcher, Buttermilk Meek. He was fat and "slow as a movieless Sunday" but regularly whacked home runs over the short right field fence at Chamberlain Field. The aging slugger gave the boy a pair of socks, making him the envy of his friends. Mary Lou McGill, always fostering her son's health, set large quantities of buttermilk before him, emphasizing what it had done for Meek. Decades later Ralph found Meek running a billiard hall in Los Angeles and learned that his hero's favored beverage was beer not buttermilk.[21]

Despite their relative isolation, in the early 1900s white Chattanoogans enjoyed cultural attractions as well as sporting events. The city boasted an opera house and theater. A variety of performers stopped there during road tours to give concerts and plays. Ralph became stagestruck and kept a huge scrapbook about faraway Broadway. He served as an usher whenever the Welsh Choir sang. The boy also watched with fascination when evangelists on "the sawdust trail" came to town. These revivals sometimes climaxed with mass baptisms in the river near the Market Street landing. The whole McGill family turned out when Buffalo Bill's Wild West Show or traveling circuses came to town.[22]

Ralph's neighborhood gang began to explore a unique aspect of his hometown—its Civil War past. The majority of East Tennesseans had opposed secession, and his loyalty went to the Union. So unlike most regional leaders of his day, he never suffered from the "Lost Cause" syndrome. During the civil rights movement he infuriated readers by playing the role of contrarian and declaring that the South was on the wrong side of history just as it had been during the Civil War.

The boy learned that President Lincoln and his generals focused on East Tennessee in their strategy to divide western resources of the Confederacy from the east. All troops could approach Chattanooga both from the Tennessee River and several railroad lines. In September 1863 a fierce battle was joined in a tangled, wooded area near Chickamauga Creek. For two days its waters ran red with blood. Total casualties mounted to almost 34,000. Federal reinforcements, headed by General U. S. Grant, fought the Confederates several more times before forcing their retreat into Georgia and occupying Chattanooga.[23]

Eyewitnesses to the battles, the occupation, and especially to the guerilla warfare that raged thereabouts made a deep impression on Ralph. His pastor at Central Presbyterian Church, the Reverend Dr. Thomas H. McCallie, was the only clergyman to remain in Chattanooga during the summer and fall of 1863. He and his wife held prayer services in their home and helped care for the wounded who poured into town. McGill's family told vivid stories about their support of the United States government. The most active Unionist in Hamilton County was a relative, William Clift. He was sixty-seven when war broke out, but his efforts were worthy of someone thirty years younger. He trained a militia to resist the secessionists. For over two years he fought skirmishes and sabotaged the Confederate cause. After the battle of Chickamauga Clift carried messages back and forth between Union generals in East Tennessee. During one mission the old courier was captured by a Confederate officer who happened to be one of his sons.[24]

The most frightful stories Ralph heard centered on the guerillas or "bushwhackers." Acting on their own, they perpetrated acts of cruel vengeance for both sides. Homesteaders in Hamilton County and other parts of East Tennessee suffered mightily from such marauders. As long as Confederate military authorities controlled the area, Unionist families like the McGills whose loyalty stretched back to Revolutionary battles stood at risk. Victims of these roving bands suffered theft, arson, or worse. Once Chattanooga fell to Federal troops, guerillas wreaked a terrible revenge on supporters of secession, confident that East Tennessee was unlikely ever to fall under the protection of the Confederacy again.

As a boy Ralph also heard relatives give high praise to Abraham Lincoln whom they always called "Old Abe." President Lincoln had, after all, saved the cause for which McGills had fought since the battle of King's Mountain in 1780. Ralph soon realized that his birthday was only a week earlier than that of the sixteenth president. He studied about all the famous Americans born during February. In his mind, Lincoln stood above the rest. The Civil War leader became a lifelong idol. Coupled with admiration for "Old Abe" was scorn for slaveowners and the antebellum institution they had defended with rhetoric and then with arms. Where he grew up, McGill said, slaveowners were blamed for much suffering. In East Tennessee even Confederate veterans stopped short of a defense of slavery.[25]

His own father, like so many in East Tennessee, was a staunch supporter of the party of Lincoln, and the boy adopted his loyalty. He did not formally change until he was thirty-five and working for Clark Howell's *Atlanta Constitution*. Ralph described Ben McGill as being "dogmatic in his views." Along with Calvinism, Republicanism formed the elder McGill's world view. A quiet hardworking man, he prized the values upon which the Grand Old Party was founded. This included fair-mindedness about blacks who now made up forty percent of Chattanooga's population and should, he insisted, have every chance to vote and work.

About the time the McGill family moved to Chattanooga, Republican candidates for mayor, governor, and president lost favor with local voters. Both the city and county went for Teddy Roosevelt in 1904 but did not support another Republican presidential candidate until Coolidge ran in 1924. When native Virginian Woodrow Wilson won the presidency in 1912, many southerners joined the massive swing to the Democrats, but Ben McGill remained a strong partisan of the GOP along with his son.

Ralph always accompanied his father when he voted after work at the old No. 5 firehouse. One morning Ralph went to the polling place on his own. Republicans had hired a surrey to transport elderly and crippled voters in the ward, but the black driver became lost. Poll workers drafted Ralph to be his navigator. All day he "labored lovingly for the GOP, going to the doors, ringing the bells, and then assisting the elderly or infirm residents out to the surrey and into a seat." He also made sure that some school friends saw him riding high.[26]

As he roamed the area with friends, Ralph came to love Chattanooga's setting and terrain dominated by sharp curves in the river and three surrounding mountains. He learned the river first because of trips to the McGill farm. Then one by one he explored the three mountains. Lookout Mountain, rising southwest of the city, was first. Visits to Lookout Mountain gave Ralph and his friends a spectacular view of their world. At an elevation of 2,225 feet, they could see for miles and miles. Below spread a panorama of fields, factories, houses, railroads, and river tracing the shape of a giant Indian moccasin. It was, as he said, "a good place for a boy to grow up in." He appreciated the advantages open to white southerners in urban environs. The potential of a diversified economic base with ample transportation was obvious to him from childhood. He never had to be converted to the New South ethos.[27]

Yet, from the farm upriver Ralph retained a conviction that self-sufficient agriculture was a viable way of life for people who preferred rural folkways and chose nature as the determinant of their destiny. Within a generation, the Great Valley he viewed from Lookout Mountain was altered forever. The McGill home-place along with countless other farms, churches, schoolhouses, stores disappeared under a system of TVA dams and lakes. He grieved for this lost world. His parents had made the break, however, and their son never allowed his nostalgia to blind him to the progress they sought.

Thanks to his parents' efforts, he had opportunities beyond what they could reasonably afford in Chattanooga, especially for education. Long before bringing his family to Chattanooga, Ben McGill taught his son to read. Each evening after the return commute he took the child onto his lap to look at books. Gradually Ralph learned to make out words for himself and put together sentences from the mostly religious volumes. Eventually he realized that his quiet, persevering parent was making sure that books were important to him. Although the elder McGill only attended school five months a year through the elementary grades, he was an avid reader. Like countless other Americans at the turn of the century,

Ben's obsession was that his daughters and especially his only son attend good schools.[28]

Ben took a keen interest in a school for boys founded by his pastor, Thomas McCallie, shortly after the family moved to Chattanooga. Two of the minister's sons were headmasters at the McCallie School just outside town on Missionary Ridge. To McGill, whose forebears included Presbyterian preachers and elders, the school seemed ideal. Tuition and other costs were beyond the family's tight budget, but he had already proved he could find a way to do what he thought was important. Ralph must have greater opportunity than many children in the Highland Park neighborhood and most in the old farming community. Reverend McCallie confirmed that the boy would flourish in the program built around the ideal of "educated Christian manhood." So Ben borrowed the money for tuition and fees. Starting in 1913, Ralph went to McCallie for four years, never figuring out how his father managed to repay the debt.[29]

The McCallie experience set the course of McGill's life—at least for the succeeding sixteen years. His studies and the extracurricular activities prepared him for the ambience of a good college and would propel him into the top three percent of the American population with exposure to higher education. McCallie graduates frequently chose Vanderbilt. The school's ties to the Nashville university were many and strong. It was natural for Ralph to continue his education there.

Ralph walked the two miles each way to McCallie during the school year. Since he played all sports, it was often dark when he made his way home. He was sometimes later because he stopped to visit with people he knew along the way. Ben McGill never owned an automobile. He used Chattanooga's streetcars for transportation. A neighbor who owned a two cylinder Bush treated the McGill children to an occasional joy ride. However, the family usually took the trolley when they went somewhere beyond walking distance. As an adult, Ralph maintained the pattern of walking and using public transportation begun in Chattanooga.[30]

Young McGill was already a writer when he entered McCallie. During elementary school he began to put together stories and poems. High school teachers recalled that, given the option of choosing the subject himself, Ralph always produced the most interesting writing in the class. Still, football claimed first place in his heart. The 1913 season was a losing one for McCallie School, but McGill's play at the tackle position was judged "phenomenal." His physical development still lagged. He was, he recalled, "much too light" for his assignment that fall. Nonetheless, at the December football banquet he proudly received his letter.[31]

Despite a growing circle of friends and activities, Ralph remained very shy, particularly with girls. The big exception was Rebecca Mathis. He met "Reb," as he called her, at an interschool debate with Girls Preparatory School. For the next half century one of the special places in his heart belonged to Reb. Her father was a Jewish immigrant from Germany. Her maternal grandfather first come to Chattanooga with Grant's conquering army, returning in peacetime to start a business. The entire Mathis family charmed Ralph. They introduced him to the culture of the Old World. While visiting Reb, he also learned about the imbroglio of European politics.

From this household he discovered "something I would not have found anywhere else in Chattanooga." Ralph's bond with the Mathis family further sensitized him to prejudice. He reacted with horror at witnessing Hitler's anti-Semitism and extermination policy before ever challenging his homeland's repression of blacks.[32]

The summer of 1914 closed with the shocking reality of a general European war. To most Chattanoogans these were remote developments. Then wartime demand ballooned U. S. trade. The factories of East Tennessee, particularly those manufacturing iron, went into full production. Ralph took more notice of President Woodrow Wilson, although he still identified with the party of his father and other kinfolks. He began to hate German militarism. Yet as the youth anticipated his sophomore year at McCallie, he did not suspect that World War I would undermine the outlook of his generation. Participating in school, church, and family activities, Ralph felt "good and sure about everything."[33]

He added oratory and acting to his accomplishments. His was the last student generation to receive wide training in public speaking. His voice, once described as resembling "an asthmatic bullfrog," ruled out the glee club, but the content of his orations won the day. Chattanoogan Robert Strauss had gone to New York to try to break into show business but came home periodically to coach McCallie's drama club. Strauss cast Ralph in leading roles. Their friendship continued through the Nashville years.[34]

For years a bookworm, Ralph's reading tastes now expanded rapidly. He liked both topical writers and literary lions. He grew fond of the novels of Sir Walter Scott. The pages of Scott's works filled the boy's head with images of his own Scottish forbears. The romance and heroism favored by Scott made highly satisfying reading for McGill. Rudyard Kipling was always another of Ralph's favorites. Ralph memorized the Anglo-Indian's poetry for recitations. Some of Kipling's quirky notions became mixed into McGill's developing mentality.

Later he regretted that his teachers never directed these reading binges, resulting in "large gaps" in his learning. The eclectic nature of his reading, the fact that he soon became mostly self-taught, and his Celtic preference for sentimental works probably outweighed any pedagogical influence. Nevertheless, he was sensitive about this deficiency from early adulthood. Despite his intellectual curiosity, habitual library visits, and superior schooling, his scholarly potential aborted. During his twenties and thirties he felt frustrated and inadequate as well as guilty about his parents' sacrifice.[35]

When Ralph celebrated his eighteenth birthday, he was still "young" for his age but now developing fast. His physique in snapshots showed the results of athletic training and farm work. He was muscular and strong but very gangly. For formal portraits he smoothed back his hair and adopted a self-conscious scowl. In candid shots his black hair was tousled and curly.

The dark eyes were full of merriment but with a hint of shadow. The camera gave evidence already of the sad moods that dogged him throughout life. Whenever he asked his mother about these feelings, she put them down to his Welsh ancestry. He soon began calling them his "Welsh black dog," warning any and all when the black dog was upon him.[36]

Today his mother might have sought medical advice about her emotional son. His behavior patterns do meet some but not all current diagnostic criteria for a "mood disorder"—dysthymia, once known as depressive neurosis. Since a physician cannot give McGill the required "mental status exam," or test for an underlying medical condition, diagnosis is conjecture. Unlike most dysthymics, he generally functioned at a high level even though pessimism was often his psychological style of relating to the world. Also he enjoyed extraordinary support from family and friends.[37]

He faced his final season of prep school football with great anticipation. He was captain the 1916 McCallie squad. With luck he might make the All-City first team. Still a lightweight, he became obsessed with building up his legs. He and another player rode their bicycles over two hundred miles to Atlanta and back. The journey gave him a glimpse of the bustling city that would eventually become his home. As Ralph came of age, Atlanta grew enormously. From 90,000 residents in 1900, the population swelled to more than 200,000 in the census of 1920. Even Tennessee's capital, Nashville, magnet to a vast hinterland, inevitably judged its development against that of Atlanta.

Commending McGill as an All-City player, a newspaper story called him "one of the most aggressive linemen in the city." It noted one aspect of his complex personality. Despite the boy's "lack of weight," he outplayed heavier opponents in every game. He was "a loyal sort of player, always in the game, never hurt and quick-thinking—the kind of athlete in whom a coach can place full trust." The boy was elated. He might have been an invalid. Instead, he had become a jock. His mother was proud but could never once watch him play in a game.[38]

His senior year flew by. He wrote stories and poems for the literary magazine and edited the school newspaper. His oratory won the city declamation medal. Despite such success at oral and written expression he was a restless and inconsistent student. He began to question Reverend McCallie's sermons as his devotion to the McCallie sons' teaching slackened. The prep school's ethos consisted of the same bracing virtues that Ralph encountered at Central Presbyterian Church. Like other white Protestants of the prewar era, Ralph's body of received truth was homogeneous and uplifting. As a church member in good standing and sometime Sunday School teacher, the teenager seemed to be internalizing these beliefs. Beneath the surface he had problems with this disciplined, devout Calvinism. For the next thirty-five years he struggled with disbelief and dissolution until he could reintegrate some of the old virtues.[39]

He took a deepening interest in world affairs. An avid newspaper reader, he kept up with the course of the war and President Wilson's efforts as peacemaker throughout that election year. Ralph's interest in Wilson was partly due to the McCallie brothers' admiration for him. Ben McGill was chagrined over his son's fascination with a Democrat. Nevertheless, Ralph's political loyalties were in transition. His mother had always insisted that she would be a Democrat when women gained the right to vote.[40]

As Ralph's senior year climaxed, the United States entered the Great War that had engulfed the world throughout his idyll at McCallie. A wave of patriotic spirit swept Chattanooga. The city prepared for an influx of troops since it would serve as a principal Army training center just as in 1898. Some of Ralph's friends enlisted. The McGills talked with their son about his options. His parents wanted college for Ralph as much as he anticipated the experience "with a deep indescribable yearning." His football coach, Lewie Hardage, was most enthusiastic about Vanderbilt. So he decided to follow President Wilson's urging that young men continue schooling until their draft boards called them.[41]

In June he said a fond farewell to the preparatory school on Missionary Ridge. The honors he took home from graduation ceremonies with his diploma bespoke fulfillment and also promise. The progress he had made since ninth grade more than justified his parents' hopes and sacrifice. He seemed to exemplify what the McCallie family had in mind when they founded the school—to produce regional leaders with noblesse oblige. Social prominence was not in his background, but he came from solid stock. His people knew who they were. His father, now an officer of Snow Heating and Roofing, was apt to take advantage of opportunities, open to change, and determined to better his family. If as the faculty assumed, Ralph continued on his present trajectory he could become one of their real success stories and join the elite of his generation of southerners.

2

VANDERBILT LINEMAN AND LEATHERNECK: 1917-1921

THE RAILROAD TRIP FROM CHATTANOOGA TO NASHVILLE WAS barely a hundred and forty miles. To that physical journey one must add an immeasurable psychological distance when in September 1917 Ralph McGill rode the night train to begin a new life at Vanderbilt University. The train rocked along through the dark, heading northwest towards the center of Tennessee, but Ralph was too excited for sleep. Arriving in Union Station at daybreak, he traveled out West End Avenue by wagon. He expected to study medicine. Four years later he and his proud family could hardly bear the bitter loss of this hope.[1]

Later that first day Ralph with the rest of his classmates heard the welcoming remarks of Chancellor James H. Kirkland. Leading Vanderbilt from 1893 to 1937, Kirkland was approaching the crest of a remarkable career when Ralph arrived. During his dozen years in Nashville, he watched Vanderbilt grow into a top southern university. Kirkland used his influence to promote regional progress through education and social uplift. The chancellor's efforts included no challenge of "southern racial norms" except a "campaign against lynching."

Welcoming the freshmen of 1917, Kirkland took pride in the fact that America's recent entry into World War I had not interrupted the trend of increased enrollments. McGill's class was no smaller than the last previous ones had been. The war was a dominating factor on campus nonetheless. Vanderbilt sponsored and trained an infantry unit made up of undergraduate men. Many of the first year students who listened to Kirkland's speech would become fulltime soldiers within the year. McGill was one. The stirring patriotism and support for President Wilson he had encountered at McCallie School was vastly intensified on the Nashville campus.[2]

Success that fall came first on the gridiron. Coach Dan McGugin—a living legend in sports parlance—took to Ralph when he appeared on Curry Field for his first football practice. McCallie coach, Lewie Hardage, had played for Vanderbilt and told McGugin of McGill's desire to be part of "the powerhouse of southern football." McGugin saw that Ralph was "not very large but he was intensely in earnest and he never failed to exert himself to the utmost." The 1917 team was shorthanded since some upperclassmen had opted for military service. McGill became a varsity guard though he only weighed one hundred fifty-two pounds. The campus newspaper once noted that he was knocked cold in the second quarter but "proved that he was game to the core and reentered the fray, putting up a good brand of ball for the remaining periods."[3]

By the time McGill met McGugin, the coach was second only to Kirkland in popularity. McGugin was not just Ralph's coach. For several years he parented the young man. Then their relationship evolved into a bond of old fashioned friendship. The mutual affection was deep and lasted until the coach died in 1936. Initially McGugin played a role similar to the McCallie brothers and Ben McGill combined. The coach was an authority figure who helped him maintain self-discipline, keep financially solvent, and find his way in Nashville society. In later life McGill reminisced about McGugin's scholarly traits and his learning. However, the coach's style of inspiring men affected him most as a player.[4]

Lettering in football at Vanderbilt three times became one of the primary identifications of McGill's life. He was living out the chronicles of his favorite boyhood fiction heroes: Dick and Frank Merriwell. Their creator, Gilbert Patten (writing as Burt L. Standish), wanted to guide young male readers into worthy adulthood by means of sports. He shaped plots in which life mirrored the game and successful athletes grew into strong, virtuous citizens. The Merriwells' adventures at prep school and at Yale challenged readers to adopt their code of loyalty, fair play, and perseverance. On occasion the Merriwells (and Patten himself) went out of their way to support Jews and Negroes. Like Patten, McGill developed into a public enemy of the Ku Klux Klan.[5]

McGugin always saw to it that any football player needing financial help found jobs. Ralph had a hometown benefactor who advanced part of the cost but needed to finance the balance of his freshmen year himself. He became a waiter in the dining hall, took a laundry route, and held down other occasional jobs. McGill later construed his college experience to have been that of a poor boy who was on the periphery. "I had almost no money," he wrote, "and my wardrobe was meager." He claimed to have been "a thin, shy, worried youngster" who suffered "terribly from self-consciousness." The claims had only a nub of truth since he readily gained respect and popularity among the genteel, able men and women of the Vanderbilt community.[6]

Yet they were part of a lifelong penchant for projecting in person and in print the image of Ralph McGill as a poor outsider. This struck friends as odd since he had advantages beyond the dreams of most white male contemporaries and virtually all African Americans, but eventually this tendency helped him relate to the truly disadvantaged. When the fraternities sized up the freshmen in McGill's class for possible membership—a process known as "spiking"—he became a Sigma Chi. Thereafter their house became his favorite haunt. Fraternity brothers—many of whom were fellow football players—were his closest friends. He filled pages of his scrapbook with momentos of Sigma Chi.

Also that fall the Class of 1921 elected McGill its president. Looking over clippings announcing this event, Ben and Mary Lou McGill felt enormous gratitude and pride. Their sacrifices had been worthwhile. Ralph's strong start gratified the McCallie family and school staff. During the weeks since he climbed off the train and hauled his belongings to campus, he had successfully established an identity among undergraduates that numbered well over 500. His shyness was real, but those meeting him that autumn saw other strong, very appealing traits.[7]

One was his eagerness. He was almost twenty years old when

he entered Vanderbilt and had substantial school and work experience. Yet his boyish excitement fooled people. In retrospect Coach McGugin thought, "He was very young as college men go." He remembered "just a slip of a boy eager to grow, eager to find out all that he could about this big, new world." Not only in college but as long as he lived, friends marveled at his childlike openness. Enemies accused him of naivete.[8]

Much as he would have liked to have spent all his time playing football, McGill's purpose for being at Vanderbilt was to become a doctor. In the biology lab of Professor Edwin E. Reinke he made a friend but failed to master any material. Reinke, who played a key role in Vanderbilt's medical school admissions, knew the amiable youth was not cut out for a career in medicine. Later Ralph claimed that financial hardship forced him to abandon the dream. In reality, low grades sidetracked the plan. The field fascinated him all his days. He read and investigated medical science endlessly.[9]

He was more successful in the English class of Professor Edwin Mims. Mims had built Vanderbilt's strongest liberal arts department, but his literary canon ended with the Victorian era. Modern works were anathema to him. Mims assigned long passages of poetry to memorize and Ralph excelled. Years later he could still recite these. The oral tradition—love of telling stories, saying poems, acting, or declaming—was part of his Celtic heritage.[10]

Freshman English with Mims set McGill on fire to be a poet. The flames smoldered but did not die for years. With all his being, McGill desired a visitation from the Muse. He kept trying but ultimately "never got anywhere with poetry." Prose was to be his metier. Initiation into Vanderbilt's literary honor society only set him up for more frustration. He remained convinced that his gift was destined to take literary rather than journalistic form even though *The Hustler*, Vanderbilt's student newspaper, welcomed him to its staff.[11]

Besides McGugin, Reinke, and Mims, two black men—widely admired on campus—provided Ralph with guidance and a kind of discipline that autumn. They were Bowling Fitzgerald and Robert

Wingfield. The young man took snapshots of both and kept them among mementos of his wonderful freshman year. Fitzgerald was "Negro trainer for the football team and head janitor at Kissam Hall." Property holdings and his lifestyle placed Fitzgerald squarely in segregated Nashville's black middle class. Student athletes and the men in Kissam usually came to him for help and advice that, McGill said, "was always good."

Wingfield was head chef in the dining hall. His dignity and Christian character impressed students and faculty alike. Ralph was one among the student waiters "adopted" by Wingfield. Every month he went with one or two others to the man's house for refreshments and counsel. Like all other Wingfield "boys," Ralph cherished the contact and appreciated the concern. Both Fitzgerald and Wingfield warned him against being drawn into the low life of Nashville.[12]

Though Nashville bragged about its culture as "the Athens of the South," Vanderbilt students could find most any sort of vice downtown. Many from the rural Bible Belt saw with their own eyes the sinful pursuits hitherto only heard about in preachers' admonitions. Prohibition came to Tennessee in 1909, spawning a crime wave in the capital. Bootleggers from nearby areas furnished a growing number of speakeasies with illegal liquor. These night spots also fostered gambling and prostitution. Pornography and drugs were available, often in the very shadow of the state capitol. The huge profits to be made in liquor trafficking brought in gangsters who corrupted local politics and dramatically increased the murder rate. Nashville became a "little Chicago." The city was growing anyway. Population reached 118,000 by 1920, double that of Chattanooga. Newcomers sought jobs and schooling in the metropolis. They also found plenty of corn liquor, sex shows, dice games, and whores. As a police reporter McGill soon would write about the entire phenomenon.[13]

For now he was more interested in Nashville's entertainment events than the city's vice. Ryman Auditorium and the Orpheum Theater were his focal points. Booking agent Lula C. Naff leased the Ryman in 1914 and singlehandedly made Nashville into a major stop on the performing arts circuit. To the Orpheum came first run stage plays and tryouts by stock companies that traveled from the capital to small Tennessee towns. McGill's enchantment with theatrical and musical productions grew. True to his Celtic nature, he enjoyed being on stage more than in the audience. Touring companies usually needed extras. Vanderbilt students were glad to oblige. This practice, known at the time as "suping," gave stagestruck youths like Ralph a chance to wear greasepaint and ogle stars like those he had seen only on cigarette cards just a few years before.[14]

Another Nashville institution attracting the college freshman was the *Banner*, its afternoon newspaper. For more than forty years it had chronicled goings-on in the capital and surrounding towns. Since 1885 the *Banner* had been the personal instrument of its owner, Major Edward Bushrod Stahlman. Emigrating to Nashville from Germany after the Civil War, Stahlman became a success in business. He owned a local cotton mill and was general freight agent and vice president of the mighty Louisville and Nashville Railroad. In the *Banner* he exalted his business and political allies. More significantly, he waged a bitter conflict with his archenemy, Colonel Luke Lea who owned Nashville's morning paper, the *Tennessean*. Lea's financial and political clout matched and eventually surpassed that of Stahlman.

The major's grandson, Jimmy Stahlman, was a Vanderbilt Sigma Chi in the Class of 1916. Young Stahlman and Ralph were friends as well as fraternity brothers. In 1918 the major installed Jimmy, who had edited *The Hustler*, as city editor of the *Banner*. Other Sigma Chis worked there as well. Ralph regularly dropped by the converted furniture store at Third and Commerce where the *Banner* was published to watch the process firsthand.[15]

Throughout his freshman year the Vanderbilt campus was caught up in patriotic fervor. At the football banquet Coach McGugin's speech focused on the Vanderbilt men who were away in the armed services. A close prep school friend was injured. Ralph finished his freshman year and enlisted in the Marine Corps. Coach McGugin approved of his decision. "I will miss you greatly," he wrote, "but you are in noble work."[16]

Boot camp at Parris Island, South Carolina, was full of strange experiences. Before it ended, McGill had proved his own toughness to himself and knew that he could take it with the best of men. Initially, the drill sergeant ordered all the "hookies" among the recruits to step forward. Nobody moved. He directed boys from the Deep South that he was talking about them. So designated, they marched off to be purged of hookworm disease. It was a new sort of regional consciousness for Ralph.[17]

McGill served as a Marine less than a year, but for him those were charmed months. Just as Vanderbilt football let him enact the Merriwell stories, the Marine Corps brought to life dozens of action fantasies he had read and dreamed of. The fulfillment was flawed. He never left American soil. The adventure was perfectly safe. Thousands of miles away in the horrific combat, men whom he knew lost limbs, life, and sanity. Sensitive about such sacrifices, McGill tried not to let it show how much he had loved playing soldier. For the rest of his life, however, he was a gung-ho Leatherneck. Marines, he wrote a decade later, "know in their hearts that the army and the navy are a lot of bad drills and grease balls that can't shoot a lick. . . ."[18]

On liberty from Parris Island or Quantico with fellow sea soldiers Ralph began a pattern of binge drinking. He was far away from those who knew him as boyish and serious minded. He had always shown an antic side, reveling in pranks and highspirited but innocent adventures. Alcohol released more rowdiness. Companions discovered that he could be "a real rounder" whose hilarity led to wild behavior on occasion. Friends also found his remorse after one of these bouts could be unfathomable. A period of sobriety always followed, typical of such alcohol abuse.[19]

The 1918 armistice meant that McGill would never be in combat and was home in Chattanooga by March 1919. Eager to rejoin McGugin's team, he wanted a temporary job that would include conditioning for football as well as good wages. Returning servicemen and a looming recession dimmed these hopes. His father then offered a suggestion that was consistent with his ideas but unthinkable to most of Ralph's college friends: a black roofing crew at his firm needed a man. Would Ralph join them? The foreman, Charlie White, "was a humpbacked man, quite black, of indeterminate age." Growing up, Ralph and his sisters often stopped at their father's office on trips to the Carnegie library. So they knew most of the employees, including White.

It was one thing to join Vanderbilt men taking tea in the Nashville parlor of dignified, respectable Robert Wingfield but quite another to violate the etiquette of segregation doing "nigger work" under a black boss. That is exactly what Ralph did for almost six months. He carried bundles of shingles up the ladder to the men and helped spread hot pitch on tar and gravel roofs. "It was," he recalled forty years later, "furious, backbreaking, arm-wearing work."

On this job the foreman shared the lunch break with Ralph and invited the young man to his home. When Ralph left for Nashville, White hauled his trunk to Union Station in his truck. The two talked on the platform "since the waiting rooms were segregated." As the train left, White embraced him and handed him an envelope to open later. Inside were five dollars and a note.[20]

Ralph willingly crossed the color line to work under Charlie White, but in 1919 countless other whites feared and hated blacks as never before. During the war years African Americans had migrated North in search of employment and to escape deepening repression down South. Just as the first World War changed McGill, it gave many blacks a new view of themselves. Jim Crow became intolerable to some. Whites reacted drastically to any sign of change. That summer was fraught with unprecedented racial violence. Both races destroyed each others' lives and property in record numbers. Riots had never been so extensive or so prolonged. Thirty-eight persons died in Chicago, nine in the nation's capital.

Within hours after taking leave of Charlie White, McGill was back at Vanderbilt. He returned to a campus and a city that were changing. The number of Vanderbilt undergraduates increased from 600 to 800 over the next four years. During the Twenties Nashville's population grew from 118,342 to 153,866. McGill was changing too. Like so many other ex-servicemen, he saw rules, routine, even the college ethos in a new light. The freshman of 1917-18 was awed and eager. The twenty-one year old sophomore was self-assured as a result of the Marines, questioning and rebellious. Before the 1919-20 academic year ended, McGill was a brash campus journalist but indifferent student.

The recent war was in everyone's mind. Wartime sacrifices were linked to athletic heroism in collegiate minds even before the Armistice. At Vanderbilt the two ideals fused in Irby "Rabbit" Curry. In 1916 Curry was quarterback and captain of the football team as well as a popular student leader. His death in France launched his symbolic importance. McGugin mounted Curry's photo alongside Abraham Lincoln's portrait in his office. McGill knew Curry only secondhand but portrayed him as the epitome of loyalty. "I imagine," he once wrote, "that the Rabbit, as he went swinging down to die, was thinking of old Dudley Field, his coach, his signals, and the old black jersey that he wore. . . ."[21]

McGill proudly accepted the second of three football letters but continued to hold literary ambitions equal to his love of sport. Induction into a second literary honorary inspired him to keep writing. He had known for years that he was a writer. But what sort? An entirely new outlet opened for him in 1919 when a campus humor magazine appeared. McGill devoted great effort to *The Jade* and always took pride in the fact that Vanderbilt was the first southern university to undertake such a project. Sometimes Tom Sims, who later drew the cartoon strip, Popeye, and McGill wrote the entire copy for an issue. The two were also known as the life of any party.[22]

As a poet, Ralph fell short of the standards set by other friends, several of whom would soon participate in a regional literary renaissance. Their magazine, *The Fugitive*, was also their label. John Crowe Ransom stated in the 1922 inaugural issue that they were fleeing "from the high-caste Brahmins of the Old South." After the war Ransom, an English instructor ten years older than Ralph, introduced him to contemporary poets. The Fugitives never constituted a school of poetry but brought national and then international attention to Vanderbilt.[23]

Ralph's professional and collegiate journalism careers began about the same time. For *The Hustler* he wrote a satirical column he called "Censored." Being a controversial columnist certainly beat trying to master techniques of meter and rhyme. In the spring of 1920 *Banner* city editor Jimmy Stahlman put him to work. He often stopped by the newspaper in the afternoons. One day early in the baseball season he arrived to find a minor crisis. The telephone man who took the play-by-play from the Nashville Vol's baseball park quit. Jimmy drafted Ralph to fill in. He agreed to come every afternoon thereafter and help around the city room. On Saturdays he "worked from noon until 2:30 Sunday morning." Besides typing details of baseball games, he ran errands and worked as a copy boy.[24]

McGill got to know more and more of the *Banner* reporters and editors. Some were as interested in the new literary trends as those in his literary honorary on campus. His work for the *Banner* took him all around Nashville. He liked the city better all the time. One who increasingly suspected he belonged to the "lost generation" but could not manage Paris or even Greenwich Village was happy to "make do with what we had in Nashville and at Vanderbilt."[25]

Yet home was still Chattanooga. He relished being with his parents and three kid sisters. He remained Mary Lou McGill's favorite child. Ralph also stayed close to many prep school friends and to the McCallie brothers. Every development at the school on Missionary Ridge interested him. On New Year's Day 1920 the McCallie Alumni Association met and elected Ralph president of the body. He served with pride whenever his old school called upon him.[26]

He began to indulge in nostalgia for all of East Tennessee. Longings for the old McGill homeplace on the river intensified throughout his life. He was safely beyond any possibility of getting stuck in Chattanooga or the mountains before he began to look back so fondly. Nashville provided employment, friends, and stimulating urban pace. However, East Tennessee became "God's country." He lyrically described the vistas of mountain ranges and valley settlements. Usually he defied anyone to take exception to his label. "There never has been any humor in that phrase to the East Tennessean," he wrote one day, "and there never will be."[27]

Excess was coming to mark all his behavior. Though he was guilty about not living up to expectations from home, he neglected coursework and read for pleasure. On campus and downtown at the *Banner* he found friends who would stay up all night discussing novels, poems, and plays. A *Banner* reporter recalled that the sessions usually were more interesting when "a pretty raw quality of corn whisky" was on hand. By summer 1920 Ralph wanted and got a fulltime job at the *Banner*.[28]

The *Banner* staff worked under the watchful eye of managing editor, Marmaduke B. Morton. Major Stahlman seldom ventured over from his office building two blocks away. Morton was from neighboring Kentucky. He started working for the legendary "Marse" Henry Watterson of the *Louisville Courier-Journal*. After further experience in Birmingham and Nashville, the tall, thin editor joined the *Banner* in 1898. Morton always kept a "cane-stemmed corncob pipe in his mouth," and a cloud of smoke hovered over his desk. He made reporters toe the line and obey his rules. The first was "Never get too wise to use your legs." Men on the police beat received two other orders: get to know the undertakers who will notify you when an important corpse comes in; get to know the madams and find out who their important customers are.[29]

Like many *Banner* employees, Morton kept a loaded gun in his desk because the hateful feud between Major Stahlman and Luke Lea extended to their respective staffs. This aspect of danger tantalized McGill. "Legend had it," he recalled, "that one day the Leas would come surging up the stairway with revolvers drawn and the shooting would begin." In 1916 the *Banner* helped engineer Lea's loss of his US Senate seat, deepening his animosity. Lea was only thirty-five years old but never again ran for elective office. He became instead Tennessee's éminence grise whose power steadily grew throughout the 1920s.[30]

Ralph learned a thing or two about police reporting that

summer and the following year. The *Banner* bolstered the efforts of honest law enforcement officers as illegal liquor dealings spawned crime and corruption. Both the *Banner* and the *Tennessean* put out a midmorning edition and each wanted a front page story from the police station or some hoodlum's headquarters. McGill obliged whenever possible. Once he hid under a bed in an upstairs suite above Foutch's all-night drugstore, a favorite hangout where political deals were sealed with corn whiskey sold over the prescription counter below. That night he overheard a conversation that warranted an extra edition. Editors back at the *Banner* thought McGill's story was "preposterous." They decided not to print it. McGill recorded that the deal later "came off."[31]

Sometimes the eager cub reporter got more than he bargained for in his headline grabbing. When two rival gangs began shooting in the middle of town, he was caught on the scene. Nothing availed but to take cover under a farm wagon loaded with watermelons. Editor Morton put a 60-point ribbon on the story of how Sam Borum and his boys killed John Yeaman. When things settled down, McGill wondered what "a young aesthetic reporter" was doing crouching in the gutter "while the bullets sang and richocheted off the old stone buildings, whining and screeching like a thousand cats having their tails trampled on all at the same time?"[32]

Once Jimmy Stahlman and Morton assigned Ralph to do a series profiling the city through a police reporter's eyes. He labeled a block of Sixth Avenue between Church and Union Streets near the capitol as "the Western Front" because of increasing violence among rival mobsters. He told readers it also served as "the uptown headquarters for the army of women who come in silks and satins, with painted faces and pungent perfume . . . to fill an engagement." Ralph became furious when Colonel Luke Lea's *Tennessean* reprinted parts of his Western Front piece "in an attempt to embarrass the city administration" and influence the mayoralty race. By now he was swept up in the old fashioned rivalry and remained a partisan newsman for fifty years.[33]

In retrospect, he believed that Prohibition "made a little

Chicago out of Nashville." Whatever good came from the "noble experiment," as Herbert Hoover described Prohibition, was more than offset in McGill's eyes. He watched as the impact of state law and then the eighteenth amendment transformed the city's criminal class and also her politicians. The money to be made in supplying illegal liquor was simply enormous. In the end these profits spawned "an all-inclusive corruption" in the Tennessee capital. McGill all but ignored the positive effects of Prohibition and focused instead on the hoodlums, gamblers, prostitutes, moonshine dealers he saw on his beat.[34]

These assignments on the police beat were sobering and had longterm effects on his thinking and journalistic career. First, the experience convinced McGill that federal intervention in a social issue never worked. Flaunting of state and federal Prohibition laws was a hallmark of the Twenties. He assumed thereafter that federal action would be ineffective in other situations. This conviction flawed his editorial judgment when federal intervention to desegregate southern society loomed ahead. Second, police reporting occasionally gave Ralph the idea that he was in danger. Sometimes, for instance, vague threats circulated that "the boys" would "take care of him" if he did not stop writing about organized crime. He liked knowing that he was tough enough to keep filing stories despite threat of bodily harm. This attitude also stayed with him. When he later complained about threats, it was only that his "good right arm" was not "as good as it used to be."[35]

Police reporting rekindled his love of writing melodramas. Whorehouses and speakeasies were his settings. Climaxes were the death scenes he witnessed in police wagons and the stories he heard over corpses in mortuaries. He championed girl friends of bootleggers and victims of gamblers. He submitted tales of bizarre, cruel behavior to pulp magazines. Writing about campus doings for *The Hustler* paled in comparison with the challenge of doing pieces that dealt with real life and often with death.[36]

McGill seemed less likely than ever to complete requirements for his bachelor's degree at Vanderbilt. At summer's end he abandoned arts and sciences and entered the Law School. He wanted to work at the *Banner* every morning, and law classes met in the afternoons. Besides, enrollment in some university program allowed him to remain on the football team. The desire to do well for Coach McGugin reined in his tendency to eat and drink too much. Once the season ended, so did this constraint. He also skipped most of his classes. Writing became his only discipline.[37]

The pattern revealed how he differed from his father. Ralph decided that he took after the Welsh ancestors in his family tree. Ben McGill, now fifty-two years old, was quiet and abstinent. The son got drunk and dreamed up pranks that triggered laughter half a century later. Yet Ben's discipline gave his children a start in life far above that which he had. He sacrificed mightily so that his son might matriculate at the best university in the area. Now the opportunity was slipping through Ralph's fingers, and Ben was deeply disappointed.[38]

Father and son did continue to share one bond, the Republican Party. Ralph reached voting age while he was away in the Marine Corps. He wrote his father, "We'll vote for the next Republican together." In 1920 two Ohio men contended for the presidency. Senator Warren G. Harding was the Republican nominee. Governor James M. Cox led the Democrat ticket although President Wilson insisted that the election was a referendum on his peace plan, especially the League of Nations. On November 2 the voters rejected the Democrat Cox. The Senate shortly rejected Wilson's design for postwar security, but McGill never forgot Wilson's ideas.[39]

Despite his writings about illegal liquor, McGill decided to shore up his personal finances by supplying it to Vanderbilt students. A fellow Sigma Chi and graduate student was producing a popular brew in a Vanderbilt chemistry laboratory. During his last months on campus Ralph promoted the brandy and handled deliveries. Even though he was the junior partner, he made more money from the project than from the many other odd jobs he held as a student. McGill unfailingly damned Prohibition, but for some reason he liked to recall being a purveyor of hooch.[40]

A growing defiance of university authority also marked his final year at Vanderbilt. He admitted later to having been in a brash phase. This plus a strong social acceptance among his peers probably gave Ralph the temerity to become an editorial gadfly and begin challenging university policy in *The Hustler*. He learned that a deceased faculty member had left a sum of $20,000 for Vanderbilt to create a student lounge. The project never materialized. Thus, McGill claimed in an editorial that by ignoring the stipulation of the will, university officials were embezzlers.[41]

His defiant phase culminated in a typical prank that prompted Chancellor Kirkland to ask him to leave school in April 1921. The Sigma Chis were always looking for ways to discomfit their great Greek rival, the brothers of Beta Theta Pi. When the time for formals approached that spring, McGill stole the engraving plate for the Beta's invitations. The Betas intended to limit guests at their white tie affair to the social elite. McGill distributed bogus invitations far and wide, including a batch to some Nashville bawdy houses. The university employed detectives to get to the bottom of the practical joke. He never denied his part in the affair and seemed to accept the consequences.[42]

Major Stahlman readily gave the expelled student a permanent job. McGill professed to be satisfied at backing into a career in this fashion. He was in a tough business where reporters did themselves no harm by acting hardboiled and cynical. However, this reporter was disillusioned with himself. Not only would he miss the literary renaissance based at Vanderbilt, he would never be a college graduate. For years he did not mention the matter to friends. Behind his silence was a deep wound. In the meantime what he called his "great, happy school years" were over, and the promise of 1917 was unrealized.[43]

The literary Fugitives' reputations rose just as McGill's hopes of being an intellectual fell. Years passed before he resumed serious scholarship. In the meantime he spoofed such endeavors, as in his satirical, "I'm the Gink" syndicated column. "I'm the 'young intelligentsia' gink," he announced. "I'm up on all the latest novels that have a shady reputation. . . . I go in for all the 'deep' boys, and, frankly, they are over my head. Still I act as though I know, so I get by. Folks think I'm a nut, but I'm just super-intelligent, that's all." The plain truth was that young McGill did have strong intellect but would struggle long and hard before he found an opportunity fully to use it or even to discover what sort of writer he was.[44]

3

Sports "Ballyhoo" : 1921-1929

On the day he died, McGill told a group of schoolchildren that he became a newspaperman "just because I needed a job." He said he had never really known what he wanted to do. He liked his parttime job as a reporter for the *Nashville Banner*, he added nonchalantly, "so I stayed in it and have been in it all my life." The matchup between person and job was superb. Not long after getting established at the *Banner* he wrote that "there is no thrill in the world like the breaking of a big story in a newspaper office." He described the scene in the city room as word came of a nearby airplane crash. "Action. Reporters scurrying for coats and hats. Orders. Office boys running. Taxi cabs called and honking. Reporters . . . with that funny feeling in the pits of their stomachs trying to plan their leads as they rode. To look at horror and death."[1]

These twin outlets of action followed by writing were probably critical to his long but successful transition from college to career. McGill was a restless individual. He blamed this on the genes of Grandfather Skillern, the journalist with wanderlust who abandoned his young family. So the legwork that Marmaduke Morton gave Ralph even as a parttime reporter suited him better than Vanderbilt course work or literary endeavors. During his years at the *Banner* he both lived and chronicled the popular culture of the Twenties.

Yet he was still tied to Vanderbilt. Coach Dan McGugin was more important than ever to McGill who enjoyed all the McGugin family. For several years after his expulsion Ralph remained in campus housing on old West Side Row. He was never troubled by lack of friends or social outlets. He was well liked and he knew it.

In 1922, when he turned twenty-four, a fraternity brother gave him a surprise party at the Belle Meade Country Club. Ralph said the happy occasion was "the best birthday I ever had." Photographs at the time showed a well built man who could dress smartly when he wanted to. They conveyed an impression of openness and *joie de vivre*.[2]

In July 1922 McGill got his first political assignment. It was a four week baptism of fire for the fledgling reporter, who learned to his dismay why the *Banner* was called one of the South's "most outspoken newspapers." U. S. Senator Kenneth D. McKellar was defending the seat he won from Luke Lea in 1916. Stahlman told McGill to use any tactic to discredit McKellar's rival in the Democratic primary. On the road Ralph struggled with his assignment. His articles were weak, disjointed accounts of the campaign. They lacked the clarity and fluency that marked his work even in the early years.

The Democratic primary race culminated in Memphis, Tennessee's largest city where both candidates lived. Here McGill met Edward H. "Boss" Crump who controlled Memphis politics and eventually a statewide machine. At first the novice reporter thought Crump was an appealing, even "romantic" figure. Eventually his assessment changed. Even though the major's candidate in the senate race was Crump's man as well, Ralph returned from Memphis somewhat disaffected. McKellar's senate seat was safe, as he won a landslide victory.[3]

After a month and a half on the sports desk, McGill rejoined the political campaigners. From mid-October until the general election in early November he traveled with the Democratic candidate for governor. He was a protégé of Luke Lea. So Major Stahlman—in keeping with their feud—supported the incumbent governor, Republican Alfred A. Taylor. "Uncle Alf" was in his mid-seventies and much beloved in East Tennessee. Entertainment was the thrust of his reelection campaign. He fiddled, his sons and nephews sang, and his famous foxhound, "Old Limber," sat on the platform watching the crowd.

Stahlman's orders to McGill were the same as in the primary campaign. The effort was disastrous for Stahlman. Luke Lea's candidate began a long, productive tenure as governor. Lea expanded his power base and, whenever possible, used this influence against Stahlman. Contrary to McGill's later claims, he covered no more political campaigns until 1928.[4]

As 1923 began Ralph expected to do a variety of reporting, including some legislative stories, but by mid January he was the *Banner*'s sports editor. Stahlman gave him the job when Jim Ray left Nashville to work for the *Atlanta Journal*. McGill had written his first major sports stories in autumn 1922 when Vanderbilt celebrated the opening of Dudley Field, a modern football stadium seating 20,000. Like so many other institutions of higher learning, the university succumbed to the growing enthusiasm of sports fans. On Saturday afternoons millions of Americans paid to watch college football games, generating annually more than $21 million for the schools. Vanderbilt's new stadium symbolized a commitment to big time sports.[5]

By 1923 it was obvious that a "golden age of sport" had come for both amateur and professional athletes. Much as he wished sports to be a field of honor rather than a business, McGill was both witness and midwife to this transformation. The sports "ballyhoo" not only enriched athletes, it also sold newspapers. Ralph's livelihood depended on the Stahlmans' circulation figures, and he saw to it that *Banner* readers learned as much as possible about their sports heroes.[6]

Besides reading the enlarged sports pages, more and more American households bought radios. Baseball announcers like Graham McNamee acquired a following that grew by the thousands weekly despite fears of club owners that radio broadcasts would harm attendance at games. The opposite occurred. The same was true of football. After listening to exciting descriptions of action on the gridiron, people who never heard the words, "alma mater," thronged to the new stadiums. Wild public enthusiasm for Red Grange and other gridiron heroes moved some colleges to pay more attention to gate receipts than to scholastic standards.[7]

Gambling on college games also increased in popularity. Coach McGugin made gambling the theme of his speech at the 1923 football banquet. McGill reported the speech, adding more information about the scandal. He said that only one southern city had more trouble with sports gambling than Nashville. The "vultures" hung around at both college and high school football matches to take bets. They openly worked crowds attending baseball games in Sulphur Dell. Gamblers wrote anonymous letters to sportswriters and circulated false rumors about players in an effort to influence the odds. McGill deplored the corruption of college sports by the power of money.[8]

It was hard for McGill to accept the reality that all student athletes could not play, as he had, for "the real love of an ideal." Many players were not even students. During his years as a sports editor college athletics slipped further and further away from the framework he cherished. Ralph believed that through sports students could receive strong moral training. Preparation for games demanded effort and taught endurance. The contests called for courage, sometimes heroism. He construed victories as the athlete's reward for accepting the disciplines and demands of the code. Defeats strengthened moral fiber.[9]

McGill spent one-third of his career in the ranks of journalists whose words made heroes and heroines out of athletes who seldom lived by his cherished and outmoded code. In the early years he enjoyed the assignments. He treated readers to jocular articles that amused as they informed. His distinctive style was as easy to read as it was for him to compose. Sometimes money's corruption of sport disturbed him, and his biting tone jarred readers. Occasionally he forsook sports and wrote about subjects that would interest any intelligent, well educated newsman. The way McGill mastered his new job is strong testimony to his intelligence and writing ability. Those same gifts guaranteed that he would outgrow sportswriting and endure frustration and dissatisfaction until he received a new challenge.

Yet in 1923 the new editor was a novice. Ralph was familiar with the Vanderbilt sports scene and had campus contacts when he needed background material. It was more difficult to write about professional sports. The *Banner* used some syndicated stories, but Ralph scrambled to collect material about base-ball—both major and minor league—as well as wrestling and boxing. Readers also expected to keep up with their favorites in the popular amateur sports of golf, tennis, and swimming.

McGill provided much of the copy but had some staff assistance. John C. Cooke specialized in covering horses and racing. E. B. "Ebe" Stahlman II, and Lewie Little also wrote sports. McGill knew that photographs and newsreel footage contributed mightily to the phenomenal popularity of sports. Staff photographer Bill Barr had a talent for dramatic action shots that McGill exploited. The two were ingenious about rushing photographic plates back to Nashville from assignments out of town. After the 1926 Vanderbilt-Georgia Tech football game in Atlanta, Barr traveled the nine miles from Grant Field to Candler Flying Field in the sidecar of a Harley-Davidson motorcycle. He then flew to Cowan, Tennessee, where he transferred to a Hupmobile 8 for the final ninety miles of the journey. The "record-breaking achievement" got a prominent place on page one the next day as did any scoop of the *Tennessean*.[10]

Soon after starting the job, McGill began a daily signed column, "The Sport Aerial," complete with a drawing of antenna wires. Shortly thereafter came his first taste of reader reaction. Irate fans who took exception to his writing telephoned the city room. Letters—many of them anonymous—arrived at his desk. It was an exhilarating experience. He gave angry sports fans the same tough message he sent to displeased gangsters when he was on the police beat: he welcomed controversy. Stirring up hornets' nests became one of the principal satisfactions of his career.[11]

With the coming of spring McGill concentrated on the national pasttime. Nashville's professional baseball team, the Vols, belonged to the Southern League. Manager Jimmy Hamilton worked nonstop to acquire from major league teams or other minor league organizations the personnel to win a pennant. The *Banner*'s new sports editor soon became a fixture at the Vols' ball park, Sulphur Dell. In fact, some players viewed him as a kind of giant good luck charm. The press box was a hot "little hutch" on the roof of the grandstand. When McGill was absent, they claimed, games went badly. Ralph was never able to enjoy watching baseball as he did football. Some days the "tarry smell of the roof, the dust from the field, and the ubiquitous odors from the dump" made the job unbearable.[12]

Sulphur Dell was located on the site of Nashville's original settlement where in the mid-eighteenth century Frenchmen began trading with Indians. Both sought the abundant wild game that "licked" the salty water of sulphur springs near the banks of the Cumberland River. A century and a half later baseball players splashing around at the often flooded Dell were still getting tastes of malodorous water. This offered McGill good chances for bad jokes. He once asserted that ball park hot dogs were made from water spaniels.[13]

His funniest early columns were about baseball. Emotionally attached to his own playing days, he could not joke about football which he described in elegiac style. Once he combined his knowledge of scripture with baseball whimsy. For a thousand words he drew comic possibilities from a verse in the book of Judges when "southpaws first broke into sport columns." Seven hundred lefthanded warriors from the tribe of Benjamin went to the forefront of a battle in 1406 BC. Finding that many lefthanders with control, said McGill, was "a much more remarkable feat than parting the Red Sea or healing the blind." The day likely went against the forces of Benjamin because the southpaws "lost control about the third inning and had to be jerked."[14]

He kidded about superstar Babe Ruth. Each spring Nashville offered its residents annual glimpses of "the Great One" during exhibition season. Ralph enjoyed watching Ruth "pushing his dogs" around the swampy outfield of Sulphur Dell and joked about why he never hit home runs in the park. Ruth worked with disadvantaged children. McGill championed the same cause, urging Nashville civic groups to bring these youngsters to watch Ruth bat and field at Sulphur Dell.[15]

Colleagues and readers saw a different side of his complex nature in August 1923, when Jim Ray, his predecessor and friend, died in an Atlanta hospital after a freak automobile accident. A hearty, gregarious man, Ray had been a favorite around the office in Nashville. Ralph appreciated Ray's guidance in covering sports as much as he loved his banter. His profound grief was puzzling but a response that friends and colleagues learned to expect. He wrote about death with acuity whether the subject was a stranger or someone he knew. McGill always said his Celtic ancestry caused this overreaction to sad events. It was also evidence that he bordered on being dysthymic.[16]

He exhibited other behavior patterns often linked with the mood disorder. Besides being an insomniac, he ate and drank to extremes, especially on out-of-town assignments. His weight ballooned. He became a fat person who craved food and made meals into a celebration. He offered wry discussions of dieting in his column but kept overeating. The *Banner* ran photographs of their annual staff outing. One year some men in bathing suits formed a human pyramid for the camera. A caption made sure readers did not mistake the sports editor for one of those "Jap wrestlers."[17]

He often partied at a group of summer "camps" on a high bluff overlooking the Cumberland River. Some residents lived in their camps year around, but most came on weekends or for the summer. Writers, professors, musicians, librarians found there a compatible community and a local variety of Bohemianism. McGill cherished memories of telling stories on outdoor summer evenings "reclining in hammocks and on cots." He never forgot strolling out to look at the city lights of Nashville twinkling below in the valley. The sportswriter's friends remembered his more uproarious side, especially after he quaffed plenty of "white lightning colored red." He loved describing hangovers when he came "to the office on Monday morning with his nerves on his coat sleeves."[18]

Contrary to true dysthymics, he amazed everyone with an easy execution of work even on his worst days. Marmaduke Morton was a stickler for having the *Banner* staff at their desks by seven in the morning. Sometimes Ralph arrived hungover without breakfast or with shirttails flying. Regardless of condition, he sat down and began typing. He did his own "Sport Aerial" column first then worked on feature articles and stories about upcoming games. Even if frustrated or depressed, his output never slowed.[19]

McGill's first work on a sensational national story came in February 1925 when a youth named Floyd Collins became trapped in a cave in nearby Kentucky. A Louisville reporter filed dispatches that made Collins into an obsession from coast to coast. The rescue effort became a media spectacle. For two weeks the isolated area swarmed with hundreds of the working press, rescue crews, and curiosity seekers. A tent city sheltered the workers from the freezing weather. National Guardsmen tried to maintain order along the rutty road into Cave City, six miles away. The story was on page one of every major newspaper in the country. From Nashville came Ralph McGill to give *Banner* readers a full account of the tense, futile work. Collins died before rescuers could extricate him, then a slide sealed his body in the underground passageway.

McGill explained in painstaking detail the various ways that drilling crews tried to reach Collins. He quoted confident experts who vowed they would bring the victim out alive. Bill Barr came to photograph the bleak terrain, tents, and the *Banner*'s stout and stalwart correspondent. McGill sat on one crate with his portable typewriter balanced on another. He wore high boots and a long raincoat. His press card was tucked into his huge hat, a cigarette dangling from his mouth. The caption said he had not had three hours sleep in the past twenty-four. Back home editors praised his tireless efforts in notes introducing his pieces.

When the story ended, an ironic McGill reflected on what the modern media—both radio and press—had created. "Had Floyd Collins stepped in front of a train or met death by ordinary accident," he said, "he would have never been known." A "bizarre" combination of circumstances made him into "a national figure." The scale of the rescue work stunned McGill: "A half million dollars was spent in his behalf, a hundred men gave their labor and

risked their lives to free him . . . all in vain." Ralph knew the
potential for mass reaction on his own beat, the sports world. Now
he saw firsthand how media could create a giant reaction to the
most obscure happening. Cave City, Kentucky, returned to its
customary quiet, and McGill prepared to go home. However, he
knew it was only a matter of time before he would be swept up in
another such frenzy. He did love being part of a big story.[20]

In early July 1925 James G. Stahlman took over full management of the *Banner* from his grandfather, taking the paper in a
more reactionary direction. That summer was long and hot.
Tennessee wilted under the sun and from the international
publicity of the Scopes trial taking place in Dayton, Tennessee.
The media circus dwarfed the Floyd Collins coverage a few months
earlier. To McGill's dismay, Stahlman sent another man to cover
the three week proceedings and kept him writing about baseball
and golf tournaments. He visited the army of media professionals
encamped in Dayton then left for vacation in Biloxi, Mississippi.[21]

McGill's description of interstate auto travel to Biloxi is as
much a part of the Twenties as the Scopes trial. Mile after mile
they crawled through mud that "had the adhesive qualities of a
sticking plaster and the slippery qualities of a loose piece of soap
in the bath tub." Road signs were sparse and easily missed,
especially in the dark. Driving at night when "every pedestrian is
a holdup man" and "the marshall is never to be seen" was unnerving. Thankfully, the car broke down only twice along the way to
the coast. Despite such hazards, Americans were in love with
motoring. By decade's end there would be almost one car per
family throughout the nation.[22]

Even on vacation, McGill always went after a story. Besides
deep sea fishing in the Gulf of Mexico and eating, he wrote a series
of long articles on illegal liquor coming into the coast. The
government might be planning more aggressive enforcement of
Prohibition, but rumrunners were not worried. The "daredevils and
thugs" told him that stricter policing would just drive up prices
(and profits) of their often deadly products. One said, "I've got
enough buried in these rivers and swamps to last me a year or so,

and by that time . . . they will have eased up a bit." The cynical and successful bootleggers depressed him. He concluded that the government was just wasting time and energy.[23]

McGill was free to write anything he liked for his personal column, "The Sport Aerial." Reviews of books, concerts, and plays began to appear. These were pointed reminders for Jimmy Stahlman and Marmaduke Morton that McGill had intellectual interests beyond football, baseball, and golf. Stahlman knew that the talents of his fraternity brother could be put to good use beyond the *Banner's* sports pages, and he usually assigned McGill stories on a crime or a catastrophe rather than features.

In late 1925 McGill did a memorable sob story, a genre he still enjoyed. Feeling abandoned by her gangster lover, an ice cream parlor cashier shot herself and was laid out at her parents' house awaiting burial. Distraught, the gangster hurried back to Nashville, kissed her cold lips, then blew "himself into eternity." When reporters stopped by a whorehouse near the *Banner* offices "to buy the girls a drink, they were still shedding tears over McGill's heart rending story and he was the hero of the hour."[24]

He began a second daily column which he called "I'm the Gink." Quite brief but running on page one, the column became so popular that McGill syndicated the feature in August 1925. Initially Republic Syndicates placed "I'm the Gink" in twenty-four newspapers. The pieces overflowed with every craze of the Twenties from Mah Jongg to movies. He offered shrewd, sardonic commentary on urban manners and trends. He did vignettes from the office, the boardinghouse, or the streetcar ride back and forth. Many Gink columns reflected changing relations between the sexes.

He attributed many of his own foibles to the Gink. The Gink loved chasing fire engines. The Gink bummed cigarettes off people. The Gink talked too much while playing bridge. The Gink took up more space on the streetcar seat than he should. The Gink diagnosed and doctored all his friends' ailments. The Gink stopped to weigh himself at every outdoor scale on the way from the office to the lunch spot. The Gink tried every diet that came along.[25]

McGill generally ignored sports news of special interest to Nashville's African-American community. In fact, the *Banner* ran many more such items on its general news pages than McGill ever included. On the rare occasions when black groundskeepers, cooks, or other menials he knew appeared in his column, they were slow, shuffling, and spoke in ungrammatical dialect. He did admire some black athletes, particularly those who kept old fashioned sporting ideals and avoided sham. He discussed these men as fellow human beings not racial stereotypes.

Middleweight boxing champion, Theodore "Tiger" Flowers died in November 1927 and got a better eulogy than McGill would have given most white fighters. McGill had followed Flowers, an "obscure Negro laborer" from Brunswick, Georgia, as he became a world champion and an idol of Harlem. Flowers was "a sincere Christian" who lived by the tenets of his faith. "There was no Hokum about the Tiger," he continued. "He tried hard, and there was never lack of action when he was in the ring. He was in a business wherein there was much sordidness and underhanded play. When he died, there was no smudge on his name. . . ."[26]

In August 1928 he wrote about Sam Langford, "the Boston Tarbaby," in the same straightforward style. McGill believed Langford was "probably the greatest heavyweight the ring ever knew," and sports historians have ranked him very high. Langford "knew what he was up against in his day" with the "color line" drawn against him but exhibited dignity, shrewdness, and employed humor against whites who baited him. McGill offered several anecdotes to explain why he admired Langford. Apparently beaten in one fight with Tiger Flowers, Langford "chopped him on the jaw—just a little chop that traveled no more than eight inches." Flowers was "out an actual five minutes."[27]

By contrast he neither knew nor admired participants in the 1925 football game between Fisk University and A and I State Teachers' College. The only players he praised were some he identified as "colored" versions of selected Vanderbilt stars. He dwelled on the uninhibited behavior of the fans, especially the "dusky girls." Halftime was a scene of "wild pandemonium," but

Fisk's unexpected victory brought even wilder celebration. The crowd tore apart the goal posts and all the decorations. He reported seeing one huge Fisk guard "with a piece of the colored paper in his big muddy paw." In his elation, the guard "forgot all his school English." " 'Boy, I sho am gonna send dis to my gal' " the man shouted. [28]

By now McGill had established a lifelong pattern of deliberately trying to provoke his readers. He lambasted sports fans: "There is really nothing more tiresome," he wrote, "than arguing with some dumb duke who apparently thinks he has the whole of football's lore stuffed away in his cranium and knows what it is all about, so to speak." His scornful coverage of boxer Jack Dempsey brought more reader reaction. Dempsey's huge crowds and gate receipts epitomized sports as mass entertainment and big business. He had also avoided service during World War I. McGill regularly called the champion, who had wed Hollywood actress Estelle Taylor, "a movie star by marriage."[29]

By 1927 an occasional bitter note crept into his comments on the opposite sex. "The wonderful thing about women," he wrote, "is not that we can't get along with them or without them, but that we get along in spite of them." What readers did not know was that his emotions were torn by a special woman in his life. She was Louise Stevens from the Belle Meade section of Nashville. From the summer of 1926 to late 1928 he and "Steve" had a love affair that eventually led nowhere. Both found other life partners but treasured memories of their relationship.

Steve came into McGill's life when ambition was starting to gnaw at him. Their romance produced contradictory feelings. Her encouragement made him hopeful of a fresh start or new direction. However, her affluent background convinced him that he could never provide all that she deserved. She, on the other hand, valued his tender devotion more than a big salary and preferred his serious mind to status. The sweethearts mingled easily with each other's social circle, but Ralph worried about their long term happiness.[30]

As he struggled to free himself of sportswriters' argot and find a different niche in newspaper work, his best pieces were sensitive observations of the natural world. The prose was fresh and flowing, hinting at his giftedness. He was beginning to cover meetings of foxhunters. A great dog lover, he learned all he could about Tennessee's famed fox hounds. In Louisville's train station in August 1927 he spied a cargo of Walker hounds. "The baggage man," he wrote, "let me climb in and talk with them. . . . They were not cowed or frightened by the noise in the station as most dogs would have been. . . . I always think of Cromwell's Round-heads when I see fox hounds—solemn, serious and absolutely devoted to one religion—chasing foxes."[31]

The sport was usually associated with wealthy Americans, but he knew it in Tennessee as "the great democracy," claiming a variety of folk. He went to the town of Dickson in October 1927 to report on a week long convention of hunters. He told of seeing a large red fox just before dawn and the casting of the hounds. "Red Russell, as Chaucer called him, stood there in the road, eyed the shuffling horses, their hot breath making wraiths in the cold air, and then walked nonchalantly into the bush." Red foxes usually eluded the hounds. Grays had less courage and cunning. Watching from a hilltop later, he saw a pack turn a gray fox into an open field of sage: "There was red on the brown leaves to match the red of the sumac. Rarely does Red Russell go down beneath snarling hot teeth."[32]

The feat of the decade—Charles A. Lindbergh's solo transatlantic flight in May 1927—brought a lapse into ballyhoo: "There may not be immortality for most of us. . . . Nevertheless, there must be some arrangement whereby great souls like those of . . . Lindbergh live on forever." Aviation had enthralled him since he saw his first airplane from the playground of a Chattanooga elementary school. He promoted any flying feat that advanced Americans' progress in manned flight. He was proud that Nashville was about to open a metropolitan airport.[33]

In 1927 McGill was on the road far too much to suit even a man who said he liked nothing better, but on the day after Christmas he was summoned to the most unusual assignment of his *Banner* career. A terrible gun battle erupted on Christmas night in the tiny town of South Pittsburg just west of Chattanooga. City police fought county police aided by other men. Six were killed and four wounded. Both sides denied starting the battle. Some claimed it began as an ambush. For a year a local stove works had been deadlocked with powerful unions over owners' desire to have an open shop. The unions' strike virtually shut down the company. Even deeper conflicts over power, money, family status preceded the months of strife. Now unemployed union men filled the ranks of county police. The city, claiming lack of protection, hired "special men" as its police.

McGill's accounts were first rate. He gave vivid word pictures of events and explained the bitterness behind the tragedy. More violence threatened. State troops came along with Tennessee's adjutant-general. They set up a 37 millimeter gun and imposed an evening curfew on townspeople. Then in an extraordinary turn of affairs, McGill intervened in the dispute. Beginning on December 28, he spent five days going from one faction to another with the adjutant-general. Finally the negotiations brought about an agreement to elect a replacement for the slain sheriff. The stove works reopened, and state troops left in a few days.[34]

Word of McGill's role as mediator spread across the state. In mid-January the mayor of South Pittsburg traveled to Nashville for conferences at the state capitol. He made a public statement praising the sports editor. McGill briefly saw himself in a new light. He never forgot the dynamics of conciliation and how it felt to be a mediator. He also felt he lacked the background for this kind of reporting. Even without the strain of negotiating, writing the complex South Pittsburg story almost overwhelmed him and left him confused about unions. The dark side of human nature always fascinated him. He had shown a knack for describing tragedy stemming from weakness, passion, even evil in individuals. In South Pittsburg he encountered tragedy rooted in social and economic forces rather than just personal conflicts.[35]

McGill knew he was vulnerable to seasonal depression which in 1928 was worse than usual. The work in South Pittsburg had drained him. Nashville's frigid January weather broke records. Just ahead lay his thirtieth birthday. Birthdays had always intensified McGill's sense of failure, causing him "to check up and discover what should have been done with the years that are gone and what hasn't been done." Now he was out of shape, stuck professionally, and indulged too often in "communing with a charred keg." A warm celebration did little to break the winter doldrums.[36]

At least in 1928 McGill wrote some political stories after a long hiatus. In April he was in East Tennessee's Happy Valley for the eightieth birthday celebration of Republican Alfred A. Taylor, former congressman and governor. Three thousand people and fifteen hundred autos converged on the isolated area. Ralph offered lyrical descriptions of wild violets and redbud trees blooming on the mountainsides. In fact, Elizabethton, where the Taylor clan resided, was a factory town. Less than a year later workers at one of the rayon manufacturing plants would walk off the job. Under the guns of National Guard troops, workers and managers in Elizabethton plants would contend over wages, working conditions, and union membership.[37]

During the summer the Stahlmans took McGill off the sports desk and sent him on the road for five weeks with Senator Kenneth D. McKellar who sought the Democratic nomination for a third term. The primary campaign reached a climax in Memphis, McKellar's hometown. Throughout West Tennessee the newspapers controlled by Luke Lea's interests claimed that their enemy, Boss Ed Crump, would rig the election in Memphis and all of Shelby County. McGill's final days of political reporting in Tennessee were consumed with a defense of Boss Crump and assurances that their accusations about "the activities of 'the machine' . . . are so much hooey." McGill's dispatches placed McKellar in the political pantheon just below George Washington. The senator won by a landslide, but Ralph went back to reporting baseball.[38]

Summer 1928 he began dating the woman who would later become his wife, Mary Elizabeth Leonard, known to all as "Red." Her family had come from McMinnville to Nashville where her father practiced dentistry. Mary Elizabeth went to Ward-Belmont and Peabody Colleges with hopes of becoming a dietician. Ill health ruined her plans. She had suffered debilitating attacks of kidney disease from age three. Then in her late teens she developed tuberculosis. Her stay in a sanitarium lasted only three months, but she was bedridden for more than two years. She was working in her father's dental office when she met the sports editor.[39]

From the beginning McGill was strongly attracted to Red Leonard. Whether because of periods of invalidism or her temperament, she went at life full tilt. She was a free spirit. No intellectual pretensions weighed her down. Social decorum did not inhibit her. The Leonards were a solid Middle Tennessee family, but as one friend observed, "She didn't give a hoot." She had a keen sense of humor that could be sharp on occasion. No one, including Red herself, expected that she could ever take the place in his life Louise Stevens had held. Even after Ralph became more interested, Mary Elizabeth wondered if he were still in love with Steve.[40]

McGill's interest in his Nashville beat was fading as fast as his attraction to Atlanta sports was growing. For years he arranged a stopover in the Georgia capital whenever possible. He complimented Atlanta sportswriters extravagantly—especially the work and character of Ed Danforth. Now Georgia Tech would play for the national championship in the Rose Bowl against California. Like millions of other Americans of his generation, Ralph longed to experience firsthand the allure of California. His wish came true, as Tech chose McGill and another sportswriter to accompany a trio of Atlanta reporters to the West Coast. On December 20, 1928 the special train pulled away from Atlanta's Terminal Station. The entourage reached Pasadena on Christmas Eve.

The Yellow Jackets did triumph, but everyone remembered a fluke play rather than the victors. The California center, Roy Riegels, recovered a Tech fumble, spun around and ran almost all the way to his own goal line before a teammate pulled him down. Over one hundred thousand souls in the Rose Bowl stadium and millions more listening to their radio sets never forgot how "Wrong Way" Riegels "lost" the game for the Golden Bears. McGill was as proud as he was irate over Riegels's fame: "They always had the prettiest girls, the finest whiskey, and the fastest horses down in Dixie. And now they have the greatest football team and the championship of the nation. . . . The supermen of the effete West turned out to be just a couple of other fellows. . . . "[41]

Ralph's trip grew longer and longer. He had been gone nearly three weeks when the team returned to a heroes' welcome in Atlanta. The Stahlmans gave him permission to remain in the Georgia capital several more days to participate in the victory celebrations. He stepped off a Nashville-bound train late on Saturday, January 12, and went directly to a favorite haunt of *Banner* reporters. He learned that starting Monday morning the paper would have him covering the most sensational murder trial ever conducted in Davidson County.[42]

For the next six weeks McGill sat in the courtroom composing on a special silent typewriter a nearly verbatim account of the proceedings. He thus joined the ranks of reporters who throughout the Twenties titillated millions of Americans with details of murder trials. This killing was not as gruesome as some that mesmerized the masses. Nevertheless, the trial gave McGill a front page byline in southern newspapers for weeks. To him the assignment was an ordeal, but it fed his growing fame. Countless southerners had enjoyed his accounts of the recent California trip and Rose Bowl. Now they learned that he was a virtuoso with "sob stuff" as well as sports.[43]

From mid-January to late February 1929 McGill's noted capacity for prodigious output was pushed to the limit. In addition to producing melodramatic daily reports of the trial, he continued to do "Sport Aerial" columns and for one month reviewed the productions of the Ralph Bellamy players during their Nashville repertory stint. It was harder and harder to unwind or even find time to sleep. Word of a "hung jury" and mistrial came during a record snowfall that paralyzed Nashville. April 15 would launch a retrial. His mood darkened.[44]

In the meantime, Ed Danforth called late one March evening to say that he was moving from the *Atlanta Georgian* to the *Atlanta Constitution* and wanted McGill on the sports desk with him. He knew that his friend likely would accept the job offer. In fact, Ralph hung up without inquiring about salary and had to ring Ed back immediately. Danforth, an Atlanta newsman since 1916, was only a half dozen years older than McGill but recently had become his mentor and sometimes father confessor. On several occasions Ed and his wife, Betty, had provided a bed and solace when Ralph needed to get away from Nashville. In the Danforth's tiny apartment he poured out his frustrations with the Stahlmans' refusal to move him from sports into straight reporting.[45]

The Danforths were aware that McGill's romantic dilemmas might ease in a new location. "I don't trust my resolutions at all when I'm around you," he wrote Steve, "I don't know where you got all that power over one man, but you have." Ed and Betty liked Steve but understood why Ralph felt that the romance was doomed. They now watched his growing involvement with the feisty Miss Leonard. Like everyone, including Red herself, the Danforths puzzled over his attraction to two such different women.

The personality of his new sweetheart buoyed his spirits especially when sadness overtook him. Ed's sister died in early August 1928 and was to be buried in Hopkinsville, Kentucky. Accompanied by Mary Elizabeth, Ralph joined the funeral party aboard a train in Nashville. Betty Danforth soon noticed that she was wearing one blue shoe and one brown shoe. Red flippantly tossed aside a faux pas that would have mortified many females as wellbred as she was. McGill relished her saucy attitude.[46]

Nashville readers opened their newspapers on Sunday morning, March 31, to discover that "good old Mac" was leaving. For his leave-taking Ralph composed a farewell version of the "Sport Aerial". The gigantic column paid tribute to the Stahlmans and *Banner* reporters. McGill's tendencies towards sentimentality and loyalty were never more obvious. He was able to be so gracious because he was leaving. His memorable moments from eight years included Vanderbilt football games, the police beat and performances of artists whose concerts or plays he had reviewed. He recalled sensational disasters he had covered from Floyd Collins to the recent murder trial. Not a single word appeared about Tennessee politics or the three assignments that took him briefly on the campaign trail. Publicity that made him out to be largely a political commentator and reporter for the *Banner* came years later.

The *Constitution*'s welcoming story conveyed all that McGill brought to his new job. Reprints of his stories had made him "home folks" to Atlanta readers even before the recent Rose Bowl and murder trial series. Other reporters in the Georgia capital were well acquainted with the caliber of his work. The preceding August O. B. Keeler gave an apt appraisal in the *Atlanta Journal*: "He invariably sets down exquisite English, which is something most of our latter day sports scribes cannot be bothered with. . . . his views are at once firm and temperate." The owners of the *Constitution* knew it was a coup to gain a newspaperman of his talent and potential.[47]

He was also a person eager for a fresh start. Danforth understood the mixture of attraction and revulsion behind the precipitous decision to relocate. McGill left no doubt of his feelings about Nashville in a long letter to Steve. "I love the place," he wrote, "but it was doing things to me, tearing at me and submerging me because it was insidiously easy for me. It was binding me in little debts and false security so that I wonder I had the courage to leave." He arrived at Atlanta's old Union Station carrying two suitcases. As always, one was full of books. Emotional baggage not visible to passersby on Forsyth Street that morning would weigh him down for many more years.[48]

4

ATLANTA AND HARD TIMES: 1929-1936

McGILL AND DANFORTH JOINED THE SHOP OF CLARK HOWELL SR., the *Constitution*'s owner and publisher. The *Georgian*, which Danforth had left, was an afternoon paper owned since 1912 by William Randolph Hearst. Hearst added an edge to the longstanding (and sometimes bitter) local competition between Howell and the James A. Gray family, owners of the *Atlanta Journal*. The fact that McGill and Howell were fellow Welshmen augured well for the sportswriter's ambition. Despite McGill's becoming a Democrat and cultivating regional scholars, still Howell never saw him as a serious journalist.

Howell was born into a chaotic world in September 1863 when his mother was fleeing Yankee armies. His family spearheaded Atlanta's recovery after the Civil War and were enthusiastic adherents of the New South creed. He graduated from the University of Georgia in 1883. He began long tutelage first on Northern papers then with his father's *Constitution* under the legendary Henry Grady. When Grady died prematurely in 1889 at age thirty-nine, Howell replaced him as managing editor. Upon his father's retirement in 1897, Clark became editor-in-chief. Four years later he bought controlling interest in the paper.[1]

McGill's professional destiny was in the hands of the Howells—Clark Sr. and Jr. from 1929 to 1950. They used the *Constitution* very differently than the way the Stahlmans utilized the *Banner*. The Stahlmans functioned as part of an old-fashioned machine that featured bosses and gutter politics. By contrast, Atlanta was developing a new political mode when McGill arrived. Throughout his life there partnerships between top white businessmen and black leaders kept on track the city's ambitious schemes

for becoming first the capital of the South and then a national city.
Sometimes the coalitions were stable; often they were ad hoc and
uneasy. Clark Howell intended that his newspaper try to keep
corruption or political infighting from disrupting the "Forward
Atlanta" ethos.[2]

By 1929 "Papa" Howell—as he was known around the
Constitution's old red brick building at Forsyth and Alabama
Streets—was a national figure in Democratic politics as well as
journalism. He organized and was a director of the Associated
Press. Howell entered the Georgia House while in his early
twenties. During one term he was its speaker. At the turn of the
century he served in the state senate for several years, becoming its
president for a time. In 1896 Howell began record-breaking tenure
as a member of the Democratic National Committee.

Howell assumed Grady's pattern of promoting sectional
progress and national reconciliation in speeches throughout the
country—a practice that McGill later emulated. At the Chicago
Peace Jubilee in 1898 he shared the platform with President
William McKinley. In 1895 he arranged for Booker T. Washington to speak at the Atlanta Cotton States and International
Exposition. The black leader's address became a national paradigm
of race relations for a generation. Known as the "Atlanta Compromise," the speech emphasized that blacks would accommodate
their lives to segregation. White allies would foster any remaining
legal rights and oversee gradual economic progress.

The thorny issue of race foiled Howell's ambition to become
Georgia's governor in 1906. His run for this office coincided with
the regional campaign to eliminate African Americans from civic
life, jobs and to control their private existence with strict caste
laws. Despite the *Constitution*'s coverage and his record of public
service, Clark Howell and three other candidates lost to Hoke
Smith, whose campaign focused on race. Howell and Smith had
previously been rivals when Smith owned the *Atlanta Journal* before
the turn of the century. After 1906 Howell worked as a party
power broker rather than office holder. At the very time he hired
McGill, Howell was maneuvering New York Governor Franklin D.

Roosevelt ahead of Al Smith, the disastrous 1928 standard bearer.[3]

Howell knew Ralph wanted to cover politics but was more concerned with upgrading the *Constitution*'s sports coverage. Staffers noted that their rotund new colleague was at work within an hour of arriving. He could use the Danforths' Murphy bed temporarily and thus postpone looking for a room. So he took his first assignment from Ed—an Atlanta Crackers game with Toronto. The baseball park was a favorite congregating spot for Atlantans. Covering the Crackers, McGill would get to know many of the white politicians and businessmen who promoted his new hometown. He especially enjoyed Mayor James L. Key and future police chief Herbert Jenkins, Key's bodyguard.[4]

Atlanta's booster spirit went far beyond anything McGill had known before. For reasons all their own, Atlantans believed their city was unique in the region. They bragged that Atlanta was different from "the usual, typical southern town," which amused transplants like journalist Don Marquis of the *Atlanta Journal*. "Being from the North," he joked, "the thing that struck me was the likeness. . . ." The dark side of the region did touch the city. In 1906 a dozen died in race riots. Leo Frank, a Jewish businessman accused of murder, was lynched in 1915. Even so, Atlanta's habitual self-promotion appealed to McGill. He quickly joined the effort and began supplementing his salary with public relations work.[5]

The physical contrast between Nashville and Atlanta reinforced McGill's sense of a fresh start. Atlanta was not only bigger but had a different character. The upcoming census would count 270,366 souls there versus 153,866 in Nashville. The Georgia capital's downtown contrasted to the riverfront streets he had walked for a dozen years. When McGill arrived, Atlanta was working to reconcile railroad traffic, the city's economic foundation, with automobiles that would determine the future. The solution was to elevate downtown streets over the old "railroad gulch" with a series of huge viaducts. He discovered that Atlanta also meant to beat Birmingham as the hub of air travel in the South. Inaugural flights in and out of the new terminal often included McGill who urged his readers to become passengers.[6]

One of his fondest hopes that first spring in Atlanta was to recoup his personal finances. McGill was hopeless at managing money—a behavior pattern that disturbed him. He confided to Steve, "Rather pathetic and condemnatory commentary on my passing from Nashville was that I left in debt after working there that long and with nothing to show for it." He had tried a budget before but now resolved to try harder. He reported to her that he had "saved $110 in two weeks." If his romance with Mary Elizabeth Leonard did result in marriage, Ralph wanted to start with a nestegg rather than debts.[7]

Dr. and Mrs. Leonard doted on their only daughter who had spent all her twenty-four years in the shadow of serious health problems. The young woman handled these with verve. When Red was not sick, she was unstoppable. Ralph would have both to provide for Mary Elizabeth and to keep up with her. In 1929 he was unaware of both the extent and the implications of her health problems. He was starting over in a new city and eager to have such a lively wife. Nor could Red Leonard foresee the hardships of marriage to a journalist with a terrible case of wanderlust. She ohly thought about making him happy.[8]

They decided to be married on the Vanderbilt campus during Labor Day weekend. Ben, Mary Lou, and three daughters came from Chattanooga. The family was surprised that Mary Elizabeth had brought Ralph's long bachelorhood to an end but glad to see him settle down. The contrast between Ralph and his lean, quiet father at the same age was striking. At thirty-one Ben McGill had been married for three years and fathered three boys of whom only Ralph survived. When farm duties permitted, he was earning a little money in the Soddy coal mines. Ralph had attended the best of schools and then enjoyed the Roaring Twenties with no family burdens and relatively little work pressure. All that was about to change however.[9]

After the wedding the newlyweds boarded a train for Atlanta and their comfortable apartment just off Ponce de Leon. Its location was convenient to Ralph's trolley downtown and also for

Julia James, a sixteen year old black high school student he hired before the wedding. Atlanta's legal efforts to segregate neighborhoods failed, but mores were enough. So Julia joined an army on long daily streetcar trips from black West End neighborhoods to Five Points downtown then northeast and northwest to jobs as menials in white homes.

For four decades Julia James Crawford was the McGills' cook, companion, and mainstay. In 1929 Ralph already excelled at cooking, but Julia had yet to learn. Neither forgot the first time he asked her to fix breakfast. After he discarded the mess and showed her how to prepare eggs properly, Julia knew she had an unusual employer. "He was always with me when I had trouble," she stated. "I will never forget when I was in the hospital. He stayed in the operating room with me and when I overcame the anesthetic and looked up he was there."[10]

As football season approached, Danforth made the most of McGill's experience as player and sportswriter while Ralph scouted Georgia Tech and Georgia. His friendship with Tech Coach Bill Alexander was already strong and destined to grow. He predicted that 1929 would be a great year for the Yellow Jackets' coach. He had much to learn about Harry Mehre, once an All-American center for Coach Knute Rockne at Notre Dame and Georgia's head coach since 1928. On October 12, 1929, the university was to dedicate its new Sanford Stadium at Athens. Yale would be the Bulldogs' opponent that day—the first Ivy League team to visit the state. McGill chronicled the mounting excitement and began a lasting association with the witty Mehre.[11]

His account of the "frenzied throng" of 35,000 cheering the Bulldogs to the first southern victory over the Ivy Leaguers dominated the *Constitution*'s front page on October 13. Then economic catastrophe recaptured the headlines. On McGill's wedding day the stock market broke sharply. Wall Street seemed to recover. Then in October stock selling almost defied description as the long bull market collapsed. President Hoover and a chorus of leaders assured Americans that the country was prosperous despite the panic. Coach Mehre's Bulldogs continued to win, but readers could not enjoy McGill's witty pieces for wondering what economic disaster would come next.[12]

Meanwhile the enduring pattern of the McGills' married life emerged. Ralph traveled constantly. Mary Elizabeth and Julia kept things humming at home. In early 1930 he made the first of many trips to Dover Hall, a hunting lodge near Georgia's Sea Islands. He wrote vivid accounts of visiting sportsmen, particularly Wilbert Robinson who managed the Brooklyn Dodgers from 1914 to 1931. More intriguing were the African Americans living in the coastal area. Older ones gave McGill firsthand accounts of slavery and a South altogether different from East Tennessee.[13]

Younger blacks revealed how vulnerable they were. In 1930 McGill's readers met Angus, "a colored boy who went along to lug the game bag" on a bird hunt. Angus was recently released from the chain gang. He had found an item worth only the price of a movie ticket but was accused of stealing and sentenced to eight months hard labor. Some details explained why Angus vowed, "I ain't going back on dat gang again." McGill's Angus had a comic side and dialect that Joel Chandler Harris, a *Constitution* legend and creator of Uncle Remus, would have envied. However, the piece had a serious point.[14]

Not every young black man finding himself in trouble with "de Man" was as lucky as Angus. Local lynchings were increasing. During this period the *Constitution* gave such crimes the condemnation they deserved. That summer seven white men were tried in Atlanta for lynching a Morehouse College student, Dennis Hubert. He was mistakenly accused of flirting with a white woman. In the aftermath of Hubert's death, a mob burned down the home of his father, a respected Baptist minister. White citizens of all religious callings united in a plea for restitution.[15]

McGill was acquainted with several members of the Atlanta based Commission on Interracial Cooperation (CIC) that now stepped up its exposure of lynchings. The sincerity and good intentions of CIC members were no match for racial prejudice and violence. Nonetheless, they created a commission to recommend ways to prevent these murders. Arthur Raper, a CIC staff member, and Morehouse College professor Walter Chivers conducted the study. McGill knew Raper from his days as a Vanderbilt graduate student in the mid 1920s. Both were friendly with (and McGill a former roommate of) another Vanderbilt academic, John Donald Wade, who came home to Georgia at this time.[16]

While in Nashville, McGill had scorned individuals who worked for the CIC but sensed that the sports ballyhoo that had provided his professional identity for a decade was waning. He believed that newspapers would tell more and more about the South's problems—now compounded by deepening depression. Somehow he must be part of the effort. Yet his assignments were more limited than they had been in Nashville.[17]

Despite McGill's discontent, Atlanta sportswriters in 1930 were the envy of their fraternity. The phenomenon of Bobby Jones brought an outpouring of ballyhoo. After Jones won both the British Amateur and British Open championships in June, he received a hero's welcome in New York City. His triumphal return continued at the U.S. Open where he claimed a third title. Atlantans planned a welcome home to match the New York reception. The celebration on July 14 surpassed any in the city's history. Abandoning prolixity, Ralph wrote, "It is time, I think, to forget adjectives. The name is enough." Jones then won the U.S. Amateur tournament. With an unprecedented "Grand Slam" of golf championships, the twenty-eight year old attorney retired. For McGill and countless others, Jones remained the quintessential sportsman of their generation.[18]

Celebrating for Jones was brief because it was harder and harder to ignore bad times in Atlanta. Throughout the Twenties the city had an influx of poor people fleeing rural troubles. Pressures on city services and social agencies mounted. McGill knew the 1929 crash made everything worse, especially for blacks. The issue of black employment became inflammatory. In 1930 a white supremacy group calling themselves, "American Fascisti," decided to force every black employee out of work as long as whites were unemployed. In Nashville McGill had periodically written funny pieces about Mussolini's fascists, but the *Constitution* treated their violence as seriously as lynchings.[19]

After nearly two years at the *Constitution,* Ralph finally wrangled his first story outside sports. In February 1931 he covered a debate between his former Vanderbilt professor, John Crowe Ransom, and Georgia textile executive, William D. Anderson. In a recent manifesto titled *I'll Take My Stand,* Ransom and other "Agrarians" had attacked an industrial, urban New South. Their essays varied but favored a subsistence economy practiced within a highly traditional culture. McGill knew several of the contributors, including John Donald Wade, quite well. The book intrigued him.[20]

Emory was the third forum where Ransom pleaded the cause of agrarianism. McGill's long astute article showed how each debater refused to take the larger view. Ransom wanted southerners to return to a lifestyle without money or radios whose tantalizing commercials made them into consumers. McGill reported that Ransom wanted people "to actually touch stone, earth, and wood and to know the infinite variety of nature." Anderson contended that the aesthetic sense Ransom imagined was not possible for a tenant on a hardscrabble farm. Also agriculture would never produce the money to pay for needed schools, hospitals, social services. Neither speaker mentioned race relations.[21]

McGill received no followup assignments to the Agrarian debate but kept in contact with Cullen Gosnell whose Institute of Citizenship at Emory sponsored the program. The publicity about the Agrarians strengthened McGill's hunch that this growing regional self-consciousness would be a big story during the Thirties. His literary hopes had ended a decade earlier as the Fugitives (some now Agrarians) gained national recognition, but through Gosnell and colleagues McGill resumed an educational process interrupted when he went on the sports beat. These professors were tutors as he struggled to learn about economics, political science, and history.[22]

McGill was fortunate that his contacts were not limited to business boosters but included professional students of regional development at Emory University, also Atlanta University and the

Commission on Interracial Cooperation. With his reporter's penchant for picking brains, he grasped an emerging alternative that gave the lie to the Agrarians' retrogressive vision yet was fairer, more comprehensive than what many businessmen wanted. McGill asked these regionalists what they thought of *I'll Take My Stand*. His friend, Arthur Raper, gave the Agrarians short shrift. In Raper's judgment, they were "talking about something that didn't exist."

Raper offered McGill a different perspective on regional problems like lynching and sharecropping. He was a valuable source of information as the sportswriter worked to fill the gaps in his education. Raper published the findings of the CIC's lynching study at this time. The massive book, entitled *The Tragedy of Lynching*, argued that the crime was rooted in economic competition between poor persons of both races rather than the customary explanations. Raper supported federal laws against lynching, but the CIC never did. In the end his book "changed nothing."[23]

McGill held long conversations with another member of the CIC's lynching commission, Julian L. Harris. He was the son of Joel Chandler Harris and a colleague at the *Constitution* from 1930 to 1935. This crusading journalist won a 1926 Pulitzer Prize for attacking the Klan in his own Columbus, Georgia, newspaper. Much as Harris hated lynching, he doubted that national legislation would be any more effective here than Prohibition laws had been. Southerners cited the failure of Prohibition time and again to buttress their opposition to federal action against a problem they considered local. Later as an editorial writer, McGill reacted like Harris rather than Raper.[24]

When the *Constitution* won a 1931 Pulitzer Prize for exposing municipal corruption, McGill was off repairing his own finances with a free lance writing project. He spent five weeks in Young Stribling's Ohio training camp before the fight with world heavyweight champion, Max Schmeling. Convinced that the Georgia boxer would win, McGill was writing Stribling's biography for a fat commission. The only Atlanta journalist on the scene, Ralph also wired the *Constitution* long, fascinating accounts and anticipated his windfall.[25]

As usual on trips, McGill enjoyed himself to the utmost. Stribling's father described why he liked the sportswriter: "He bounces out early in the morning, goes for a swim in the lake, eats enough for six men at the table three times a day, helps the office force in getting out mimeographs, writes special dispatches when the publicity staff is snowed under ... tells stories for the great delight of other newspapermen." All this energy and high spirits evaporated at ringside, however. Schmeling won on a technical knockout. The biography was canceled, and—according to a fellow journalist—McGill turned into the "'saddest and maddest fat man you-all eva did see.'"[26]

Ed Danforth moved back to Hearst's *Georgian* in mid-July, and Papa Howell promoted McGill to sports editor. He began a daily personal column that he called, "Break Of Day." For the next seven years he delighted readers with writings that were witty, fast-paced and drew upon his encyclopedic knowledge of American sports. Even more appealing than the column's masterful style were his shrewd observations of human nature. At age thirty-three McGill still aspired to write political commentary and economic analysis. Meanwhile he oversaw expanding sports coverage at the *Constitution* and enlarged his personal following. It was not the job he wanted, but he made the most of it.[27]

In 1932 McGill witnessed Atlanta's African-American political power in action. Without black support his friend, Mayor James L. Key, would have lost office in a recall vote. Visiting Paris, the mayor told a reporter what few southern politicians were willing to say publicly—that Prohibition was a failure. Key was an officer and Sunday School teacher in a large Atlanta Methodist church. Shock waves rattled the congregation bound to abstinence and reverberated throughout his hometown.

Not content with starting one brouhaha, the mayor proposed weakening Blue laws to allow Sunday movies and baseball games. The proceeds would go to the city's depleted relief funds. There was no denying that Atlanta needed drastic measures to help the growing numbers of hungry, homeless citizens. But Mayor Key's suggestion challenged the prevailing mores of an overgrown Bible Belt town.

McGill thought both the mayor's controversial stands were correct and said so in the *Constitution*. Years before in Nashville he had written contemptuously of Sunday Blue laws. He always opposed Prohibition. Now the need to find new sources of relief moneys strengthened his conviction. Ralph used sarcasm to abet the mayor's case. "Civilization goes on in Tennessee," he wrote, "despite the playing of Sunday baseball. It takes the boys out of the backrooms and puts them in the bleachers."[28]

McGill rarely mentioned black athletic events in the *Constitution*'s sports pages but now he understood blacks' role in local politics from his friends at city hall. Negro residents were barred from participating in the all-white, predominating Democratic primary but could vote in city bond referenda, special elections, or canvasses such as the recall demanded by Key's enemies. The mayor's earlier work to provide schools and some services for the black community saved his career.[29]

In the midst of a giant 1934 publicity stunt, McGill described a different aspect of Georgia's racial dilemmas. A 516 car cavalcade from Atlanta to Savannah celebrated new highways and honored the state's capitals. Sitting with his typewriter on his knees in the back of car number 21, McGill watched Negroes in cotton fields. By now he knew that "the coming of good roads and machines and a new manner of thinking and living" would destroy the old cotton culture and profoundly affect black Georgians. What, he asked readers, would become of them?[30]

Family pressures distracted his effort to understand this change. As in any strong, durable marriage he and Mary Elizabeth had to put up with each other's foibles and frailties. After three years of marriage he knew the negative side of the quality he most admired—her honesty. Red spoke her mind even in situations that did not call for it. If Ralph was the object of her commentary, he just said, "Aw, shut up, Mary Elizabeth." Not every individual she upbraided was as tolerant of her unruly tongue as her husband, however. Some thought she was a loudmouth whose outspokenness could interfere with Ralph's ambitions.

Yet the more fairminded in the McGill circle knew that Mary Elizabeth's loyal and generous nature made her a rarity. They also came to understand that Red's indomitable attitude was her way of coping with a lifetime of serious illnesses. Even Ralph had not grasped how precarious Mary Elizabeth's health was until after they were married. Despite recurring attacks of kidney stones, she threw herself into the process of getting established in Atlanta. Both wanted children. She never became pregnant. Lacking children of her own, Mary Elizabeth cooked for sick friends and befriended newcomers. She tried to help anyone she found in trouble. Also, since Ralph refused to take the wheel of a car, she became his chauffeur. For four decades readers knew her as "the lady who drives me."[31]

Mary Elizabeth gave Ralph—the erstwhile bachelor—plenty of leeway. She accepted his long, drawn-out trips for the paper. She tolerated a drinking binge when cronies from his single life came to town. For decades his use of alcohol followed a similar pattern of long periods of sobriety punctuated by an episode of heavy drinking. These often occurred far from home because he never drank while at work. Thus, some swore that McGill never drank while others insisted he had a problem.

Everyone from his wife to total strangers was flabbergasted at how strong drink changed Ralph's personality. Legends grew up around his drunken pranks and the struggles to get him home and into bed. Sometimes he blacked out before friends succeeded. The remarkable thing about McGill's drinking during these years was not quantity but his wallowing in guilt afterwards. Some decided he drank just to suffer afterwards.[32]

Professional frustrations throughout the Thirties were a factor in these episodes, as were the financial problems that dogged him. His hopes for changing from a debtor to a saver vanished with marriage and onset of the depression. After three paycuts in short order, the McGills were often left with little or no cash. Papa Howell reduced costs at the *Constitution* in every possible way. Yet the moribund state of the paper's payroll was due to more than the depression. Howell was in financial trouble even before hard times hit the country. Now the paper sometimes paid employees with grocery orders from stores that advertised but could not pay for their ads. Even so, the McGills knew how fortunate they were. Growing numbers of unemployed Atlantans were just going hungry or lining up daily at the municipal auditorium to receive a handout of soup and bread.[33]

Clark Howell believed America's hopes for recovery lay in electing Franklin D. Roosevelt to the presidency in 1932 and used all his power and influence to promote the candidacy of the New York governor, a frequent resident of Warm Springs, Georgia. So the Howells set off a mammoth celebration in Atlanta when Roosevelt swept the election on November 8. For the first time in forty years the *Constitution* staff rolled Henry Grady's miniature brass cannon onto the street and fired a salvo that set off railroad and factory whistles all over town.[34]

Two weeks later the president-elect arrived at Warm Springs to rest and make plans for his administration. Roosevelt broke the national mood of paralysis at his inauguration declaring, "that the only thing we have to fear is fear itself." His New Deal created unprecedented activity in Washington. Eventually it affected every household in the land. As one of FDR's earliest and most enthusiastic partisans, Clark Howell and his staff publicized every detail about the "Squire of Warm Springs."

McGill became part of the coverage in June 1933 with a huge Sunday feature on Roosevelt's farm in Meriwether County near Warm Springs. Attacking the longstanding crisis in American agriculture, particularly in the South, was a top priority of Roosevelt. The Agricultural Adjustment Act aimed to help farmers by setting parity prices for many crops, reducing production and giving subsidies. McGill wrote that after eight years running his 2,000 acre Georgia farm, Roosevelt would succeed at agricultural reform. The assignment thrilled McGill but showed he was unable to analyze farm problems.[35]

He finally got to meet the President in late 1934. En route to Columbus for the Auburn-Georgia game, the car's rear axle broke at Warm Springs. The visiting chief executive just happened to be talking with reporters. Afterwards McGill shook his hand and wrote: "When we ... see the warmth and humanity of this man, we can understand again that every crisis produces a great man to solve it. This one has produced Franklin D. Roosevelt." At age thirty-six McGill set aside his East Tennessee Republican heritage and fixation with Lincoln. He probably would have supported the New Deal to curry favor with Howell, but the fabled Roosevelt charm completed his conversion. Democrat Mary Lou McGill exulted to the family, "Ralph's come over to my side now."[36]

Chances to report on politics still eluded McGill, so in 1933 he used an opportunity to visit Cuba and become a "foreign correspondent." The North American Newspaper Alliance syndicated his series on a Cuban revolution. The new American ambassador, Sumner Welles, and Cubans revolting against dictator Gerardo Machado were his chief sources. Cuba was a U.S. protectorate, but Roosevelt wished to stay out as part of his "Good Neighbor" policy. Welles later came under attack from some Cuban factions, prompting McGill to mail a fiery defense to President Roosevelt. Welles was gratified, and McGill learned about cultivating government sources.[37]

The experience and a return visit in 1935 taught him about the economic forces fomenting revolution. Most of Cuba's income came from the sale of sugar that fell in 1930 with high U.S. tariffs. U.S. protectionism plus a brutal, corrupt regime were, he saw, behind the revolution in Cuba. He now understood how collapse of international markets and higher prices for manufactured items had ruined southern agriculture. To his chagrin, most readers still thought he was just a sportswriter. Decades later he remembered the sting when an irate fan complimented him on a football story then added, "But what in the hell do you think you know about tariffs on cotton?"

Such reaction was understandable. After more than a dozen years, McGill had a unique reputation in the South. He wrote better copy than most working in straight news. Operators of the wire at football games knew that while most writers marked all over their work, McGill would give them clean copy. He sat down and produced "a tremendous flow of words" that was easy to send. Reading his work was as satisfying as watching one of the era's champion athletes. Papa Howell's circulation race with the afternoon *Journal* and *Georgian* was too close to lose that.[38]

Clark Howell Jr., newly promoted from business manager to vice-president and general manager of the *Constitution*, worried constantly about finances. Around Atlanta Clark Jr. was known as "the Major" because of distinguished service in World War I. He had entered the Army from Harvard Law School and anticipated joining an Atlanta law firm after service. However, the First National Bank insisted that he begin managing the paper or they would not renew Papa Howell's loans. Swayed by family loyalty, the Major assumed responsibilities on the *Constitution*'s business side while his father continued to mix journalism and politics.[39]

Papa Howell was especially concerned with mediating between FDR and Georgia's fractious governor, Eugene Talmadge. The governor began resisting federal programs and grew determined to keep New Dealers out of Georgia. By the time Talmadge won a second term in 1934, his explosive style had fragmented Georgia's Democratic establishment and rattled windows as far away as Washington. In early 1935 Talmadge publicly vilified the president. Georgia, Roosevelt's favorite locale outside Hyde Park, stood to benefit enormously from federal largesse provided Talmadge could be stopped.

Sometimes the U.S. government federalized Georgia relief efforts but could not always avoid direct confrontations. In July Papa Howell—who now had a federal appointment and Washington office—arranged a meeting at the White House between Talmadge, the president, and other officials. At stake was $9 million in highway funds. Howell's efforts as honest broker backfired. Afterwards Talmadge blew up before reporters, calling FDR "a damned communist" and screaming at the distraught Howell. In a followup letter the editor warned White House staffers that Talmadge intended to run for president in 1936.[40]

By then McGill was preoccupied with personal troubles and

sorrows. His father's health began to fail in 1934. Ralph's travel schedule was hectic, but he often detoured through Chattanooga. He felt guilty at not providing his parents some financial support but was always in debt himself. Coca-Cola president Robert W. Woodruff became a friend and source of income, using him as a free lance writer for the company magazine.[41]

In the spring of 1935 Mary Elizabeth decided to begin making her own contribution to their budget. She became one of Rich's "personal shoppers" for distant customers. The job suited her. She combed Rich's to fill orders from across Georgia. Her high spirits were also due to a pregnancy that promised after long years to complete their family. She was so sure of carrying the baby full term that she began calling Ralph, "Pappy." Her frequent back-aches were, she declared, to be expected when a thirty year old pregnant lady traipsed around all day in high heels.[42]

By December 1935, however, the expectant parents knew the pains meant serious illness. Mary Elizabeth's lifelong kidney disease, now complicated by toxemia in pregnancy, threatened both mother and child. The doctors hospitalized her, hoping to control matters until Red could safely deliver the baby. New Year's 1936 brought vile winter weather to Atlanta and heartbreak for the McGills. Ralph rushed home from the Sugar Bowl to face the dreaded medical crisis. On January 6 doctors delivered a baby girl prematurely. For a couple of days Ralph watched tiny Elizabeth's vain struggle for life. On January 10 he carried her casket to a simple graveside service in Westview Cemetery.[43]

Surrounded by kinfolks and friends who loved them, Ralph and Mary Elizabeth struggled with their loss. Elizabeth's death was all the more devastating since they knew that another pregnancy might end Red's life. Ralph immediately returned to work, writing huge nostalgic columns about happy times back in Tennessee. Mary Elizabeth had to regain her health as well as deal with barrenness of both body and spirit. Adopting a baby was a possibility they agreed upon—provided the baby was born when they had expected little Elizabeth to arrive. They filed papers with an agency and left Atlanta for much needed rest and a change of scene.

Their destination was Springwood, the Thomasville, Georgia, plantation of Thomas Caldecott Chubb. McGill met Chubb and introduced him to readers in early 1933 while reporting from the Southern Amateur Field Trials in Albany. A lifelong dog lover, McGill never missed this competition that included the hunting dogs of prominent Atlantans like Bob Woodruff and Mrs. Walter Rich. Now Chubb offered them the hospitality and peace of Springwood. For ten days the grieving couple rested.[44]

Then a call from the office threw Ralph into turmoil. Coach Dan McGugin had dropped dead at a friend's house, and the sports desk wanted a statement. McGill broke down. All he could say was that next to his father, McGugin was the finest man he had ever known. McGugin believed in Ralph as strongly as anyone outside the family. He helped launch the fresh start in Atlanta. Now Ralph wired the paper a eulogy raw with pain and bitterness. He blamed "selfish, inconsiderate alumni of Vanderbilt" obsessed with winning for hounding McGugin to an early grave. Coming so soon after his child's death, the death of his good friend was a terrible blow.[45]

Back in Atlanta the McGills learned that the adoption agency definitely had a baby in mind for them. Ralph's elation was clouded by a realization that Mary Elizabeth was not getting well. Instead of vitality to care for the coming baby, by spring she had debilitating pain, fever, and more kidney stones. In the hospital her temperature soared to 105 for almost a week. The despairing doctors finally decided to operate. Ralph wrote Tom Chubb: "They found a terrible abscess and removed half the kidney and the stones which had caused that half to abscess to such an extent that it practically was destroyed anyway. How the poor kid has gone along I don't know." Forty-eight hours after surgery, Mary Elizabeth contracted pneumonia. For the second time in four months, Ralph began a deathbed vigil. Red survived, and her weary, relieved husband contemplated huge new medical bills. He had just been paid $500 for a Coca-Cola article, but, he confided to Chubb, "I'll have to be selling something else."[46]

Ralph understood that his wife faced a long and difficult convalescence but decided to go ahead with the adoption. Even before Mary Elizabeth was discharged from the hospital in May 1936 he brought home their baby daughter. Julia cared for the newest member of the household until "Miss Red" was better. They named the child Virginia Colvin after Mary Elizabeth's doctor. The family often called her "Ginger" but to her adoring father she was "Miss Virginia." No individual before or afterwards had quite the hold on his heart that Virginia McGill effected in their scant three years together. The tone of his writing changed as soon as he adopted the baby. Lilting prose signaled that once more he found life worth living.[47]

Even more good news awaited his return to the *Constitution* after cruising the Atlantic with Georgia Tech's naval ROTC. Papa Howell granted McGill his first real political assignment in over seven years. Gene Talmadge gave up his notion of opposing President Roosevelt in 1936. On July 4 he announced his intention to replace Richard B. Russell in the U.S. Senate. Russell could not have been more different from the spellbinding politician known as "the wild man from Sugar Creek." Talmadge's biographer contrasted them: "Gene [who] stirred men's souls and left them howling like dogs.... Neat, clean cut, respectable Dick—the kind of man you might think Gene would eat alive."[48]

The Howell family intended to utilize the *Constitution* fully against Talmadge. The once friendly relationship between Talmadge and Papa Howell continued to deteriorate. While McGill was at sea, the Democrats met to renominate FDR. At the Philadelphia convention Howell regained a place on the Democratic National committee from the apostate Talmadge and resumed mending fences. Stories that he had made a "deal" with Gene for the seat infuriated Howell. "It is preposterous," he exclaimed, "to anyone who knows me that I would ever enter into any trade with Talmadge whose principles I unalterably oppose." In the final weeks before the September primary, Russell was running scared. Howell ordered McGill to cover several of the senator's appearances and bolster his campaign against Gene.[49]

That summer McGill worked feverishly on the campaign trail. He would turn thirty-nine next winter with ambitions that had welled up in him since McCallie unfulfilled. For months he had been on an emotional roller coaster and hardpressed by debt. When Papa Howell gave him a break, he compressed all these frustrations into verbal ammunition. Talmadge came into his sight, and McGill fired again and again. His versions of these rallies began by praising Russell and ended in damnations of Talmadge.

Even the rabidly partisan Major Stahlman would have quailed at printing such stories in his *Banner*. Senator Russell, according to Ralph, was Georgia's favorite son "who has kept the faith and never betrayed his state, his party, or his friends." Audiences "know him to be telling the whole truth and not half truths." Talmadge, on the other hand, was "a traitor and a deserter and one who would wreck his own party and his own state to satisfy his own insolent ambition."[50]

McGill worked in enough particulars for the governor and his cronies to go after him. According to one account, Talmadge's closest friend, John Whitley, twice beat up the sportswriter. On the second occasion Whitley supposedly stood over the bleeding reporter and vowed, "'McGill, the next time I see you I'm gone have a pistol, and I'm gone kill the hell outta you.'" Threats or even sensing danger always excited McGill. In this instance the newspaperman proved what a powerful weapon his typewriter could be. His interpretation of the governor's record and rhetoric darkened the Talmadge pyrotechnics and deflated the demagogue himself.[51]

The 1936 primary campaign launched a decade of strange chemistry between the politician and newsman. Papa Howell, who had a scant ninety days left of life and work, allowed the enmity to grow. The *Macon Telegraph* answered McGill's coverage with an editorial, "Crooked Newspaper Work." Talmadge then circulated the Macon editorial widely as a campaign ad. Howell let Ralph compose a scorching rebuttal that ran on the *Constitution*'s editorial page. In the end the voters dealt Gene the worst defeat of his career. His popular vote was 134,695 to Russell's 256,154. The governor won only sixteen of Georgia's 159 counties. Talmadge never forgot who was to blame for his "whuppin'" and vowed to return the favor one day.[52]

Although McGill and Talmadge were the strongest of opponents, the two nonetheless showed admiration for one another on occasion. This confounded McGill's associates. Maybe the old fashioned sportsman was just saluting a worthy foe. More likely McGill was remembering and regretting the excesses of 1936 when Talmadge was not the only loser. He was sports editor for two more long years.

While McGill was dynamiting Talmadge's campaign, another kind of explosion knocked Atlanta sky high, transforming the lives of his good friends, John and Peggy Marsh. Peggy became an instant celebrity that summer as Margaret Mitchell, author of the newly published *Gone With the Wind*. Ralph and Red McGill's house on Fifth Street was only a few blocks from the Marshes' Crescent Street apartment fondly known as "the Dump." Peggy and Mary Elizabeth were close. Both couples were part of the circle—mostly newspaper folks—that gathered regularly for convivial conversation and corn liquor. Ralph's well deserved reputation as a raconteur was no match for Peggy's. Her chatter and high spirits were legendary in Atlanta.[53]

Spurred by ambition and the need to pay on his debts, Ralph wrote about Peggy's turbulent notoriety. A quarter century later he offered in print observations he dared not make in 1936: "Candor compels one to say that the most loyal friend would not have believed that even by rubbing an Aladdin's lamp could she have written the book." The Sunday *New York Times* ran his long profile on October 4, 1936 with no byline. Disappointed, McGill could not imagine how the global *GWTW* phenomenon would later help his career. In the late 1950s he gained fame and national syndication partly because of his Atlanta dateline and the book he doubted Peggy wrote.[54]

On November 14, 1936, Clark Howell Sr. died at Pine Hill, his Atlanta home overlooking Peachtree Creek. Word reached McGill in New Orleans where the underdog Georgia team was leading

Tulane. Those in the press box watched as "slowly, he pulled the running story out of his typewriter and cranked in a clean sheet of copy paper . . . his thick, square hands hovered for a moment over the keyboard and then, with two fingers . . . he began to write." The Morse key operator tapped out a 2000 word eulogy that ran on page one and, according to Harold Martin, "went into a thousand scrapbooks." Georgia Tech Coach Alexander knew the sportswriter as well as anyone in Atlanta and remarked in 1934, "If you want to live in the memory of your fellow men, arrange for old, fat sentimental McGill to write your obituary." Paean done, the sports editor resumed writing about Georgia's victory.[55]

Dealing with another death in a period fraught with crises was bound to trigger a reaction in a man ruled by his emotions. That night on the Pullman heading north to Atlanta, some reporters were talking in a nearby compartment. No sooner had one offered a strong opinion than he was jumped from behind by "a bear in pajamas," determined to thrash him into a retraction. Later the victim was awakened by his assailant, now tearfully begging pardon. Harold Martin climbed down from his berth to receive an abrazo and formal introduction to his future boss and friend, Ralph McGill. Some of the tears that night were for Papa Howell. He probably wept too for Dan McGugin and for his lost child. McGill was also known to sob over career uncertainties. As Major Howell took over his father's newspaper, what would become of the frustrated sports editor?[56]

PART II:

1937-1957

5

"THE MOST IMPORTANT DAY OF MY LIFE": 1937-1940

THE YEAR 1937 WAS A TIME OF CONSTANT MOVEMENT FOR MCGILL. He traveled greater distances than ever before. He also connected with a group of men who provided momentum away from sports, but conflicts and tragedy almost ruined his promotion. Celebrating Georgia Democrats' return to the Roosevelt faction, Major Howell took a large group to the inauguration. He included McGill, who was eager to contribute feature articles and debase Talmadge, now home on the farm nursing his wounds. McGill wrote that everyone in Washington wanted to meet Georgia's new governor, E. D. Rivers, and congratulate him for defeating "the vicious opposition which had sought to sully the democracy of Georgia." Rivers took office promising to remove barriers Talmadge had placed against federal programs and also to give the state its own "New Deal."[1]

Roosevelt's inaugural challenge to help "one-third of the nation, ill housed, ill clad, ill nourished" still inspired McGill when in early February he did two long articles on Dr. Edwin Embree's agricultural reform ideas. Embree was president of the Rosenwald Fund and co-author of *The Collapse of Cotton Tenancy* with Will Alexander and Charles Johnson. The book focused on farm tenancy in Georgia. The Bankhead bill pending in Congress included many of their recommendations. McGill's friend Arthur Raper also investigated how Georgia tenants and sharecroppers fared under early New Deal programs like the Federal Emergency Relief Act and Agricultural Adjustment Act. Raper knew these laws were inadequate and passed along his findings to Alexander, in hopes of seeing the Bankhead bill enacted into law. All wanted tenant farmers moved to better land, given loans and a chance to become owners.[2]

Will Alexander liked McGill and understood his frustration. Alexander was a former minister who worked for interracial cooperation through the CIC in Atlanta and later served in New Deal agencies. After the *Constitution* ran Ralph's Embree articles, Alexander and others suggested that he apply for a new Rosenwald fellowship as a way of finally getting out of sports. Alexander and Embree had set up the awards through the Rosenwald Fund for regional scholars, journalists, and other professionals who might be in a position to influence public opinion.[3]

McGill was utterly pessimistic about his chances of gaining a fellowship. His poor college record still pained and embarrassed him, but he prepared and mailed the required material. Louisville editor Mark Ethridge later recalled the Rosenwald panel's reaction to McGill's application package. Ethridge had gotten to know Ralph while working at the *Macon Telegraph* and with other board members thought "he was far too intelligent and too socially conscious" to spend the rest of his career on the sports desk. They chose him as a fellow in hopes he could "break the cycle of sports writing" and finally "come into his own."[4]

Unaware of their confidence, McGill kept on his beat. He covered several golf tournaments, including the fourth Masters in Augusta. In March he accepted from Governor Rivers a political appointment that haunted him for years. The legislature created a new State Athletic Commission to regulate boxing and wrestling events. The expenses of the body were met by fees, licenses, and 10 percent of gate receipts. Ralph hoped that heading the commission would help pay his debts. The post generated very little income for the great amount of time it required, however. When scandal later tainted Rivers's administration, McGill's enemies smeared him.[5]

On April 16, 1937, the McGills received notice of his Rosenwald fellowship for six months' study in Europe. The *Constitution* announced his "high honor" in the same issue that reported Margaret Mitchell's Pulitzer Prize for *GWTW*. The paper gave him a leave of absence at half pay but required him to furnish a large number of stories about his travels. The Rosenwald stipend was only $1,500. McGill began exploring the possibility of loans. How could he assume more debt with old hospital bills still unpaid? Bob Woodruff found a way to help. He wanted a history of the Coca-Cola company to sell at a bottling convention. Ralph agreed to write the booklet for a nice fee.[6]

Then, pressured by family troubles and self-doubt, McGill fell victim to his "Welsh black dog,"as he always called his melancholy moods. Virginia was sick. Doctors wanted to know why, among other problems, her thymus was so enlarged. Ralph and Mary Elizabeth canceled plans to take the baby to Europe in November. Instead he arranged for his parents to keep Virginia in Chattanooga. As summer began, Red had a bad fall and injured her arm. Her mother, Octavia Leonard, was making one of her extended visits. Ralph worried about the effect the two women had on one another. He considered his mother-in-law to be a neurotic, who in turn was beginning to worry about her daughter's drinking.[7]

He tried to lose his worries in extra work. He made several talks for Emory's Gosnell on farm tenancy in Middle Georgia then left for the Kentucky Derby, stopping on the way back to see his parents. In late May he flew to New York City. He again accompanied a Georgia Tech naval training cruise in June. Feelings of inferiority grew stronger. He wrote Tom Chubb, "I'm tired, haven't been sleeping well, and have decided I can't write a line and will never be able to do anything but this newspaper drivel."[8]

Beginning his Rosenwald study in Denmark in December, Ralph had several letters of introduction that led to widening contacts. He began by studying cooperative marketing of Scandinavian farm products. His articles about reforming American agriculture were naive. He said his interest in co-ops stemmed from watching Georgia farmers peddling hampers of beans, peaches, or corn from door to door without access to a central market. He ignored the reality that Georgia farms produced mostly cotton for world markets and not local produce. He also presumed that rural families would choose to return to or remain in the country rather than live in cities like Atlanta. Yet for eight years he had rubbed elbows with wretched farm refugees flooding the Georgia capital. They lacked almost everything to subsist and were confounded by urban life. Most still preferred Atlanta to the oppression they endured as tenants or sharecroppers for rural landowners.

After visiting prospering Danes on their farms, in schools, factories, and at home, he wrote that education was the key to their strong society. Literacy was universal. The people were lifelong learners. Innovations in agriculture filtered out from the universities to individual farmers at a community folk school. Visits to Norway and Sweden confirmed his impression. Back home he had seen farmers shun suggestions for improving their hogs and chickens because they could not read the simple pamphlets offered to them. He already knew that the driving force in Ben McGill's life was offering his children educational opportunities. After Scandinavia the link between southern backwardness and widespread illiteracy became a major theme of his writing and speeches.[9]

In February 1938, soon after Ralph turned forty, the McGills decided to visit Germany for two weeks. The train that sped them to Berlin brought McGill to a fateful encounter. Adolph Hitler, the Nazi dictator, addressed his Reichstag or parliament on February 20. Along with thousands of Germans, McGill and his wife witnessed the parade to and from the speech and stood listening to Hitler's three hour harangue—amplified beyond the Opera House to the packed streets. Ralph's schooling had included enough German to let him understand the speech. His understanding of the event, however, went beyond translation to a deeper grasp of its impact.

Late in the day they returned to the Hotel Nordlund where he composed a letter to Virginia. He promised that when she was grown, they would read the letter together "to check on history's judgment of Hitler." After sixteen years as a sports writer, McGill knew about mob psychology. He had reflected in print and with friends about the effect an athletic spectacle had upon crowds of spectators. He also recognized how an authority figure could twist and manipulate the virtue of loyalty he prized. Everything that he saw that day and later in Germany and Austria made perfect sense to him. He sat down at his typewriter and began confronting readers with something they needed to face: totalitarianism.

In Virginia's letter and his articles McGill asserted that another war was inevitable. He and Mary Elizabeth talked to some young SS troops lining the parade route. Later he interviewed more men in the elite Nazi guard. The strength of National Socialism, he said, lay in its young recruits. These fellows had once been hungry, alienated, despairing of the future. Hitler gave them work, hope, and confidence in his cause. Nazi leaders were willing to employ violence, and McGill feared that the youthful troopers he met would soon be fighting to enlarge Hitler's Third Reich. Having witnessed Hitler's effect on the crowd and heard his fury, the Atlantan wondered if any government possessed the will or the power to resist what he knew was a demonic force loose in the world. "It is a dangerous period," he wrote Virginia.[10]

In his speech Hitler warned the world of his intention to control the destiny of seven million Austrians and three million Germans living in Czechoslovakia. The fate of Austria was already sealed in McGill's mind though the formal takeover would not occur for weeks. His reporter's adrenalin at this big story overrode any interest in agricultural reform. What he wanted most was to be present when Hitler actually entered Austria in triumph. Try as he might, McGill could not get permission to enter Austria with the Nazis in mid-March. The law that Hitler signed reuniting these Germanic peoples was to be submitted for popular approval on April 10. McGill was determined to cover this plebiscite.[11]

In the meantime the couple went to England. Ralph's articles explained to *Constitution* readers Britishers' attitudes towards German rearmament and aggression. He listened to debate in the House of Commons over which was the greater menace to European security: Nazism or Communism. He told his readers that Hitler's incessant use of the Communist "bogey" was a phony tactic to conceal his own intentions. There was no genuine Communist threat to the Third Reich. In truth, he reported,

Germany carried on quite a bit of business with the Soviet Union. Above all, the democracies of the world should not think they had to choose to support either Communism or Fascism against the other.[12]

On April 3, McGill left Mary Elizabeth ill in London and started for Austria. He traveled through Belgium, Germany, and finally reached Vienna shortly before the plebiscite. He was carrying verbal messages for two Jewish families from friends and relations now safe in England. They had explained something of the racism practiced by the Nazis. He would soon learn much more. The sportswriter saw Jews and other "undesirables" dragged out and forced to scrub the streets while Nazi guards jeered. In the market he watched soldiers turning shoppers away from stores and stalls owned by Jewish merchants.

He located the two families. Soldiers had terrorized them, ransacking their homes and offices. A dignified lawyer broke down and cried when McGill brought news of relatives he would never see again. Ralph drank tea with the eighty-two year old mother of one refugee as she told how the Nazis had taken all her valuables. Soon they would return to evict her. "She was," he wrote, "a cultured woman who spoke five languages, who knew the operas and music." Memories of the family of Rebecca Mathis Gershon swept over him. Those cherished boyhood friends could suffer such a fate. He sent Reb a long letter full of shock and foreboding.

People in regions dominated by the Third Reich were losing not only culture but freedom of thought. In Germany and Austria McGill saw bookstores emptied of all save propaganda material. Loudspeakers blared slogans that passed as truth for a full eighteen hours a day. Nazis told newspaper editors to be thankful that the state controlled what information they could put before readers. Otherwise confusion would reign, and the old postwar troubles would return. Under Hitler's direction the Germanic peoples were moving forward again. Always the focus was on the young. Ralph talked with mothers who trembled at songs their children were learning about blood, iron, and torturing Jews.[13]

The days in Vienna produced memories that never left him. He had witnessed a kind of madness on those streets, ablaze with red banners and swastikas. He evoked his deepest images to explain its effect upon him—a "Damascus road experience." "I took an oath," he always said, thereafter to fight hatred, intolerance, prejudice. McGill did not experience a conversion like St. Paul's, but the sportswriter's career did change as drastically as that of the apostle after his Damascus road encounter.[14]

In fact, when the sportswriter encountered the Nazi aggression and persecution of Jews in 1938, he was primed for a "calling." For over sixteen years he had endured an identity crisis. His family and the McCallies reared McGill to believe he was destined to succeed and to make a difference. Their expectations easily fed into his competitive, restless nature. His own failings plus circumstances at the *Banner* and *Constitution* thwarted all their hopes. Then he went to Europe.

The stories that McGill sent back to the *Constitution* showed talent and potential far beyond his present job. Early in 1938 he received a letter from Francis W. Clarke, executive editor of the paper and brother of former Ku Klux Klan leader Edward Y. Clarke. The letter hinted of a transfer from sports to the editorial department. Then in February Clarke died suddenly. Had the idea of a new job died with him? The answer was waiting upon McGill's return to London. Clark Howell Jr. wrote that he was still mulling exactly how to rearrange his staff. Typically, he asked for suggestions and advice. The Major was leaning towards making McGill editorial director with added responsibility for a daily column on the editorial page. His nine year rut ended.[15]

The unexpected opportunity coming at his milestone fortieth birthday gave McGill a renewed sense of destiny. Being a Rosenwald fellow and seeing Europe was, he wrote Bob Woodruff, a dream come true. He regularly sent notes of appreciation for the part Woodruff played in the sabbatical. "I have tried not to be an ass on this trip," he confessed, knowing that his taciturn mentor would chuckle. "I'd like to do big things," he wrote Woodruff shortly before he heard from the Major. "Anyone with ambition would." He had no inkling of the conflicts and grief that the 1938 "calling" would bring.[16]

The "Damascus road experience" left McGill feeling that democracy was very fragile. Both Germany and Austria had written constitutions after World War I. "But there was also hunger and want and despair," he wrote, "and when you have those conditions you have a ground ready for the harvest of the dictators." Thereafter, McGill assumed that economic disaster always caused social chaos, including violence. The Nazis' main victims were Jews; at home blacks were the scapegoats. He began to think the American South must experience prosperity in order to improve race relations.

In 1938 he saw that laws were no guarantee of freedom. If a people no longer supported their laws or ceased to find meaning in their government, these would fail. Hereafter this notion sometimes distorted his thinking, especially when he recalled the flaunting of Prohibition during the 1920s. Finally, he took issue with those who claimed that Roosevelt was subverting democracy in the U.S. Having seen real dictators, he argued that New Deal programs prevented many young Americans from falling prey to "alien and subversive influence."[17]

Back in Atlanta, Ralph and Mary Elizabeth fetched Virginia home from Chattanooga while the paper ran columns that he had mailed from Europe. McGill and Clark Howell readily arranged his transfer out of sports. On June 17 McGill became executive editor of the *Constitution*. He was to have "complete charge of the news, sports, and society departments." Howell added that McGill would "also write a daily column for the editorial page, on any subject he sees fit" and a variety of feature articles. The Major left the editorial page where it had been since Clarke's death—in the hands of Ralph T. Jones, "a dry and bloodless Englishman." Howell changed his own title to editor and publisher.[18]

Ralph's elevation confirmed his status as the *Constitution*'s best writer but started management problems that persisted for three decades. The Major had correctly gauged that McGill's talent and drive would transform the sportswriter. Yet Howell was wrong to expect Ralph to oversee the staff of three departments. The man "who as sports editor could not bring himself to fire, or even strongly rebuke, an incompetent colleague," would be no help to the Major. McGill had neither interest in nor aptitude for management. He had never handled his own affairs successfully. How could he give direction to editorial policy or reporters?[19]

McGill's promotion had another regrettable aspect. He falsified the realities of his earlier career to make it seem that he was well qualified for the new job. The announcement on page one credited him with covering state and national politics at the *Banner* for years. He kept enlarging claims of past political reporting. Eventually they obscured the reality that he spent one-third of his career in sports.[20]

It was too tempting for McGill to embellish his qualifications in 1938. He was always sensitive about lapses in his education. Through years of frustrated waiting, McGill had magnified the status of the editorial staff versus the sports desk. Two and a half years before his promotion he wrote: "There always has been a famous man in the old front office on the fourth floor of the *Constitution* building." James R. Holliday, secretary of his idol, Henry Grady, was still around the *Constitution* when McGill arrived in 1929. He pressed Holliday for every detail the old man could recall about Grady. He admired Papa Howell almost as much as Grady.[21]

McGill made an auspicious start to the latter two-thirds of his career. He called his new daily column, "One Word More." At first he devoted more attention to international affairs than to matters closer to home. He made the most of his recent firsthand experiences abroad and the mountains of material he brought home. His Emory contacts coached him in politics and economics.

Occasionally the tone and content of the new editor's work was so "highfalutin' " that old sportswriting buddies could not resist parodying the piece. Ed Danforth never understood why his former protégé looked beyond the *Constitution*'s sports desk, needling Ralph in print and predicting privately that he would never measure up to the likes of Grady and Howell. Some old *Constitu-*

tion hands also joked about his early efforts to create a new print persona. The thin-skinned editor smarted at their refusal to take him seriously. His recent Damascus road experience coinciding with the providential job opportunity strengthened his sense that it was "meant to be," however.[22]

Was he influenced by other editors in the South early in his career change? Since he regularly discarded correspondence files until his secretary stopped the habit in the 1950s, it is difficult to gauge. Unlike McGill, many owned their newspapers and had well defined views of the New Deal. Hodding Carter, whom the national media often paired with him during the 1950s, completed purchase of the *Delta Democrat-Times* in Greenville, Mississippi, just as Clark Howell promoted his sports editor.[23]

Almost immediately after McGill's promotion a national political storm cloud broke in his own backyard. The New Deal was beset by conservative foes in both the judicial and legislative branches. When Roosevelt's 1937 "court packing" scheme to alter the judiciary failed, he aimed to reshape Congress in the 1938 elections. He also wanted to see legislative opponents of court packing defeated. FDR's friends and political allies in his adopted state learned to their dismay that Georgia's influential senator, Walter F. George, who opposed court packing was on the "purge" list. The president intended to campaign against George on home ground.[24]

The purge campaign and presidential visit to Georgia distressed McGill. Even though he never participated in the New Deal like editors Mark Ethridge and Jonathan Daniels, he wanted Roosevelt to regard him as an ally in the Fourth Estate. Instead he was obliged to join most other Georgia newspaper editors in objecting to the president's interference. McGill tried to soften his opposition to the purge with extravagant praise of Roosevelt, "a great humanitarian who . . . saved this country." Yet both he and the Major knew the White House would not forget their betrayal. Sure enough, Roosevelt wrote Jim Farley that he was furious with "the mossbacks like Clark Howell of the *Constitution*."[25]

The controversy revealed McGill's tendency to waffle. This pattern of reversing himself, long a source of jokes in his circle, would undercut his editorial effectiveness for the next thirty years. During these early years out of sports he often muddled in print—first exploring one side of a question then trying the opposite. Sometimes on whim, Ralph composed bunches of paired editorials, arguing just as hard for as against the issues. Such feats left the staff wondering what convictions he really held.[26]

In some of his earliest editorials McGill asked readers to regard him as "liberal." He soon stopped, realizing it jeopardized the paper's shaky finances and did not fit his persona as a writer. For thirty years thereafter he was irrational about labels. His link to the Southern Conference for Human Welfare illustrates the problem. In November 1938 the first SCHW assembled in Birmingham, drawn in part by Roosevelt's recent claim that the South was "the Nation's No. 1 economic problem." McGill's name was on the list of sponsors, "a who's who in southern liberal organizations." It was the editor's first such public association.

FDR hoped the meeting would focus on ending the poll tax. This fee, levied on potential voters, aimed at disfranchising blacks but eliminated some poor whites. Most SCHW delegates aimed wider. Then conferees' attempts at integrated seating and a resolution against Jim Crow got more media coverage than their many reform ideas. With the specter of racial mixing raised, some whom McGill admired dropped out of the SCHW. Simply by lending his name to the SCHW in 1938, McGill was attacked as a radical. Years later when a Communist element in the SCHW discredited the organization, McGill denied attending the 1938 meeting. He probably was in Atlanta at an annual football game played on behalf of a crippled children's hospital. During his first year at the *Constitution*, he created the slogan of the benefit game, "Strong legs will run that weak legs may walk." It was his favorite bit of public relations, and he tried never to miss the Thanksgiving Day game.[27]

In 1938 he also raised the hopes of local reformers that they had a new recruit in the struggle against backwardness. Rebecca

Mathis Gershon, now widowed and devoting much time to such groups, was often his entreé. She was a lifelong confidante who understood his ambition. Knowing that Ralph was sensitive towards underdogs and good hearted, Reb nudged her friend towards social activism. At her urging, he made a talk to the Citizens Fact Finding Movement of Georgia. He also praised the CFFM's efforts in his column. Under the spirited leadership of Josephine Wilkins, the CFFM exposed social evils and economic exploitation in a statewide publicity network. Wilkins, Gershon, and other CFFM leaders soon realized that McGill was the most widely read journalist in Georgia. They cultivated him.[28]

It was easier for McGill to attack the Ku Klux Klan than relate to social activists. In the late 1930s the "invisible empire" attacked labor organizers and Communists as readily as its old foes—Catholics, Jews, and Negroes. Early in 1939 Atlanta prepared for dedication of the new Cathedral of Christ the King. The adjoining rectory once housed Imperial offices of the KKK. So when Wizard Hiram W. Evans sold the property to the Roman Catholic church to pay back taxes, many Klansmen turned against him. Evans sealed his fate by attending the consecration service at the cathedral. McGill had put his friend, Bishop Gerald O'Hara, up to inviting Evans. In his column the next day McGill commended the Klan leader for accepting the Bishop's invitation. He asserted that the KKK was now all but gone. Atlanta, he wrote, had no place for intolerance.[29]

McGill's observation was wishful thinking. It would take more than such statements to advance his crusade against prejudice and hate. KKK power was increasing. Atlanta and Georgia government continued to harbor many Klansmen and conform to its purposes. Even Ralph's political benefactor, Governor Rivers, had KKK connections strong enough to make him unacceptable to FDR as an opponent for Senator George in 1938. Shortly after the cathedral consecration, aldermen voted down a ban on hoods in public. Evans sold his stake in the Klan to James Colescott and told McGill he was relieved to be out. The new Wizard reopened the robe factory in Atlanta and sold plenty of advertisements in the Klan magazine to the city's leading businesses.[30]

Clark Howell supported McGill's scathing attacks on the Klan and pleas for improving Atlanta slums. The Major was a decent man who considered himself a progressive. If McGill occasionally leaned too far left, Howell assumed he was new enough at editorial work to be gullible. Openness was his most appealing trait, both personally and in print. The Major had worries enough keeping solvent. Surely he had not created more problems for himself by elevating the popular sports writer. Howell counted on Ralph's close friends from the business community to keep him mindful of the *Constitution*'s role in the "Forward Atlanta" ethos and the dangers of rocking the boat.[31]

For the next decade none was more important in this regard than Bob Woodruff. McGill knew how much he owed Woodruff. He valued having the benefit of Woodruff's advice and took pleasure in his company. Ralph saw the Coca-Cola president regularly both in Atlanta and at Ichauway, his south Georgia plantation. Unlike some businessmen, Woodruff had a social conscience. Ralph watched this sense of *noblesse oblige* evolve into philanthropy of massive proportions.

In his early tenure McGill did not understand that the political conservatism of Woodruff and other businessmen was a boundary of their friendship. If the editor crossed that boundary in print often enough, most opposed him and eventually ostracized him socially. Atlanta's mayor, William B. Hartsfield, for example, thought nothing of storming into McGill's office in a tirade if an editorial displeased him. Few businessmen were as fond of McGill—and as tolerant of his foibles—as Woodruff was.[32]

Ralph soon admitted to friends that the new job was confining. Except for speaking engagements around the state and visits to his parents, he was deskbound. He missed the constant travel that went with covering sports. Even if he had not transferred from sports, he would likely have stayed close to home the spring and summer of 1939. His daughter was beset with one spell of sickness after another. When she came down with scarlet fever, he relieved the horrors of the McGill household's critical bout of the fever in 1914. Each evening he hurried home from the paper to sit with the child, reading books and singing. Even after the quarantine period, she was not bright, funloving "Miss Virginia." When she fell and hurt her knee, the doctor ordered new tests. Ralph and Mary Elizabeth then faced the unbelievable fact that the daughter they adored had leukemia.[33]

The McGills sought every medical treatment they could discover. Ralph's college friend, Merrill Moore, brought her case before doctors at Harvard Medical School. The staff at Egleston Children's Hospital in Atlanta agreed to use experimental therapy on the three year old. In early November Virginia received new blood in a transfusion that took 24 hours and constant monitoring. "We are clinging to hope," her anguished father wrote Tom Chubb. Weeks later he communicated the outcome: "The hope which the doctors held out didn't materialize, and it is only a matter of time." In December Ralph and Mary Elizabeth watched the life go from Virginia. The vigil was all the more painful because they had left their baby for six precious months of their short time together.[34]

In a cruel parallel Atlanta was building to a crescendo of celebration as the McGills sank into grief and remorse. On December 15 the city hosted the world premiere of the film version of *Gone With the Wind*. It was Mayor Hartsfield's coup and a way to show the world what a great city he led. The extravaganza was, in the words of a Margaret Mitchell biographer, "like winning the Battle of Atlanta seventy-five years late."[35]

Normally Ralph and Red would have reveled in being part of Atlanta's *GWTW* mania—made all more memorable because of their friendship with the author and Ralph's new importance. In his column McGill begged Atlantans who failed to get tickets to the ball to donate to the childrens' charities. "There will be lives saved and lives soothed," he wrote. Not in his family, however. The night of the premiere Ralph rented an ambulance that took Virginia downtown to see the lights and crowds. He rode beside her stretcher, pointing and talking softly. Four days later the three year old died.[36]

The same edition of the *Constitution* that carried Virginia McGill's obituary included an editorial headed, "Welcome Governor Cox." It signaled a business change that would affect McGill even more than the death of his daughter. James M. Cox, former Democratic governor of Ohio and candidate for the presidency in 1920, bought both the *Atlanta Journal* and the *Atlanta Georgian.* He closed the latter. Hearst had lost over $10 million running the *Georgian.* Cox had no intention of repeating his folly. Major Howell had been in a tight circulation race with the *Journal* throughout his tenure. The governor's arrival on the scene made it even harder for Howell's newspaper to compete and for McGill to risk controversy.

The sixty-nine year old Cox had his eye on Atlanta long before 1939. His Ohio base included Dayton and Springfield newspapers. In 1923 he bought the *Miami Daily News.* In both Ohio and Florida, Cox owned powerful radio stations. Acquisition of the *Journal* brought him WSB, Atlanta's 50,000 watt station. Cox saw his beachhead in Georgia as "a rare opportunity." He knew many Atlanta leaders and admired the city's business ethos. Through the years he had remained close to his running mate on the 1920 Democratic ticket, Franklin D. Roosevelt. The president sent a warm letter welcoming Cox to Georgia, "my other state." Cox, a lifelong liberal, came to town with banners unfurled. He served notice on Atlanta the first day he was publisher that the *Journal* would take strong stands. "To try by vague and pointless preachment and evasion to please everybody is bad faith." The new executive editor of the *Constitution* was learning that the hard way.[37]

McGill decided to take his shattered wife away from Atlanta for a while. They drove to Louisiana, touring the region made famous by "Evangeline" and arriving finally in New Orleans. There they carried out a sorrowful mission. Virginia had New Orleans roots. They called on her maternal grandparents to share something of what the child had meant to them. Travel did not seem to help Mary Elizabeth start the recovery process. Ralph had his job. It challenged and stimulated him even before Virginia's death. Now he worked to forget.

He also drew strength from his mother and father. Mary Lou McGill had lost two little sons of her own. She had taken Virginia to her heart. From the deep bond between mother and son came consolation and help. Ben McGill loved his only grandchild almost as much as Ralph did. Virginia was the key to their establishing a new relationship. She was the focus of Ben's life during her six month stay in Chattanooga. Red took no such solace from her mother or any kinfolks, for that matter. Within weeks Ralph knew that his wife was going through a breakdown.[38]

Mary Elizabeth's illness was a fresh ordeal for Ralph, but in 1940 no editorial writer could put the world on hold for family problems. The European war that he always predicted was underway. A presidential election loomed. How would the Democrats resolve the third term dilemma? Their party leader was firmly entrenched in the White House and keeping his own counsel. Georgia politics were in turmoil. Governor Rivers's pledge to bring a "little New Deal" to Georgia without new taxes promised financial ruin. Rivers was also linked to corrupt state contracts. Talmadge left nothing to chance as he moved to recapture the governor's office. Bob Woodruff insisted that Ralph come to the Woodruff plantation, Ichauway, in late January, and he welcomed the chance to rest.[39]

A column from this visit had readers flooding the *Constitution* for months with requests for copies. In Woodruff's living room, lighted only by a fire, blacks sang spirituals for the guests. One song, "Yonder Come Day," helped Ralph deal with Virginia's death and Mary Elizabeth's breakdown. He wrote that he was not a religious person just "a man who was afraid and lost and hurt." From the song he realized that real light followed utter darkness. God's part in the suffering of his wife and daughter always haunted McGill, but he survived each and every dark time until finally he outlived their power over him.[40]

He returned to work and attacked the Ku Klux Klan which now viewed McGill as a special foe. They paraded on the sidewalk outside the newspaper to protest his editorials. KKK activity in Atlanta kept growing. Some chapters became vigilantes. Tipped off that certain individuals drank too much, beat their wives, or were just shiftless, the Klansmen flogged the person. These beatings, often with police looking on, increased during 1939. Some Klan initiations included kidnappings or terrorizing citizens. The inductees made sudden appearances in full regalia to carry one or several persons away with them. Another favorite show of power was for robed Klansmen to march into a church service, present an offering, and march out.[41]

Incidences of what McGill called "Klan justice" went unpunished until March 1940 when they beat a man named Ike Gaston to death. Atlanta newspapers gave the murder such publicity that authorities could not avoid action. Indictments and ensuing trials brought some Klan floggers to judgment. McGill, who knew that the sadistic attacks could break out again, employed a variety of verbal weapons against the KKK. These ranged from imaginary monologues to sarcasm to cold fury.

The *Constitution*'s police reporter, Keeler McCartney, gave McGill information to lend veracity. Not that he needed help. From his chilling experiences in Germany and Austria he knew what to expect from totalitarian personalities. After 1938 McGill always linked Nazis and Klansmen. He was not surprised when Fritz Kuhn, the American "Führer" collaborated with Northern KKK cells. The editor regularly called Kuhn a fool and ridiculed his work as he did the Klan's shenanigans. He appealed to Georgians to use their common sense and reject all hatemongers.[42]

Yet it was fear rather than common sense that controlled many Georgians as the 1930s ended. Change seemed to be sweeping them towards an uncertain, ever darker future. Most of McGill's readers had already endured far more changes during the decade than they wished. They sought scapegoats and lashed out at those they perceived as agents of unwelcome change. Such notions plagued voters as they prepared to choose a governor in 1940.

Eugene Talmadge dominated the race. Heretofore the wild man from Sugar Creek scorned organized campaigns. With the advice and efforts of his son, Herman, he now created a network that included the entire state. He even reversed himself and sought votes in places "where the streetcars ran." McGill had no doubt that "ol' Gene" would reoccupy the governor's office in early 1941.[43]

The editor was not sure who would be president. He often wrote about Roosevelt's administration as if it were already history. He never was associated with the New Deal and gave it mixed reviews. He called for an end to the Works Progress Administration but found other initiatives like the Tennessee Valley Authority worthy of praise. He said that some New Deal policies, such as those relating to labor and farmers, were sound in principle but were implemented by bureaucrats who often were "arrogant and dictatorial." He believed the strongest legacy of the New Deal was to give Americans "a new awareness of our duties towards society in general." He said that would endure whatever the outcome of the election.[44]

How, he wondered, could he best foster this new awareness? Personal tragedy had deepened his compassion. Once he might have hinted that unfortunates were partly to blame for their trouble. Now he supported almost any downtrodden soul. Sometimes his pieces were vague, emotional pleas. More often he offered statistics to prove the need and went on to summarize proposals for reform. His strongest pleas were for diversifying agriculture, particularly marketing hogs and cattle. The change might increase income of farm families. More importantly, it might slow their exodus from the land and ease relief problems of these refugees in cities like Atlanta.

In mid-April 1940 he did attend the second assembling of the Southern Conference for Human Welfare in Chattanooga. On the trip back to Atlanta, Arthur Raper recalled, McGill and others "philosophized" about what the South could do to assure a future better than its immediate past. They had just heard Will Alexander warn in a speech that progress would be slow and difficult.

Alexander also asserted that "the South's problems would have to be solved by Southerners." That would be McGill's position for the next twenty years.[45]

This penchant for distrusting outsiders ran throughout the region's history. Now it focused on organized labor. Although labor representatives were prominent during sessions of the second SCHW, they were often at risk out in the field. Union organizers were a favorite target of Klan floggers. Mill owners especially considered them a scourge. Years later McGill recalled that a favorite tactic against textile union proselytizers was to send "hired evangelists . . . thundering that the people must choose between God and the CIO." The editor himself was never keen on unions.[46]

Whatever support Ralph gave to CIO organizing efforts was due to his friendship with Miss Lucy Randolph Mason. In 1937 this fifty-five year old Virginia aristocrat moved to Atlanta as public relations officer for the CIO. "Operation Dixie," their organizing drive in the region, faced opposition across the social spectrum. Newspaper editors were integral to Mason's struggle to win acceptance for unions in the South. Mason fascinated McGill. He wanted to discover what impelled a female whose ancestors signed the Declaration of Independence and fought in America's wars to lead a cause that respectable southerners called un-American, even Communist. The two occasionally lunched together, visited each other's offices, and corresponded.

Mason had set out to convert the *Constitution* editor. Early in their acquaintance she described McGill as "a bitter foe of all CIO unions." Despite this attitude, she considered him an "open minded, fine man." She admired the way McGill took after the Klan. By summer 1940 "Miss Lucy" perceived a gratifying change in the newspaper's attitude. The *Constitution* had gone from "raw hostility" to neutrality as the CIO fought for members and recognition. The *Atlanta Journal* had always been more favorable to unionism, she noted. McGill soon dashed Mason's hopes. He expressed skepticism and even made attacks (he later regretted). Atlanta was more resistant to unionism than his hometown of Chattanooga or Birmingham, or even Mason's Richmond were.[47]

Ralph was temperamentally unsuited to assume the crusading stance which "Miss Lucy" and other liberals envisioned for him. When Mason died in 1959, he wryly admitted that she had made "several hundred men feel like fools." He was one. He had waited too long to jeopardize his promotion with a truly unpopular stand. When new at the job, he was confused by the complexities of economics or politics. He always focused his editorial attention on Georgia but was collecting data from a growing body of regional experts. It would be years before he showed the expertise that marked his sports stories.[48]

What he perceived as his obligations to the *Constitution*'s broke owners also held him in check. McGill knew that pleas for federal aid to education, food stamps, or consideration of African Americans' legal rights brought negative feedback to Clark Howell. Aware that many fellow editors owned and controlled their papers, he always reminded friends that he was just an employee at the *Constitution*. In time he became Howell's claim to fame. Yet he insisted that he had no job security. When he drank too much at social functions and his inhibitions dropped away, he sometimes insulted an important Atlanta businessman. By the end of the evening he was telephoning colleagues predicting that he would be out of a job tomorrow.[49]

6

HENRY GRADY'S HEIR: 1940-1945

MCGILL TURNED WARTIME UPHEAVALS INTO CAREER ADVANCES that began when a Georgia crisis brought his first appearance in a national magazine. Eugene Talmadge won the governorship in 1940 just as the editor predicted. What no one had expected was his ringing praise of his old foe. McGill asked readers to take Talmadge at his word, that he wanted "merely to be a good governor." He gave Gene high marks as a campaigner. "Much sweating spadework" lay behind the victory. His son Herman deserved credit for this, wrote McGill, adding that young Talmadge's political future "looks like a sure bet to me." Such editorial compliments may have been a way of bowing gracefully to the inevitable or of taking the long view. McGill correctly observed, "Nothing could be worse for Georgia than an obstructionist campaign."

Why he went beyond these thoughts to rewrite the record is inexplicable. McGill claimed that Talmadge had not been "disloyal to the party" though that was his reason for attacking the governor earlier. Gene had taken the law into his own hands. He had matched and perhaps exceeded the outrageous behavior of other demagogues in the political sphere. He played havoc with state government, defying reasonable men to try and stop him. Why did the popular *Constitution* editor not warn Gene that the Georgia of the 1940s could not bear a repeat of these shenanigans? Instead he anointed Talmadge as the man of the hour. It was not the last time that he gave Gene accolades rather than the verbal warning the governor deserved.[1]

McGill's analysis of national politics and international affairs was clearer than that of the governor's race. He agreed with the

Democrats' breaking precedent and "drafting" Roosevelt for a third term. The war was his reason. He never budged from advocating preparedness. He saw the war as a global conflict where Axis conquests might spread from Europe and Asia to the Americas. He was not an early interventionist but urged the U.S. to offer greater support to the British in hopes that they could hold out. McGill expected Hitler to conquer the Soviet Union. He gave Republican nominee Wendell Willkie credit for waging a strong campaign. He predicted that Willkie would make a good president if he beat FDR. He rejoiced in Roosevelt's triumph, however.[2]

He returned from a two week tour of defense plants in June 1941 just in time to watch Governor Talmadge singlehandedly wreck Georgia's higher education system. The editor reneged on all compliments he had paid the governor. No one has ever fully explained why Talmadge went on the attack against the state's colleges and university. McGill may have come close. Talmadge, he wrote, had regained office in 1940 by what were for him rational means. Still obsessed with winning a senate seat after two failures, maybe he thought Georgians relished a taste of "ol' Gene."

Whatever triggered his rampage, Talmadge showed how far he would go to protect the state from the influence of "furriners." The dangerous ideas he accused them of importing concerned race relations. His first victim was dean of the university's education school, Walter D. Cocking. Marvin S. Pittman, president of Georgia Teachers College in Statesboro, was second in line for removal. In each case the "evidence" that they favored "race mixin'" came from a fired or disgruntled staffer. Talmadge launched his attack from the university's Board of Regents where the governor sat *ex officio*. Initially a majority of the regents tried to stop the governor. Infuriated, Talmadge resolved to purge the board and appoint men who would fire any suspect educators.[3]

Clark Howell Jr. had been a university regent since 1934. One June morning the governor came to the *Constitution* building and marched into the publisher's office. Months ago the Major had made a token offer to step aside. Talmadge demanded that he do so. When Howell demurred, the governor refused to leave without a resignation letter. Gene glared while the Major complied. Some Talmadge advisers had warned the governor against tangling with Clark. They reminded him that supporting the university system was a point of pride in the Howell family. If provoked and humiliated, the Major would turn the *Constitution* into a powerful weapon against the Talmadge administration.[4]

Now assured that the replacement regents would vote his way, the governor opened their July 14 meeting to the public. McGill stood in the throng that packed the capitol house chamber to watch the firing of Cocking and Pittman. Despite strong evidence to the contrary, Talmadge claimed the educators were subverting white supremacy. He kept shouting, "They ain't a-gonna do it." The governor prevailed and proceeded to widen his purge. Media in Georgia and across the country lambasted Talmadge's baseless attack on academic freedom.

Survey Graphic was eager to run McGill's account since Talmadge used an issue of the magazine as evidence that Pittman believed in Communism and racial intermarriage. After describing recent events, the *Constitution* editor interpreted their meaning for *Survey Graphic* readers: "The roots go back to the writing of freight rates and the tariff laws for a conquered section of the nation." Many of both races were trapped in poverty and backwardness, but the whites turned to demagogues like Talmadge. Like other southern leaders unsure about how to alter race relations, McGill reiterated complaints about the South's colonial status on every occasion.

He went on in the article to draw a parallel between the South and Nazi Germany. Just as economic chaos and poverty helped Hitler come to power, "a soul-sickness" existed among poor southerners. They supported a Talmadge, a Huey Long. The pattern of book burning, "slander and smears," and "anti-Semitic propaganda" was the same he observed in Europe three years before. It dominated his thought patterns. "How close is the tie-up," he asked, "and who backs them?" Talmadge was especially venomous towards the Rosenwald Fund from which flowed "Jew money for Niggers." The governor vilified Rosenwald's Edwin

Embree who had sponsored McGill and taunted the editor as "Rosenwald Ralph."[5]

McGill had been settling into his editorial position gradually. He offered no pat solutions to any socioeconomic dilemma, including race relations. He asked whites to show fairness and grant Negroes their legal rights. Yet by late 1941 he despaired of progress in this regard. What bothered him most was that whites' fears seemed unwarranted. As he said, nothing threatened segregation. He sometimes praised individual blacks—especially the cadre of strong ministers who led congregations in Atlanta but never hinted that initiatives for racial justice would come from within the black community. Like so many paternalistic whites (including other southern editors), he assumed that his race would continue to control the issue.[6]

He was shouldering heavy personal burdens that often distracted him. Just eight months after Virginia's death, in August 1940, Ralph's father died in Chattanooga. Ben McGill was seventy-two and been in poor health for six years. His final spell of suffering was brief. Ralph and his dad long ago gave up trying to understand each other and simply bonded in great affection. Ben outlived his disappointment over Ralph's expulsion from Vanderbilt. The son learned to appreciate the struggles and hopes that underlay his father's sternness. His mother still doted on him. No family kidding fazed Mary Lou McGill, shining with pride and joy in her "good, smart, grand son."[7]

Added to these sorrows was Mary Elizabeth's illness. He continued to send his wife out of town, hoping that restful stays with friends and family would help. He saw no encouraging signs that she would be her old self anytime soon. Perhaps if they were a family again, not just another childless couple. Against their Atlanta adoption agency's advice, they took home a boy from a Macon orphanage near the anniversary of Virginia's death. James was going on four and had had a rough start in life. In early 1941 Ralph wrote Tom Chubb that the boy "makes life a little more interesting." But Virginia was irreplaceable. Mary Elizabeth and Ralph sadly concluded that the boy should go back to Macon.[8]

For Red McGill this was a deeply troubled time in their long marriage. After two more aborted pregnancies, she felt fate was cruelly denying motherhood to her. An expert cook, she brought feasts downtown to Ralph and his colleagues at the paper. Sick friends and neighbors received nourishing meals from her kitchen as long as they needed them. Newcomers to town met her bearing a special dish.[9]

Her husband could not take much encouragement from such generous gestures that were offset by unwise drinking. Given the seriousness of her health problems, Mary Elizabeth probably should never have used alcohol. Even a small amount had an exaggerated effect on her behavior that was sometimes boisterous. Both she and Ralph were aware that her family history included alcoholism. After a few social occasions when Red appeared unable to hold her liquor, Atlantans who did not know her or understand her ordeals gossiped cruelly about the *Constitution* editor's wife.

Friends and family saw his dilemma but said little to him about this latest trouble. While Mary Elizabeth did not get the help she needed, throughout the 1940s Ralph had a guardian angel of sorts. When he was tied in knots or went on a binge, Bob Woodruff saw that he got enough time away from Atlanta to overcome his misery. Woodruff knew he was struggling with pressures at the paper and liked his efforts to make meaningful commentary on Georgia's problems. He believed the editor would eventually decide that alcohol was no way to cope with his problems, and he was right.[10]

The Japanese attack on Pearl Harbor December 7, 1941, lifted both McGills onto another plane of existence. The second anniversary of Virginia's death and their failed adoption of James were set against the dark backdrop of world war. Ralph admitted that combat zones were no place for a fat, middle-aged journalist and had a very different war than he had in 1918-1919. He served on the local draft board, promoted war bond drives, and urged civil defense upon Atlantans. Red volunteered at a nearby military hospital. So both became war workers "for the duration," as everyone said.

The war took away essential commodities but brought economic prosperity. Georgia became a massive training ground for the armed forces. War production facilities sprang up. Leading the list was Bell Aircraft's $15 million bomber plant north of Atlanta. As construction began, McGill went up to Cobb County to have a look. His long feature story emphasized what the plant would mean in coming years. Thousands of Georgians would build B-29s at undreamed of wages. Yet he also recognized the impact of industrializing. He interviewed some of the 140 families uprooted from the site and described the historic landmarks that bulldozers destroyed. Like many of his generation with rural nostalgia, he remained ambivalent about the price of progress in the South even if it fought both poverty and the Axis.[11]

Spring 1942 brought the Metropolitan Opera's annual visit to Atlanta and a special new female in McGill's life. She was Ruthanna Boris, a young dancer in the company's ballet corps. Both stagestruck and a balletomane, Ralph watched Boris dance in "Carmen" with enchantment. He also realized that, as the opera unfolded, his painful attack of bursitis vanished. He hurried backstage afterwards to thank the ballerina for the cure and to escort her to a party for the company. Tired and bored, Boris intended to skip the event. Something about McGill's openness changed her mind. By evening's end, they were friends.

Ralph kept in touch with Ruthanna thereafter. He encouraged her through periods of professional and personal turmoil. At first she was baffled that a prominent editor treated her, barely out of adolescence, as an equal. In time Boris accepted and relied on his support. She sensed too that his letters and visits to her soothed his own frustrations and sorrows. Like Reb Gershon, the ballerina filled a void in his existence that was hectic but sometimes desolate. Boris saw something of a dancer's kinetic energy in the aging football player but worried that binge drinking might drain this vitality.[12]

As spring warmed into summer, McGill spent two weeks at Harvard University under auspices of the Nieman Foundation. Professors and administrators from President James Conant down briefed the fifty visiting journalists on as many aspects of the war as possible. The war was cutting so many Americans loose from their roots, scattering them across the globe. For at least five years Ralph had been preparing himself to understand and comment upon change. The former sportswriter knew the world was his beat now.[13]

McGill returned to Atlanta with trepidation about the upcoming governor's race. Governor Talmadge's attorney general, Ellis Arnall, was his principal opponent. Support was building for Arnall from Georgians who were angry and embarrassed over Talmadge's assault on education. By now all the state's institutions of higher learning were pariahs as far as accrediting agencies were concerned. The governor's defiant cry that "We credit our own schools down here," rang hollow with many voters. Academic freedom seemed to be the issue. McGill begged the politicians to leave "racial matters" out of the campaign. He was wasting words. Arnall was as strong a segregationist as Talmadge. However, Gene's shenanigans allowed Arnall to beat the governor without ever having to prove that he was.[14]

McGill threw himself into the campaign with abandon. As the September primary neared, invective poured from his typewriter. He compared Talmadge with Hitler. Both repeated lies until people believed them. Like the German leader, the Georgia governor surrounded himself "with trash." With our youth "going off to fight against dictators," he asked, why "nurse a small one at home?" As he later bragged to Westbrook Pegler, the *Constitution* hit Talmadge "with everything we had." Ralph thought of his old football days. "I was trying to lead interference," he wrote Pegler, "and getting kicked in the shins and gouged and otherwise punished." Nothing stimulated the newsman as much as a political donnybrook unless it was a physical threat.[15]

A few days after he hailed Arnall's victory over Talmadge, McGill won a prize of his own. He became editor-in-chief of the paper and top occupant of the fourth floor office suite. Clark Howell Jr. took the title of president and publisher then rejoined the Army. Bearing the rank of Lieutenant Colonel, Howell closed up his Atlanta home and headed for Mississippi with his wife, Margaret. The beleaguered publisher was looking forward to active duty. Between Talmadge and Cox, whose *Journal* now surpassed his paper's circulation, he was wrung out. He sent a uniformed photo back to Atlanta inscribed to Ralph, "who's keeping the home fires burning, thank heavens."[16]

Howell's financial woes and McGill's weak editorial direction dampened those flames during the 1940s. The building that had housed the *Constitution* for nearly sixty years was decrepit. One of the presses regularly caught on fire, wafting smoke to the upper floors. The newspaper had talented, popular writers like Harold Martin and Celestine Sibley. Lamar Q. Ball and M. L. St. John covered politics ably. Yet the staff was always too small and underpaid. The *Constitution*'s desperate financial condition bothered even the most loyal on occasion. The only bathroom on the sixth floor had a razor hanging from the wall on a string. A note read, "For wrist slashing." Such black humor aside, the staff tolerated the mess and enjoyed great camaraderie.[17]

Shortly before Howell promoted Ralph and left, the two men published the *Constitution*'s huge seventy-fifth anniversary edition. It was a tribute to Atlanta and Georgia as well as a celebration of the paper. In his column that day Ralph confided that whenever he stayed late to work, he always stopped at the three busts of Henry Grady, Joel Chandler Harris, and Papa Howell before leaving. He put his hand on the shoulder of each journalist and said goodnight. As far as he was concerned, they were still around and his role models.[18]

Ralph's sentimentality enclosed a kernel of truth. He used Grady's old rolltop desk. He absorbed every detail of the famous editor's life. Now a half century later McGill was Grady's heir and the South's most widely read editor. Would he possibly become his generation's spokesman for yet another New South? While fairminded white southerners of the 1880s contented themselves with calls for racial justice and concentrated instead on modernizing the economy, now legal challenges to segregation were advancing in the courts. The impending racial revolution would have confounded even the self-assured Grady and almost swamped his heir.

McGill asked that race relations remain on hold until the war was won, but challenges to the status quo kept coming. In October 1942 southern black leaders met in Durham, North Carolina, to consider the war's effect on their race's oppression. Participants included Atlanta University's Dr. Rufus Clement and the president of Morehouse College, Dr. Benjamin Mays. Both men worked tirelessly to make the university complex "an oasis" where Negroes did "not suffer the injustices that the person who had to make his living in the city did." Mays ordered his students to stay away from segregated events: "I did not want them to go up in the 'buzzard's roost' to see anybody's show, to see any theatrical performance. . . . I said, 'Even if God Almighty came to preach at a white church I wouldn't go to hear Him.'"[19]

The Durham conferees addressed racial discrimination throughout southern society. Their report called for an end to devices that kept blacks from being citizens—the poll tax, white primary, all-white juries. They deplored violence and brutality, especially at the hands of law enforcement officers. They recommended removal of barriers to economic and educational advancement for blacks. Without insisting that segregation must go immediately, these leaders demanded that opportunities become "equal." The report emphasized the contradiction that World War II set before Americans. How could the nation ask Negroes to die in a war for freedom and yet deny their rights solely because of their race?[20]

The Durham Conference challenged McGill's current editorial stance. He thought it made no sense to discuss an end to segregation at this time. He believed that a long era of economic prosperity would precede changes in race relations. So he feared a repeat of the kind of social turmoil that Talmadge unleased in Georgia. Over the next half dozen years, the gap between his editorial stance and legal realities would widen. Yet McGill differed from some prominent whites. He was a learner and, unlike the true standpatters, open to change. This quality of mind plus his 1938 vow kept him moving along.[21]

He waited two months before commenting upon the Durham conference. He had been counseling both races to think the best of one another, knowing that segregation "must be maintained." He asked whites to take heart that Axis agents had no luck recruiting Negroes to betray the U.S. He urged blacks to believe that they were making unprecedented progress. He acknowledged discrimination but insisted that southern Negroes suffered less than members of their race in other sections of the U.S. Overall, African Americans were better off than minorities around the world.

He made the first of many attacks on the NAACP's executive secretary, Walter White. Even though White was moderate, he unsettled McGill who called him "an officious show-off" with no real appreciation of southern black leaders who "aren't political exhibitionists such as he." By contrast, he called the Durham conferees realistic and reasonable. He asked southerners to discuss their report "calmly and intelligently." As always, he assured white readers that no one was talking about "social equality," which, his readers knew, implied sexuality.[22]

Fellow Georgian and writer Lillian Smith found McGill's approach contemptible. By now Smith was "all out" against segregation. Unlike him, she felt it was "the right time to speak out clearly and unequivocally for racial democracy. . . ." Whereas McGill urged gradual change in the 1940s, Smith anticipated revolution. The two not only contrasted; they feuded. From her mountaintop in north Georgia, Smith saw McGill as "hedging on all things that may offend his big-business buddies. . . ." In Atlanta the editor knew most businessmen shunned his racial conciliation but kept trying, certain that Smith's fanaticism did more harm than good.[23]

On March 28, 1943, McGill got a chance to play mediator before a radio audience of twelve million souls. He appeared with two scholars on the University of Chicago's Round Table. Doing the broadcast was unnerving but an unprecedented opportunity. He said the South wanted to become fully part of the nation but was hindered by its colonial status. He deplored this economic discrimination, especially unfair freight rates. It was a favorite ploy of regional apologists. However, McGill's claim about the South yearning to reconnect to the union did not sit well with listeners. Southern ideology held that the section was too different to conform to national patterns.

McGill's comments about blacks during the broadcast were riskier and showed that the Durham Conference was affecting his public position. He stated flatly that the war had raised Negroes' hopes of gaining "all civil rights—the right to be a person, the right to have equal opportunity—all the rights, I think, that any of us enjoy." In another part of the broadcast he reiterated that poverty was the root of southern racial troubles. Prosperity would help. McGill said that his view of human nature made him doubt that federal action alone could solve southern racial problems.[24]

In Atlanta he also tried to conciliate when racial tensions flared, particularly on crowded streetcars and buses where whites could demand all the seats and space they wanted. McGill employed effective literary devices when he wanted to influence rather than just entertain. He described a conversation with an angry visitor who had come to the *Constitution* offices to vent his spleen. He had used this technique since Nashville days. In fact, his willingness to hear out anyone who called or dropped by his office was known all over Atlanta. Whether the reported conversation was real or imaginary, it brought frustrations and fears into the open. McGill made points as part of a dialogue without pontificating. A second technique was to throw out food for thought as if he were talking in a reader's ear. In such columns his persona could have been a neighbor talking at the back fence or someone waiting his turn in a barber shop. McGill imparted his points as a casual and friendly exchange.[25]

Beyond the confines of the paper, editor McGill was becoming a symbolic public figure. In April 1943 he chaired a gathering of white southern leaders attempting to respond to the Durham Conference. Out of the meeting came a Collaboration Committee of both races appointed by McGill. They drafted a document that did not suit either whites or blacks but was finally adopted. The so-called "Atlanta Statement" condemned discrimination but not segregation. It was a start. The Collaboration Committee planned a followup conference for June 16 in Richmond. McGill sent the letters inviting thirty-three leaders of each race to attend. At this point he begged off, pleading a hectic travel schedule. He has been accused of avoiding a fracas, but his excuse was true.[26]

It was also typical of McGill during this period. After waiting long and working hard, he was enjoying a measure of fame. He never liked to turn down anyone. So he took on too much outside his demanding job. He was neither well organized nor good at compartmentalizing his life. It was impossible to follow through on all his promises and good intentions. In late 1942 he contracted with Alfred A. Knopf to do a book about the South. Such an accomplishment would fulfill youthful dreams and mark him as a serious student of the region. The effort failed. He later confessed to Knopf that the material he sent "was so bad that I hardly had the heart to try again."[27]

If regular duties and outside obligations were not enough, McGill started traveling again. He hated being deskbound, but the editorial job, family troubles, and wartime restrictions combined to keep him home. It was bad enough to lose the freedom he felt far away from home. Even worse was watching everyone else go off to war. Once Ralph broke the five-year "grounding," he traveled constantly for the rest of his life. In June of 1943 he went to Florida then Cuba. For ten days he wrote one long, nostalgic travelogue.[28]

His high spirits flowed from the happy secret that he would soon go to Great Britain. He reported firsthand what the Brits and Yanks stationed there endured before a second front was launched across the channel on D-Day. U.S. crews making daily B-17 bombing raids included many Georgians, and McGill brought them the sights and sounds of home, especially his home. "Coming to town every morning, the bus makes a turn not far from Buckhead and you can look out and far down the street and you can see Atlanta high on a hill . . . rising out of the early morning sun."

He walked them down Broad Street near his office with its

smells "of people, of bread, of roasted nuts, of vegetables, of meats, of things cooked and cooking, of coffee, of spices, and of fruits.... He went into department stores—High's, Kline's, and of course Rich's. Then he was a boy in Tennessee, out with his mother to buy piece goods: "I recall the men with the pencil and the large shears and how they would measure off the goods and snip it with their sharp shears. I remember the dry, clean, cloth smell of it." Then back in Atlanta, "a place of kindness and of charity and of hope and of promise. And I like it."[29]

The entourage included two Bostonians who became close friends. Laurence Winship edited the *Boston Globe*. Edward Weeks held the same post at the venerable *Atlantic Monthly*. He encouraged Ralph to write for his magazine. The Atlantan became a regular contributor thereafter. Traveling companions also observed drinking binges that were as predictable as interviewing Georgians. It was disgraceful, Ralph felt, for the editor of the *Constitution* to be seen drunk around Atlanta. Such inhibitions disappeared hundreds or thousands of miles from home. As someone observed during the homeward voyage in 1943, "He may very well be the original Old Ironsides because he can drink more whiskey than anybody I ever saw."[30]

That fall McGill established an even stronger bond than his new Boston friendships. He hired Jack Tarver of the *Macon News* as his associate editor. Tarver fascinated McGill. His leading traits were qualities that McGill possessed but often repressed. Tarver always wrote with caustic wit. He was tough. If he made up his mind about something, he did not budge or even care who disagreed with him. He rejected McGill's earlier offers to come to the *Constitution* but was ready to move to Atlanta in 1943. Tarver was nineteen years younger than his new boss, but in some way they were on equal footing. They became the closest of friends. Perhaps McGill had reached out for a colleague who completed his editorial persona. Before many years passed, Tarver also showed a hand for management.[31]

Meanwhile, the core of McGill's national readership was forming. Servicemen and servicewomen stationed in Georgia came to know and like his work. Even readers who disagreed with him admitted he was kindhearted. Throughout the war in his column he consoled the grieving. Death always fascinated him. His own struggle with grief for two lost daughters heightened this sensitivity. He tried to help, admitting his words seemed "strained or overdone or maudlin." Readers appreciated his good intentions and said so. They stopped by his office to show off homemade scrapbooks of his work. Sometimes they stayed for hours. His secretary was busy with requests for extra clips of favorite columns.[32]

By early 1944 the postwar era dominated McGill's writing. Like so many influential Americans of his generation, McGill let the immediate past shape his ideas about the postwar period. He anticipated a repeat of the interwar years whose reactionary politics and social conflict had bred totalitarian regimes by the 1930s. Georgia's problems reinforced that fear and led him to assume wrongly that it was a bad time for changing racial mores.[33]

However, McGill was not as convinced as some that the war's end would inevitably depress the U.S. economy. He had a good grasp of how the myriad of new products and production capacity might spell growth rather than depression. It would not be easy, especially if labor leaders were inflammatory. Yet after reviewing notes from briefings and conferences, the *Constitution* editor predicted the dawning of a new economic age in the South. The region finally might cast off its colonial economy, he wrote. New plants stood ready for conversion to peacetime production. Capital was available within the region rather than north of the Mason-Dixon line. Southerners had learned modern business techniques and opened up to change. The key to maintaining a sounder economy was regional planning. Urban centers like Atlanta alone could not sustain growth. Small towns and farms must prosper as well.[34]

McGill's hopes rested on social stability, particularly in race relations. If Georgia or, worse yet, the entire South descended into one of its periodic dark, violent phases, the chance to prosper might be lost. It was in this frame of mind that he served as an incorporator of the new Southern Regional Council in February of 1944. He saw the council as a bulwark against outside agitators. It would provide a framework for "friendly" Negro leaders of the region "to work this thing out with southern whites." Otherwise, "northern radicals" would seize the initiative. McGill kept apart from the SRC after its founding, he later claimed, to maintain editorial independence. Actually he was getting controversial enough by 1944 without bringing more trouble for the *Constitution*'s owners.[35]

By now McGill was familiar with every part of Georgia's nearly 60,000 square miles. He sometimes took readers along on his trips. Coming back once from Rome, he described a town "dreaming of the time when the great Coosa river project will be done; when ocean going tugs and barges will tie up at docks there where the Etowah and Oostanaula rivers meet." Through his eyes they saw "the Euharlee road, where boxwood, cherry, spruce and laurel grow." Passing Allatoona and Kennesaw, renowned for its "Big Shanty" distillery, they came into Marietta. Present municipal leaders were conservative, McGill noted, but in the last century the summer resort had been "the fastest town in Georgia." He came at last to his home.[36]

Ralph and Mary Elizabeth were now living in a tiny house on what their families jokingly called "a farm in Buckhead." After James went back to the orphanage, they concluded they would never need room for children. Mary Elizabeth was tired of renting and watched for some house they might buy. When a "for sale" sign appeared in a yard on Piedmont Road, she was ready to move. Ralph was out of town, but she went ahead anyway. When he came back, he worried that the house was too small but loved its two acre setting. He wrote Tom Chubb that way back of his garden in a "wild and protected" area his dog "blundered into a covey of quail which got up almost under my feet."[37]

Ralph spent more and more time away from Atlanta. In the summer of 1944 John S. Knight, president of the American Society of Newspaper Editors, had him persuade both political parties to add a freedom-of-the-press plank to their convention platforms.

The ASNE then expanded its free press efforts to governments across the world. In early 1945 Knight asked Ralph and two other men to make a 50,000 mile journey. The ASNE goal was a treaty guaranteeing "a free flow of uncensored news between all nations." McGill's companions were to be Wilbur Forrest, assistant editor of the New York *Herald Tribune* and dean of Columbia's Journalism School, Carl W. Ackerman. The ASNE invitation sent McGill's spirits soaring. He had a chance to see the whole world as the war entered its final phase.[38]

Then an even bigger shock seemed to cancel his trip. Mary Elizabeth was pregnant. The couple could hardly believe the doctor. Both thought she had had a successful tubal ligation when doctors decided that another pregnancy might be fatal. Now Mary Elizabeth said she wanted to try to have the baby. Ralph was undone. His wife would soon celebrate her fortieth birthday in far below normal health. Despite circumstances, she turned a deaf ear to all advice.[39]

Not only was Red McGill going ahead with the pregnancy, she wanted her husband to make the global mission for ASNE. She and Julia could handle things just fine without him, she declared. Mary Elizabeth may have been presuming upon her housekeeper's loyalty. According to Ralph, Julia's reaction upon being told the news was, "Miss Red, we is getting too old for this here foolishness." They were. Red prevailed anyhow. Ralph flew out of LaGuardia Airport on January 10, 1945. Mary Elizabeth spent the next three and a half months waiting for her fondest dream to come true. The couple's circle of friends and kin kept an anxious vigil on behalf of the absent father-to-be.[40]

The three missionaries for free news flew from New York to London. Ralph was shocked at the toll the war had taken on Londoners since his visit eighteen months ago. Between meetings he wandered the streets and sat in pubs, wondering that the Brits were still "a great, tough, resilient people." A German V-2 rocket exploded near their hotel. The liquid-fueled missile heralded a new age in weaponry. He made detailed notes. McGill, Forrest, and Ackerman crossed the Channel to Paris. He sent home stories of bravery during the occupation of France by Nazis. He found an elderly man who managed to publish a page or two of news daily, knowing that discovery meant certain death. To McGill, his work was a benchmark of a free press.[41]

In freezing winter weather they crossed the mountains into Italy. By now Ralph's companions kidded that he made Georgia connections everywhere. Even General Eisenhower's son, John, was dating a friend of the McGill family. Heading for the Vatican in Rome, Forrest wagered that at least "the Pope won't have a son who's courting an Atlanta girl." But the Holy Father concluded their audience by sharing a letter from Ralph's old friend and KKK foe, Bishop O'Hara. The journalists then turned East where the journey became more interesting but wearing.[42]

The committee's frustrating experience in Moscow alerted McGill to the difficulties that would soon mark Soviet-American relations. He could not get Soviet officials to understand that their party newspapers were entirely different from a typical U.S. daily. He took this confusion in stride, having encountered it throughout Europe. However, the deep Soviet resentment over American newspaper coverage of the U.S.S.R. depressed McGill. His reporting anticipated postwar emergence of two superpowers. He had seen with his own eyes the power vacuum that made this development inevitable. He thought that if the U.S. and U.S.S.R. dealt with one another solely in terms of mutual fear and suspicion, another war could come.[43]

The ASNE committee went on to India and then flew across "the Hump" into China. McGill wired back to Atlanta more ideas of what to expect after the war. Racial and religious passions would tear apart India and other colonial regions as they cast off imperial rule. Long sessions with Chiang Kai Shek in China convinced McGill that he was a corrupt militarist who could never pacify China and lead her war weary millions towards freedom. Disease and starvation threatened to complete the war's devastation. The suffering he witnessed everywhere overwhelmed him. He always blamed the rise of Axis aggression on chaos following World War I. Now he feared that history would repeat itself in twenty years or so.[44]

Landing at Melbourne, Australia, on April 13, 1945, the three journalists noticed all the flags at half mast. The day before President Roosevelt had died in Warm Springs. McGill had resigned himself to a transfer of power in the 1944 elections. The GOP was bound to triumph, he wrote, after the unprecedented Roosevelt era. When FDR said he would run, McGill jumped on the bandwagon. After the president returned from Yalta, McGill saw him in Washington. Unlike some journalists, McGill thought FDR was fit for a fourth term. "He is a well man," he told readers.[45]

During his work at the 1944 Democratic convention McGill had conferred several times with Harry Truman, then a Missouri senator. Now Vice-President Truman would assume the presidency with scant preparation. Ralph assured readers that Truman had "more capabilities than is generally believed." Nonetheless, Roosevelt was irreplaceable in laying the groundwork for peace.

The ASNE committee moved on to San Francisco and the organizing conference of the new United Nations. He knew collective security was essential to contain future aggressors. As a teenager he had caught Woodrow Wilson's vision of a League of Nations and never lost the ideal. He tried to be encouraging about the San Francisco conference but admitted that the Russians were tough negotiators.[46]

The pace and pressure of the trip at least kept him from dwelling on his worst fears about Mary Elizabeth. He had "only two or three periods of despondency and worry." One took hold just before the Moscow stop. Until then, he wrote his mother, he had no idea of how his wife was. There the Associated Press passed along word that she "was doing fine." He added his hope that Mary Lou "had been in touch with her." Before Ralph left Atlanta, his wife claimed he could easily return for the birth. It was Red's bravado, and Ralph knew it. "I can't possibly get back by the time the baby comes," he told his mother.[47]

His decision to abandon Mary Elizabeth during this critical period gnawed at him. He hated being forced to choose between his wife and a chance that was as wondrous to him as the pregnancy was to her. After sixteen years the odds seemed to be against their being parents. Her insistence on carrying the baby to full term despite her kidney attacks and against the wishes of her family vexed him sorely. During a time when the couple should have been closest, they were separated by continents and oceans. It was as if these distances matched a widening emotional gulf in their marriage. Was this the way to begin parenthood?[48]

Realities soon swallowed up his questions. Tarver wired him in Fiji, "Baby boy, weight six pounds seven ounces, born Caesarean, 8:42 A.M., Wednesday, April 25. Looks like you but is healthy." McGill was forty-seven years old and about to hit his professional stride when Ralph Emerson McGill Jr. arrived. Later both father and son acknowledged that this shaped their relationship. With Julia's unfailing help, Mary Elizabeth made the most of motherhood. She seemed to be her old self again, her relieved husband observed. The baby's arrival set off conflicts within McGill, however. He returned to Atlanta with a fresh vision of his work. This warred with his delight in their new son.[49]

On the trip he saw the whole world and made contacts any newsman would envy. He gained a platform for his ambition that bypassed his limitations at the *Constitution*. Always learning through observation and conversations, Ralph wrote with new mastery. He analyzed the presidency with an elan never possible during his hero worship of FDR. He approached Truman and succeeding presidents as an important southern editor not a local sports writer. Back from the tour, McGill wired a reminder to the White House that he was "one of the original Truman men" and promised support. For the rest of 1945 the editor visited Washington every few weeks. War ended in Europe in May. He agreed with Truman's decision to use two atomic bombs against Japan, especially because the horror might deter future wars.[50]

As Ralph watched the government turn to postwar problems, he could not bear only to comment from a desk in Atlanta. He wanted to be part of the process. Those watching his bad mood and increasingly heavy drinking saw how torn he was. Neither fatherhood nor a role in this new establishment would come his way again. On October 16 he became a special advisor to the State Department for the press and wire services. Such commitments snowballed. They meant that Ralph Jr.'s earliest memories were of goodbyes. Try as McGill might, he could not make increasing absences up to the child. A little boy could not fathom why covering important people and events mattered so much, especially when his mother was ill. One day father and son would face each other as strangers.[51]

7

"THE SOUTH IS IN A DILEMMA": 1946-1949

As events in the south outran McGill's stand on race relations, he often escaped abroad, gaining invaluable news sources. He began 1946 with a long trip to Germany and the Middle East. Herbert Bayard Swope asked him to do a comprehensive study of the Palestine question for the Overseas News Agency, building on his expertise from the 1945 ASNE mission. Swope promised to pay him well and to give the resulting articles "wide exploitation." Howell, Tarver, and others at the *Constitution* knew that he was miserable. His columns from abroad—which would avoid the quandary of race relations—were sure to help the paper in its losing circulation race with the *Journal*. Julia was capable of caring for both Mary Elizabeth and the baby if need be. He could depart without the excess baggage of guilt and conflict that he carried from Atlanta in 1945. He accepted immediately.[1]

This was also the first of many "missions" McGill sought from the U.S. government. Before leaving he contacted William Benton, assistant Secretary of State, to ask if his articles would be of interest to the department. Benton intended to use the reports to gain funding for new overseas information programs. He directed U.S. diplomats to help the Atlanta editor whenever possible. So McGill traveled as a private citizen but had ready access to U.S. officials everywhere. He put his knack for public relations to use often in the early postwar years. This ploy brought him closer to the centers of power.[2]

McGill's first dispatches were from Nuremburg where the Allies put leading Nazis on trial as war criminals. He had seen some of these men in 1938. From the spectators' gallery he peered through field glasses as if to penetrate their masks. He doubted that any court proceedings could encompass the enormity of their evil. This Nuremburg visit reinforced his 1938 vow to fight hatred, prejudice, and intolerance. In Germany he also described problems that occupying forces had with Soviet troops and anticipated the Cold War for readers.[3]

During the trip McGill became a Zionist. He visited refugee camps and met survivors of the Holocaust. It would be impossible, he said, to send many of these displaced persons back to prewar homes. Then he moved on to Palestine and saw areas that Jewish agencies had bought to resettle émigrés. He knew how deeply the Arabs opposed Jewish settlements and that Arabs controlled most of the world's oil reserves. He decided that 100,000 Jews (a typical repatriation proposal) would not intrude on the Arab populations in Palestine. Still, he warned that in the future the U.S. must choose between dependence on Arab oil and pressure to support Zionists.[4]

He returned home invigorated. His nickname, "Pappy," was more popular than ever, partly because of the baby, but also because he spent so much time advising veterans. McGill had always been sympathetic to young people's ambitions. Strong, helpful men had encouraged him during his teens and twenties, and he took advantage of opportunities to do the same for others. Upon meeting McGill shortly after the war, Harry Ashmore of the *Charlotte News* noticed that he "had a great way of making you feel equals." Ashmore moved on to the *Arkansas Gazette* and then to California, but their correspondence over the years testified to a bond deeper than newsmen's camaraderie.

McGill continued Papa Howell's *Constitution* tradition of an open office door and helping hand. In his travels he told countless servicemen to come visiting after the war. Many did. Others who had never met the editor but felt they knew him through his column occasionally stopped by. Like McGill, they had seen other parts of the world and knew the South must change. His message was always the same: Why not settle in the South and work for regional progress? Harold Fleming was one who did. He grew up in Atlanta but after commanding black troops in World War II, decided against returning to segregation. On a visit to his home-town Fleming saw McGill who sent him over to the Southern Regional Council. He stayed for fourteen years, including four as the SRC's executive director.[5]

McGill took heart from the accomplishments of Governor Ellis Arnall. Despite wartime disruptions Arnall achieved much in his four year term. He oversaw modernizing of state government, including a civil service system. He improved Georgia's backward educational and penal institutions. The notorious chain gangs were outlawed as were the pardon rackets. Repealing the poll tax and lowering the voting age to eighteen increased the electorate. Best of all in McGill's view, Arnall successfully fought in court the freight rate discrimination that handicapped southern industry. The young governor, McGill exulted, had slain a dragon that had bluffed regional politicians for seventy-five years. He did not add that newfound prosperity had rendered it toothless.[6]

Arnall's success was flawed, however. Georgia was never so prosperous. Yet the governor failed to ask for taxes to sustain his reform program. Also Arnall made a national speaking tour that did not sit well with the folks back home. It was natural that one who seemed destined for higher office should seek a wider audience for his ideas. Georgians thought he made himself look good on the tour by airing too much of their dirty linen. Back home, Arnall tried to reverse a constitutional ban on a second term. He failed. The 1946 governor's race was thrown wide open.

Even if the liberal factions united behind one candidate, a force loomed that might vanquish reform and send Georgia politics back to the Dark Ages. It was Gene Talmadge. Talmadge was bitter about governmental trends during the Roosevelt era. He seemed powerless against them until fate rearmed his favorite political weapon—racism. McGill lived in dread of another reactionary period like that of 1919-20. In 1946 Talmadge sensed it coming. He would sweep back to a fourth term riding McGill's twin monsters, fear and prejudice. "There ain't another Goddamn sonofabitch that can get elected governor," he told a friend. "I been sick and it might just kill me, but I'm a gonna do it." On

April 16 he announced his candidacy.[7]

While McGill was abroad, Georgia blacks moved closer to gaining the franchise. In a one-party state the Democratic primary determined political winners and losers. Black voters could not participate in the primary on grounds that it was a private affair. A succession of court rulings in early 1946 destroyed that subterfuge. Blacks who qualified and registered would help elect the governor. McGill had hoped to wage an editorial campaign for tolerance and patience before Georgians faced changes in race relations. Once again he was reacting to rather than leading public opinion. All spring he pleaded vainly for calm and fairness in the face of white panic and rage. His frequent claims that Negroes would not indulge in "bloc" voting were not assuring.[8]

If McGill was not ready publicly to acknowledge political realities, Mayor Hartsfield was. Throughout his early years black leaders regularly visited the mayor with demands and grievances. Many blacks refused to support his 1945 reelection bid. When an all-white primary vanished in 1946, Hartsfield knew a reckoning was coming. He prepared to meet at least one longstanding demand—black policemen. Black leaders had wanted this from Mayor Key's tenure. Key refused, believing the time was not right for such a step. Key told his aide, future police chief Herbert Jenkins, to expect them while he was on the force, however. After a demonstration by thousands in 1945 and renewed pressure from Hartsfield's black kitchen cabinet, the mayor began paving the way.[9]

Meanwhile Atlanta's African-American community launched a massive registration campaign. Working block by block, volunteers added 18,000 new voters. Atlanta blacks had recently proven their power at the polls during a special congressional election in which neither the primary rules nor Georgia's odd county unit system that rendered populated areas powerless applied. The new representative would win strictly on a popular vote. Only one candidate sought black support, and in February 1946 their ballots sent Helen Douglas Mankin to Congress from the Fifth District.[10]

Talmadge used the Mankin election as proof that Georgia

needed him to ward off the "radical, Communist, and alien influences" threatening white supremacy. He proposed an elaborate legal scheme he claimed would defy the Supreme Court's decision on the primary. Then in June the high court ruled against segregation on interstate transportation, strengthening Talmadge's appeal. The former governor vowed to unload every bus or train at Georgia's borders and force passengers to buy new intrastate tickets. He assured voters he had the will and the way to keep Georgia white man's land. He concentrated efforts in rural counties, especially those with large numbers of blacks. Elimination of the poll tax would bring some poor whites to the polls for the first time. Talmadge played upon their fears. He also urged all whites to challenge any Negroes who tried to qualify to vote.

His two opponents, E. D. Rivers and James V. Carmichael, were segregationists themselves but avoided discussing these obvious threats to the status quo. Like Gene, Ed Rivers was trying to reoccupy the governor's office, promising to add to new state programs. He was the "spoiler" of the race, dividing the anti-Talmadge vote with Carmichael, the *Constitution*'s candidate. A thirty-six year old attorney, Carmichael ran the Bell Bomber Plant in his hometown of Marietta. His political experience was scant, but McGill and others touted his managerial ability and character. Carmichael pledged more good government in Georgia.[11]

As if on cue, the Ku Klux Klan—defunct for years—reappeared. Demands by the Internal Revenue Service for decades of back taxes ruined the leadership of Wizard James Colescott. New leaders of the hate group saw their chances for a revival and held a fiery initiation ceremony atop Stone Mountain in May. McGill used his tried-and-true weapon of ridicule against those "who somehow get a thrill out of wearing a mask and a robe." He noted that two candidates for governor had Klan connections. He urged Georgians not to listen to any political advice from this "evil and vicious gangster-minded outfit." Yet racial fears took center stage in the campaign. These played right into the hands of new Wizard "Doc" Samuel Green.[12]

McGill sought release from these local troubles in projects that gave him national media exposure. He was in demand as a speaker, thanks to his Overseas News Agency reports and the publicity of well-placed friends. He appeared on NBC's "Town Hall of the Air" in March and spoke to an American Federation of Labor convention in May. After years of rejection notices, he was selling work to leading magazines. Edward Weeks ran a second McGill article in the April issue of *Atlantic Monthly*. In bio lines Weeks described the Atlanta editor as a "fearless" liberal. Such introductions in print or on the speaker's platform had two unfortunate effects. They deepened Clark Howell's problems and set McGill up for future ridicule as a "Jim Crow liberal," despite his repeated claim, "I have never said I was a liberal."[13]

The governor's race climaxed in mid July. Ralph made his final pleas for common sense and progress. "Don't be caught in the spiderweb of falsehoods," he urged. Segregation was assured by state law. On election day he called for defeat of Talmadge who would only "throw the state into discord, tension, and fear." Carmichael, he predicted, would win without a runoff. McGill's man did get more votes than Talmadge. However, Georgia's peculiar county unit system, in which less populous rural counties could outweigh the political power of the urban counties, gave Gene his victory.[14]

At the *Constitution* on election night McGill commiserated with Governor Arnall and some reporters. Suddenly Talmadge appeared, "his steel-trap jaw snapped shut around a cold cigar." He shook hands with the disheveled editor. "Ralph," he said, removing the cigar, "I give you a good whuppin' this time, didn't I?" The governor-elect sat down and reminisced about the decade through which they had contended. Onlookers sensed that both men viewed their conflict more as a duel than a feud. When Talmadge rose to leave, he admitted that the campaign had taken fifteen years off his life. Family and friends knew it was so.[15]

McGill was also at low ebb. He went up to Tennessee, hoping its outlandish politics would distract him. Sitting in Nashville's Associated Press office on July 26, he got reports of a brutal lynching just east of Atlanta. The night before a gang of twenty unmasked whites had shot two young black men and their wives beyond recognition. The mob broke the arms of the women before murdering them.

McGill wired home an anguished column. The curse of Cain was truly on Georgia, he cried. One by one the twenty murderers would break under the burden of their guilt. "They cannot tie the hands of Conscience behind his back and shoot him with pistols and shotguns." In angry followup columns he confronted readers with a hard choice. Southerners wanted to solve racial dilemmas without "outside interference." If, he wrote, we make "intolerance and murder the keystone of our society," we cannot expect to be left alone.[16]

Ralph grew more and more despondent about the future. The Walton County lynchings, coupled with Talmadge's triumph and revival of the Klan, made Georgia a byword for degradation. Failure to bring a single member of the large lynch mob to justice deepened the shame. He felt a violent, chaotic spell darkening his postwar hopes. He could not even enjoy his baby son who was happy and robust.

The black moods that had plagued him from youth had never lasted so long before. Unable to sleep, he feared breaking down. In August he wrote Ruthanna Boris that he was gripped by "a very real melancholy, close to despair." Those about him decided that intervention was necessary. Bob Woodruff sent the exhausted editor to his ranch in Cody, Wyoming, for several weeks. Day after day he worked with the ranch hands, gathering in hay and moving horses. Between the hard physical labor and regular sleeping, he recovered. It was the only time depression took him off the job. Otherwise, work was "his anodyne."[17]

Soon after returning from the West, McGill wrote a stinging piece about southerners who wanted all critics to leave the region. Their line, "If you don't like it, you can go somewhere else," had worked. The South's "greatest export product" was its "best and most ambitious human beings." That out migration had to stop. He concluded, "if we love the South, we cannot ... refuse to fight to bring our standards up to those of the rest of the nation."

Throughout 1946 McGill had been ready to give up his job and relocate. This column revealed why he stayed put.[18]

Even though he complained regularly that he and his family paid too high a price, he kept "his innards on display every morning on the front page of the *Constitution.*" He headed Brotherhood Week for the National Conference of Christians and Jews. Yet blacks needed a much more powerful force than tolerance to win their struggle for rights. A hate group called "The Columbians" set up shop in Atlanta. Using old Nazi tactics, they tried to stop Negroes from relocating from the ghetto. McGill joined the civic outcry. In scathing columns he discredited the Columbians' leaders and scoffed at their threats on his life. He begged Atlanta real estate agents to meet with leaders of both races and work out a plan for transitional neighborhoods.[19]

The year ended with two calamities. On the night of December 7 the worst hotel fire in history occurred in Atlanta. The Winecoff, a Peachtree Street landmark since 1913, burned. 119 died and more than 100 were injured. Many victims were boys and girls attending a state youth conference. Ralph was early on the scene. He crossed a ladder stretched across an alley thirteen stories up and crept around the hotel before removal of the bodies. The paper ran his detailed account on page one. The piece resonated with his morbid fascination with horror and death. His lead editorial and accompanying column were measured and thoughful.[20]

Fourteen days later Gene Talmadge died at an Atlanta hospital. His last interview was with the *Constitution* editor. In his post mortem column McGill admitted that his sometime "objectivity" (some would have said apostasy) about Talmadge had caused concern. He explained it grew out of mutual respect. He revealed that twice the governor proposed that McGill write his biography. His late foe was, he concluded, "a puzzling man." The column had an incomplete quality as if he were postponing judgment. After the deathbed interview he hinted about matters Gene had confided. Perhaps after all McGill might do a Talmadge biography and in good time say what he was keeping to himself.[21]

Followers of the senior Talmadge now created a constitutional crisis that defied Georgia's best legal minds and added to the scorn heaped upon the state. The governor-elect's son, Herman, was a write-in candidate in November. If Gene could not take office, his men intended the legislature to choose Herman. After nearly twenty-four hours of what McGill described in the *New Republic* as "a mixture of legal red tape and Graustarkian drama, a coup d'etat out of a fiction-writer's plot," they succeeded. Arnall insisted that Lieutenant Governor Melvin E. Thompson was his successor whereupon Herman forcibly occupied the governor's office and mansion. The state supreme court approved Thompson, but Georgia enjoyed "three governors" long enough to become a laughingstock across the country.[22]

McGill fled Georgia's bizarre politics for long European trips in 1947 and 1948. What he saw convinced him that the U.S. must aid citizens of war torn Europe and abandon cooperation with the Russians. He thought Truman had "responded magnificently" to two years of challenge and came away from special White House briefings impressed with the president's grasp of geopolitical realities. He was even more enthusiastic about Secretary of State George C. Marshall. In 1947 and 1948 McGill testified at congressional hearings on behalf of both the Truman Doctrine and Marshall Plan. Soon he was truly a Cold Warrior, urging that the U.S. rearm.[23]

Journalists like McGill were valuable as the administration sought ways to contain Communism and reverse over a century of American non-involvement in Europe. He led a campaign for a proposed broadcast information program called the Voice of America. He was dead set against the government propaganda he had observed under the Nazis. However, the "distorted news and false accusations" beamed across Europe by Russian radio infuriated him. Even well established news agencies like the AP and UPI tended to play up sensational stories. The Voice of America might give foreigners a fair idea of how ordinary Americans lived and the values they cherished.[24]

At the same time he was seeking to counter Communism abroad, McGill and other editors began discussing what Communists might be up to at home. He deplored tactics that the House Un-American Activities Committee used investigating Hollywood and elsewhere. He always maintained that the Communist party was negligible in the South and unsuccessful in wooing blacks. However McGill, like any other southerner discussing racial change, was himself being branded a Communist traitor. So he attacked groups and individuals suspected of radical connections, hoping to disprove charges against him.

The moribund Southern Conference for Human Welfare served his purpose well. Even its leadership was torn over the issue of fellow travelers within its ranks. McGill declared that Communists joined such "reform groups for the deliberate purpose of embarrassing and defeating them." He admitted having high hopes for the SCHW when it began in 1939. Like so many others, he said, "I knew enough to get out" when Communists participated.[25]

McGill's attack on the SCHW was a personal vendetta as well as Red-baiting. Its president and one of a few salaried workers was Major Clark Howell's cousin, Clark Foreman. Foreman was among a handful of individuals whom McGill personally detested and lambasted in print. He justified these attacks because Foreman "fouled us up here in Georgia in innumerable ways." Through another relative, Foreman asked the major for McGill to make a retraction or at least "a clarifying statement." Aubrey Williams, old friend of both men, also pleaded with Ralph whom he thought smeared Foreman.

Foreman had almost given up and was considering legal action when the editor finally apologized in an early 1948 column. Yet he managed to turn the apology into another attack. "I believe I know Clark Foreman better than you do," he later wrote to Aubrey Williams, "his judgment is atrocious." Ralph added defiantly, "I have never called Clark a Communist, and even he doesn't accuse me of that."[26]

In late 1947 the SCHW sponsored a southern tour by Henry Wallace, and McGill took after him. The former Vice-President became Secretary of Commerce after Roosevelt replaced him with Truman on the 1944 ticket. Wallace opposed Truman's tough handling of the U.S.S.R. and resigned in protest. Now many old line liberals and leftists promoted him as a third party candidate against Truman in 1948. Wanting an integrated audience, Wallace gave his Atlanta speech at the huge auditorium of Wheat Street Baptist Church. Its pastor, the Reverend William Holmes Borders, was among the city's strongest black leaders. In a column McGill warned Borders to expect "a few overly ripe critical tomatoes for getting mixed up with the Southern Conference and its set of discredited professional phonies."[27]

Major Howell had far greater concerns than his cousin and the SCHW. In the decade since Howell assumed control of the *Constitution,* he had worried about competition from the *Journal* and even more about his own precarious finances. Now Howell reckoned he had to make a move or be left behind in Atlanta's postwar boom. He built a $3 million facility for the newspaper just up Forsyth Street. In late December 1947 the *Constitution* transferred operations from its decrepit home of sixty-four years, now sold to Rich's. Howell's building was within sight of the new multimillion dollar *Journal* plant.[28]

The major also tried to match Governor Cox in other media. The *Journal's* radio station, WSB, was a big attraction for Cox in 1939. So in studios atop the new *Constitution* building, WCON began broadcasting as a local affiliate of the ABC network. McGill was on his European tour at the time. He made a series of well-publicized radio reports from abroad to help inaugurate WCON. Aware that Cox would start television broadcasts in 1948, Howell laid plans for entering this medium as well. Up until now Howell had managed to keep the *Constitution* breaking even by being "notorious for pinching pennies." After the move his family and the handful of other owners faced losses. Mounting operating costs and losses vexed Howell. The situation was not lost on the prospering Cox enterprise.[29]

Given these financial pressures, McGill worried about alienating readers and lowering advertising linage by being controversial as a "nigger-loving Communist." At issue was his position on segregation. Ralph felt deeply his obligation to the Howells and other owners of the paper. Also throughout his editorial career he vowed never to get too far ahead of (white) readers. After Georgia's recent troubles he could not envision an abrupt end to Jim Crow, so he continued to urge slow change—especially making separate facilities truly equal.[30]

However, he anticipated a role as the South's conscience. His *Constitution* column of January 3, 1947, warned, "Whatever is done must meet the test of being right or wrong. . . . We must first be honest with ourselves. Laws are not enough unless they be just." Justice was integral to his life, starting with a youthful sense of fair play. Once he allowed a sense of justice to dominate his thinking on race relations, he found his way out of a wilderness of conflict and pessimism. It brought some consistency to his writing until several years later when he moved "left of center" and supported desegregation.[31]

Knowing that fear was a big part of prejudice, McGill continued to soothe anxious segregationists in letters and print. He tried to convince them that treating blacks fairly would not bring social equality with its feared miscegenation. "I am not interested in associating with negroes," he told one irate man in November 1947, "therefore I do not plan to do so. . . . if I am on a train, I do not have to sit by a negro unless I want to and I don't want to. Therefore I am not bothered."[32]

Meanwhile, he gratified his sense of justice with work that seemed promising to him but infuriated segregationists. Editorially he pushed hard a plan to give Atlanta blacks more housing. He constantly warned white southerners that they were responsible to provide equal facilities if they expected to retain segregation. Outside the paper he used fiction to express moral indignation. In late 1947 *Harper's* published his short story about a young black woman and the suicide of her despairing husband, a veteran of military service. The piece captured the essence of young blacks' postwar anguish and drew more reader response than any in *Harper's* recent history.[33]

Then racial issues moved onto the national political agenda, blowing his gradualism strategy skyhigh. In February 1948

President Truman proposed federal civil rights legislation. Truman wanted voting rights plus protection against lynching and job discrimination. McGill opposed these proposals as unconstitutional. The first two areas were local matters, he wrote, and employment was not really a civil right. He told a national CBS radio audience that the South was making progress and would continue to do so if left alone. Yet he warned southerners in print and on the airwaves that if they did not actively pursue racial justice, then they deserved federal coercion.[34]

By early 1948 McGill found that playing mediator in the emerging civil rights campaign would bring attacks from both races. Participating at an Atlanta University symposium, he faced black anger. He got off to a bad start by using the hated pronunciation, "Nigras." Then outraged students took him to task for pleading justice yet opposing the federal initiatives. At least two members of the audience encouraged him, however. They were Grace Hamilton and Will Alexander. Both knew that the editor was one of few Atlanta white leaders who would have appeared at AU. Some associates thought he risked more in the 1940s than later.[35]

Hamilton, rooted in the AU community and since 1943 director of Atlanta's Urban League, entertained McGill at her home after the program ended. "I think he handled himself as well as he could," she recalled. Hamilton understood his frustration but was glad he had witnessed the students' outrage. Alexander, a racial mediator for decades wrote the editor, "What you did is not a pleasant kind of thing to do, but...I think you did it very well." Alexander blamed some of the students' hostility on "their own perplexities." He urged McGill to keep listening to young African Americans. He did, reporting that a working class black woman had come to his office and expressed different priorities than those of the AU students. She was angered that "the white people think all Negroes are just alike."[36]

Increasing contacts with blacks made McGill into more of a hostile outsider and less of a southern apologist. By midsummer 1948 he warned that African Americans would gain their civil rights one way or another. If the states failed, then Washington would force the issue. "Let us, who love the South, realize that the trend in the world is against the southern ideas. . . . We cannot expect the rest of the nation to conform to our beliefs. . . ."[37]

McGill found much fulfillment in the late 1940s despite conflicts over civil rights. He had a small kitchen adjacent to his office in the new building and often cooked lunch for members of the staff. When they ate out, McGill rated special treatment from the restaurateur. Nothing gratified McGill more than to be counted among McCallie's distinguished alumni. In 1948 he was the school's commencement speaker. The following year he dedicated a new gym during homecoming weekend and was honorary chairman of the Fiftieth Anniversary campaign. In his youth the staff talked of the ideal "McCallie man" who used his education to make the South a better place. He had become the man. Standing beside the football field, he savored memories of a boy who "felt good and sure about everything."[38]

Thanks to the superb management of Mary Elizabeth and Julia, he was freed from household chores to play with Ralph Jr. To a friend he declared, "He is our heart." Mary Elizabeth's exuberance knew no bounds when it came to her only child. When little Ralph played with other children, she pushed him center stage. If guests came to the McGill home, she had the precocious child show off his latest "cute tricks." Mary Elizabeth began teaching him to read at age three. He remembered bits and pieces of his father's discourses that would have stupefied an average tot. Such intense parenting produced a boy not easily accepted by peers.[39]

After almost two decades of marriage, the McGills were a family at last. The three of them traveled to Chattanooga where grandmother and aunts doted on both Ralphs. Mary Lou worried about her daughter-in-law's health and the effect of a chronically ill wife on Ralph's life. High blood pressure now complicated Mary Elizabeth's kidney disease. Between attacks of stones and fever, however, she kept busy. She was the family's only driver. She wrote a column in the Buckhead paper offering recipes and cooking tips. The three of them vacationed in Florida at the beach homes of Atlanta friends. The shadows of death went away.[40]

Ralph turned fifty on February 5, 1948. During the Nashville years he always did a birthday column. This milestone got no mention other than a sour account of a doctor putting him on a diet. Nothing was new there. He once told Jack Tarver, "I must have lost a thousand pounds in my life." Withal, he remained heavyset and broad, resembling the prizefighters he once loved to cover. The most telling change at this age was a growing self-assurance in his writing. Among family, friends, and most strangers, he was still open and unassuming. Yet he went on the attack in print more often.[41]

Whereas earlier his persona as a writer bent over backwards to maintain a tone of fair play, he now lashed out, using his talent as a weapon. Sometimes the vengeance was misplaced. The intemperate columns and letters often came when he was overtired, harassed, or worried about Mary Elizabeth or *Constitution* finances. His lifelong friend, Reb Gershon, believed Ralph "always took on too much. He wore himself out." However, his biographer and friend, Harold Martin, pondered why McGill developed "strong dislikes on whim" or had "tirades of unprovoked anger against his closest friends." Family and friends accepted without understanding his paradoxical nature. Even when he failed to warn that a dark mood was upon him, they were never surprised by an irrational reaction.[42]

Once McGill achieved a certain degree of fame, he worked constantly to enlarge that reputation. He spoke all over the country. Already producing great amounts of copy for the paper, McGill drove himself to write more and more. He cultivated editors of top magazines and submitted long articles to them. He got many favorable responses but always with orders to rewrite, revise. Sometimes he stayed at the office all night to get one of these free lance jobs in the mail by his deadline. In 1947 he contracted to do a book about the Chattahoochee River in a Rinehart series on American rivers.[43]

In May 1948 the *Saturday Evening Post* published the first of many McGill stories. "Will the South Ditch Truman?" exposed for the *Post*'s huge readership the defiant and irrational mood of many southern Democrats. McGill admitted that Truman's federal civil rights proposals were mild but insisted that progress was already being made. He concluded that once more blacks voted and the Republicans established a viable southern wing a new pattern would emerge without federal coercion. His plea for time was unconvincing, given the revolt he had predicted.[44]

The editor himself had been criticizing the president all year. He preferred no federal civil rights legislation. He was convinced such laws were as unenforceable as Prohibition had been. If Washington forced them, then chaos was inevitable. He predicted the end of Truman's presidency long before traveling to Philadelphia where the Democrats reluctantly nominated Truman and the revolting Dixiecrats walked out. In September he rejected a request to serve the administration. Truman's Executive Order forbidding discrimination in the armed forces provided for an advisory committee. The president wanted the Atlanta editor to be one of the seven men. Ralph declined, blaming "our local political situation" and the fact that "complete integration" seemed "inevitable," given the other six members. Truman made only a start.[45]

McGill covered the remainder of the campaign with a kind of mesmerized horror. He worked to discredit the Dixiecrats but feared their appeal. Progress in the South seemed doomed. Truman won against all predictions. The *Constitution* editor ate crow for his readers and sent the victorious president a wire. "We will not be dishonest and say we thought you could do it . . . but we were for you ... and proud that we helped give you the majority in Georgia." When Ralph attended the inaugural in January, 1949, his accounts played up Truman's tough stand against Communism rather than his civil rights bills.[46]

The editor shifted emphasis, partly because he realized the new Congress would never enact civil rights legislation, but mostly because the anti-Communism gripping America soon worsened. The public feared Communists had riddled the U.S. government with spies and were about to claim China. Meanwhile McGill continued his sly Red-baiting at home. He still denounced HUAC, limiting his attacks to Atlanta where anti-Communism had been strong since 1932. He also hoped this duplicitous strategy would satisfy his own accusers. It did not.

McGill's primary target was Don West whom HUAC identified as a Communist long before the editor did. Their lives had strange parallels. Both were born on poor mountain farms and later attended Vanderbilt. West left with two degrees, however. Each won a Rosenwald fellowship, West while completing his Ph.D. He began teaching at Atlanta's Oglethorpe University in 1946. When West directed Henry Wallace's Georgia campaign in 1948, McGill did a half dozen columns about his Communist ties in the 1930s that had never been proved. West lost his job. In 1949 McGill renewed his attacks on Homer Chase, "the official southern representative" of the party. When criticized for Red-baiting, McGill replied that the deadly chemistry between Communists and "Kluxers" distracted southerners from the real question of justice for Negroes.[47]

1949 found Mayor Hartsfield in a tough reelection fight. McGill was regularly on the receiving end of the fiery mayor's wrath, but he viewed Hartsfield as a great asset to Atlanta. As election day neared, the editor came to his defense. Black voters allowed Hartsfield to win, reminding McGill of Mayor Key's 1932 recall scare. The election illustrated "the Atlanta style" of politics. A highly politicized black community made common cause with whites whom Hartsfield called "the decent folks," allowing the city to project a progressive image.

John Wesley Dobbs had recently merged his black Republican leadership with the Democratic councils of attorney, Austen T. Walden. The men knew that their new Atlanta Negro Voters League would exert greater pressure than the old party organizations. They were right. Hartsfield received about two-thirds of the count in black precincts. Although he carried wealthier white neighborhoods, he did not win a majority of the white vote.

When eight black police officers went out on patrol in 1948, the Atlanta style of politics was fully launched. Herbert Jenkins, schooled to expect such changes by Mayor Key, was now Atlanta's police chief. Hartsfield pushed through hiring the officers and proclaimed it a major breakthrough in race relations. In the *Atlantic Monthly*, McGill said the step proved that black political power and interracial cooperation could accomplish more than federal laws. Neither the mayor nor the editor revealed that the Negro policemen had to dress at a black YMCA, answered to a white officer, could not arrest whites or carry weapons.[48]

8

"FLEAS COME WITH THE DOG": 1950-1956

ATLANTA AND THE SOUTH WERE CHANGING FASTER THAN MCGILL could believe, but worse upheaval lay ahead. The 1950 census found 326,962 persons living in the city proper, 663,711 counting the suburbs. In 1951 new boundaries tripled the city's size, adding 100,000 to the population. Money was to be made with an ease that confounded McGill and old families like the Howells. Always a boom town, Atlanta welcomed all who would roll up their sleeves and share this ethos. Ralph desperately wanted to help black citizens benefit from the city's postwar prosperity. Even after the landmark Supreme Court rulings of the decade, he remained pessimistic that a new pattern of race relations would quickly replace segregation. As he often said during this period, "I've got ideas but not answers."[1]

His ideas included pressure from black ballots on white politicians to rectify political wrongs, improve Negro schools, and give job opportunities. These were enough to enrage most whites. In July 1949 he confided to another newsperson, "Only the fact that our situation is a little complicated has prevented me from putting on a Negro reporter who would bring his stuff into the office. He would not have a desk at the office. We are not ready for that." The editor also knew that blacks disliked the practice of separate sections for notices from the "colored community." He said he would have liked for the *Constitution* to treat their news "as news and not have it 'Jim Crow-ed.' "[2]

The complicating situation to which he referred was the possibility that Atlanta's two white newspapers might merge. Since summer 1948 a local investment firm had been secretly conducting negotiations between the *Constitution* owners and Cox family. Even

McGill suspected nothing for months. Then during a social occasion one evening, Clark Howell loosened up. Perhaps, he said, in future they would produce the papers together. McGill was both confused and worried. He wanted Jack Tarver's opinion. Tarver spent all of 1949 in South America on a Reid fellowship. Even thousands of miles away from Atlanta, Tarver understood Howell's dilemma. The new building, his television venture, plus inflationary costs made it impossible to be profitable again.[3]

McGill spent most of 1950 traveling. While he was abroad that spring, Governor Cox did buy the *Constitution*. Major Howell and the other owners took 180,000 shares of convertible preferred stock in a new corporation, Atlanta Newspapers, Inc. Cox, who turned 80 a few days after making the purchase, was chairman of the board of ANInc. Howell continued as publisher of the *Constitution* for another decade, but management of both newspapers was in the hands of a Cox man named George Biggers. Tarver put in a telephone call to McGill. He located his boss in London and gave the particulars. According to Harold Martin, "There was silence at the other end. Finally, across two thousand miles of empty sea and sky came McGill's despairing cry. 'Ohhhhh shit!'"[4]

National news coverage of the merger emphasized how Cox had surpassed Howell in the decade since he bought the *Journal*. The stories stung McGill, who wanted no part of the Cox monopoly. Red McGill was even more upset than her husband. Without waiting for Ralph to return and get the particulars, she decided the sale was a disaster. She began calling editors in various cities, threatening to picket the paper or issue some statement. By the time McGill reached Atlanta, understanding friends had calmed Mary Elizabeth down. Tarver and Ralph were still on tenterhooks. Each considered leaving the paper.[5]

At Governor Cox's request, they flew to Miami in the company plane and met with him in the *Miami Daily News* tower. He said, "'I know how you boys feel; you feel like you've been sold out.'" But Cox added that they were the reasons he bought the paper. He promised to keep hands off news and editorial policies. The two men felt somewhat better after visiting the Governor. "Back in their hotel room, McGill threw himself upon the bed, heaved a great sigh, and said, 'Well, Mr. Tarver, all our *old* troubles are over.'" In fact, Tarver's career took off. He moved from being associate editor to assist first Howell, then the president of ANInc, George Biggers. Eventually Tarver got Biggers's job.[6]

Even though he reassured the staff in writing, McGill struggled with the new arrangement. Along with other old *Constitution* hands he moaned, "Hell, we haven't been merged, we've been submerged." Perhaps it was McGill's Welsh black dog mood or his trait of fierce loyalty intensified by the *Nashville Banner*'s hateful feuds. Despite the Governor's assurances to the contrary, Ralph believed himself to be under the thumb of a hireling of his hated rival paper.

For the next half dozen years no one could convince him that Biggers did not live to torment him. The two were temperamental opposites. Biggers grew up in Kentucky. He began his newspaper career in sports, arriving in Atlanta eight years before McGill. At the *Journal* Biggers switched to management and rose to presidency of that company in 1946. He had a brusque manner and harsh managerial style. This does not fully explain the strange chemistry that developed between McGill and the ANInc president. Biggers's strong segregationist position may be the key.

A solution was to let McGill travel more and more. He had always been more columnist than conventional editor. Celestine Sibley and others at the paper suspected that he viewed himself as "a reporter first and then an editor." Sibley admitted that "a roaming, writing editor is in the *Constitution* tradition." Other newspapers often bought columns from McGill's trips, satisfying the ambitions of both Biggers and the editor while keeping them apart.[7]

McGill's tendency to flip-flop continued to exasperate his staff and confuse readers. Harold Martin recalled that one spell of reversals brought a letter complaining, "'To contradict yourself is normal. But you are now contradicting your contradictions. . . .'" Some on the staff suspected that McGill relished making these editorial shifts or treating sympathetically someone they knew he opposed. He reminded protesting colleagues that he was named for Ralph Waldo Emerson who declared, "A foolish consistency is the hobgoblin of little minds." Or he would say, "I am like Lincoln whose policy was to have no policy." Was his lifelong penchant for pranks manifesting itself in tricks on his readers? Many who knew him well were aware of a "sly" aspect of his personality. Yet he did have what Reb Gershon called a need to see "all around a person." "I have been cursed all my life," he once wrote, "with the ability to see both sides of things."

Ralph's open-mindedness towards the Talmadges also bothered his associates. His eulogizing of Gene did not sit well with many. The editor thought Herman, who won a special governor's election in 1948, was doing well and should gain a full four-year term in 1950. Many other influential Georgians agreed. Herman Talmadge was smart, able, and profiting from his father's political mistakes, seemed ready to modernize Georgia. What infuriated colleagues and readers was that McGill held his fire even when Herman deserved attack. The *Journal* went after Talmadge's corrupt vote-gathering in 1946 and garnered a 1947 Pulitzer Prize for its efforts. McGill killed stories of Herman's personal indiscretions and promoted an image of a solid family man. Mutterings about "our lost leader" increased around the *Constitution*.[8]

Despite the merger, competition between Atlanta's big dailies was keener than ever. McGill worked very hard to upgrade the *Constitution* and beat the *Journal*. He and the Major tried to discover why the *Journal* was more popular. One survey showed that the *Constitution* had less appeal for women than its rival. Another revealed that it was easier to sell the *Journal* in outlying parts of the state. The *Constitution*, it seemed, needed better photos, a livelier front page, and ads the ladies would like. At least the hated consolidation meant that they could afford improvements such as the *New York Times* wire service and Bodoni type. They moved Ralph's daily column to page one left and planned some staff changes.[9]

In the midst of such pressures at the office, McGill attempted more outside writing projects. He was determined to produce a book. He canceled vacation plans in order to try to finish his 30,000 word manuscript on the Chattahoochee River for Rinehart. In spring 1950 he gained a book of sorts after a second visit to Palestine, now Israel. *Israel Revisited* combined column material from both his Mideast trips, but the Chattahoochee River project was more than a rehash of old columns. In the fall of 1950 he finally mailed his manuscript to Rinehart. Weeks later came news that his publisher wanted a complete revision. McGill despaired of ever succeeding with a lengthy manuscript.[10]

He was becoming a frequent contributor to the *Saturday Evening Post*, which always received a great deal of reader reaction about him. At its peak the magazine had an extraordinary circulation of seven million copies a week, giving McGill national recognition before the syndication of his column. In late April 1950 the *Post* ran his account of Florida's Congressman George Smathers contesting the senate seat of Claude Pepper. Pepper was vulnerable to charges of being too far left, but McGill's focus was Smathers, whom he greatly admired. Using quotes from Smathers to oppose Pepper, Ralph avoided his usual Red-baiting style.[11]

By 1950 McGill was searching for any possible ways to discredit segregation, so he linked race relations to the Cold War. From trips abroad he knew firsthand its detrimental effect on U.S. foreign relations. He emphasized that the Jim Crow system hurt America's competition with global enemies and its work with leaders of non-white countries: "The Ku Klux Klan state of mind has been, and is, the best little helper Communism has." The editor anticipated some American politicians who rationalized their support of civil rights in terms of the Cold War strategy rather than from a sense of racial justice.[12]

In a September 1950 column McGill began discussing Atlanta school desegregation. He noted that some of the city's blacks rejected separate-and-equal schools. Guided by NAACP lawyers, they sued against segregation. He reminded readers that courts had already desegregated higher education in some locations. What of the old argument he and others used that violence would ensue if Negroes tried to integrate elementary and secondary schools? It might prove true, he said but added, "after the bloodshed the decision and the law will remain." The column anticipated his support of desegregation as the law of the land but was atypical. Usually he devoted more space in print reassuring frightened whites that segregation was not about to disappear. Fear was a big factor in racial prejudice but, by now, he should have started preparing "the segs" for what he knew was inevitable.[13]

During 1950 Senator Joseph McCarthy went from a nobody to a household word with his campaign against Communists in government. McCarthy's tactics reminded McGill of the Nazis. He condemned the senator's "vicious, reckless and unscrupulous exploitation of the nation's proper fear . . . of Communist influences." The editor defended some McCarthy victims, especially a Jewish aide to Defense Secretary George C. Marshall. The smears and lies of McCarthyism, he asserted, were doing more damage to the U.S. than the Communists.[14]

Yet McGill saw no reason to relent in his own attacks on local individuals whom he labeled as Communists or "pinkos." He rationalized that his local Red-baiting protected him somewhat from those who called him "Red Ralph" and said desegregation was a Communist conspiracy. Besides, men like Homer Chase, Don West, and Claude Williams seemed to him deserving of scorn. Some individuals protested about their rights and his unfairness. He kept after them, continuing to attack McCarthy's tactics yet smear himself. The "segs" were not fooled, but the FBI was satisfied. The bureau's first dossier on McGill in 1951 noted that, while he had slight association with suspect groups like the SCHW, he was definitely "an anti-Communist journalist," close to Atlanta's FBI office.[15]

McGill's columns about local race relations continued to dwell on possible school desegregation, but he knew even more blacks desired access to public accommodations and citizenship. In autumn 1951 suburban DeKalb County accepted its first black jurors. That summer four Atlanta Negroes brought suit in federal court after being turned away from a city golf course. He did not write about these issues. Atlanta hosted the national convention of the NAACP in summer 1951. Mayor Hartsfield welcomed the NAACP "as warmly as if it had been a meeting of the National Association of Manufacturers" and bragged on Atlanta's progress. McGill worried with good reason about repercussions of the racially mixed gathering. The Ku Klux Klan flooded the state with publicity accusing Atlanta leaders of fostering "nigger rule." The *Constitution* editor's hate mail increased sharply.[16]

McGill kept thinking of leaving the newspaper as the post-merger situation worsened. In June 1951 *Constitution* employees suffered another trauma. They had been assured of remaining in their new building indefinitely. With almost no notice, ANInc executives transferred the news and editorial staffs to the *Journal* building. A few months later managing editor Lee Rogers resigned. William H. Fields moved from the editorial desk to replace him. Longtime colleagues were not encouraged by Fields's promotion. They knew him to be distant and "dour." McGill called him a "mossback reactionary." Some reporters lost their jobs. Others left following pay cuts. Word was that the newspaper wanted a new image, "strikingly and substantially different from the *Journal*." There were rumors that the plan was to become the *New York Times* of the South.[17]

The *Constitution*'s business, circulation, photography, and production departments had long since been absorbed. Cox began a combined Sunday edition soon after the merger. Given two generations of bitter rivalry, cooperation on the Sunday paper was not easy at first. Problems also arose in production schedules of various daily editions. Jack Tarver spent more and more time working out the snags. Biggers saw how readily he grasped the essentials of running a newspaper. Tarver could even mediate when Biggers quarreled with Governor Cox. The merger was more expensive than Cox expected. ANInc lost money for months then later in the year began to show a profit when holiday ads appeared.

Clark Howell decided not to become an owner of ANInc. He sold his and the family's portion of preferred stock to the Cox family. His wife, Margaret, wanted their two sons in the newspaper business and considered buying a paper on her own for Clark III and Barrett to manage. Nothing came of her idea. The two younger Howells eventually resigned their positions at the *Constitution* and found places in the booming Atlanta business community. The Major remained on the masthead until 1960 and kept an office at the paper until he died. His attention shifted to other business affairs, however. Cox overshadowed the strong contribution that Howell newspapermen had made to Georgia for three quarters of a century.[18]

Tarver intervened often in the increasingly strained relationship between McGill and Biggers. The president of ANInc knew that McGill was their claim to fame. However, Biggers was a segregationist and narrowminded about business. Tarver regularly confronted him with surveys and circulation figures proving that McGill's "liberalism" was not ruining the paper.

Tarver was less successful ridding Ralph of his sense of being in jeopardy and unfree. Bob Woodruff had assured him of a position with Coca-Cola if he could not stomach ANInc. Woodruff's offer was both a bane and blessing. Tarver was right, McGill knew. He would never be happy away from a newspaper. However, the Woodruff offer kept Ralph unreconciled to the merger, especially when Biggers riled him. McGill always looked back on the early 1950s as the worst years of his career. He cited Biggers as the focal point of his misery, but this was also a period when Mary Elizabeth's health problems multiplied.[19]

Travel was his only solace. In late 1951 and early 1952 he spent a month in India. His trip was partly a government exchange program, but mostly he went to satisfy years of yearning. Of all the places on his 1945 ASNE tour, India was the most "fascinating, contradictory. . . ." Afterwards an amazed U.S. Ambassador Chestor Bowles wrote Truman that, unlike "most visitors who spend their time in the big hotels and at diplomatic receptions," Ralph "actually went into the villages and lived there for three weeks." Bowles considered McGill's India series worthy of a Pulitzer Prize.[20]

McGill differed from many of his globe-trotting peers in another way. He never believed in the primacy of the Atlantic community. Rather, he cultivated and visited the native leaders of emerging Third World countries, many of whom he had met in 1945. This infuriated white supremacists back home. Also, as native governments replaced colonial regimes, he opposed forcing them into military alliances. Contrary to other ardent anti-Communists, McGill doubted that Third World countries would eventually choose "our system."[21]

McGill missed all the 1951 Christmas season to go to India. He left behind a six year old son whose mother, turning forty-seven, was often debilitated with kidney disease now complicated by hypertension. Any social drinking was disastrous. Ralph never discussed his wife's problems openly within their circle and only referred to it indirectly with outsiders. In a 1953 letter to Tom Chubb he admitted that "Mary Elizabeth has had a rather rough time of it, dating from the time when we lost our little girl some years ago from leukemia." He never let that keep him home until the very end of her life. As he said upon leaving for India, "There has always been a voice in me saying, 'There is something new beyond the horizon. Go and see it.'"[22]

The 1952 presidential race brought more travel, first with General Eisenhower. Cox wondered if Ike's magnetism might impel McGill to endorse a Republican. He needn't have worried. Ralph liked Eisenhower but feared the general's political naivete. He confided to fellow editor Barry Bingham, "He seems to find rationalization of any compromise very, very easy." McGill also noted "how woefully lacking he is in many experiences . . . of the processes of government." After two weeks with Ike, the editor wired home a furious column, "Death of a Hero." He later killed the piece but believed McCarthyites would control the administration if Eisenhower won.[23]

Truman's choice to succeed him was Governor Adlai Stevenson of Illinois. The witty Democrat captivated McGill, along with many other journalists and intellectuals. After the governor's unsuccessful 1952 race for the presidency, he began corresponding with McGill. A visit to Atlanta late in 1953 sparked a friendship that deepened over the dozen years before Stevenson's death in

1965. Stevenson often sought the editor's advice while he led an eight-year opposition to the Republicans. Their mutual admiration went far beyond politics, however.[24]

McGill was in Washington for Eisenhower's 1953 inaugural. McGill felt relieved that the GOP had won. He would no longer be obliged to defend the Democrats on behalf of his highly partisan owner, Cox, and anticipated going on the attack. He also intended to pressure the new President privately and in print. Through Bob Woodruff the two had gotten to know one another at hunts and stag dinners where they communicated man-to-man. Ralph urged Ike to exert the strong leadership that his popularity and personality could command. First during McCarthy's heyday and then the school desegregation crisis, McGill watched in vain for Eisenhower to lead.[25]

His own visibility grew during the 1950s thanks to trips, prolific writing and frequent speeches. He joined the boards of the Ford Foundation's Fund for the Advancement of Education and the Fund for the Republic. By now he rationalized that incessant travel was a secret of his success. "One of the things wrong with American editorial writing and comment," he stated in a letter, "is that not enough editors get out of their office long enough to go and see even a small part of what is going on." He left too often, returning to Atlanta exhausted, often ill, facing a mountain of correspondence and tasks. In late 1952 Bishop O'Hara warned, "Take it easy, Dear Ralph. Don't shorten your life by over-work." It was wasted advice.[26]

At least McGill had a new secretary, Grace Lundy, who offset the effects of his overload. At Tarver's behest, Lundy organized his appointments. She stopped McGill's habit of letting anyone off the streets encamp in his office while he tried to work. Lundy not only coordinated his schedule but also learned how her boss wrote. An admirer of his work before she joined the *Constitution*, she relished the chance to make it better. She agreed that McGill's desire to do a reporter's legwork made him a better columnist. She familiarized herself with the background material he read before leaving on a trip. As the columns came back to her by mail or wire, she checked their factual accuracy and composition. She sent daily status reports about his family and the staff. For the next sixteen years Lundy was invaluable to him.[27]

He considered highly placed contacts even more important. He used these to promote protégés like Bill Baggs, an Atlantan who worked for Cox's newspaper, now called simply the *Miami News*. Washington sources were essential. After Eisenhower, McGill's most significant source in the nation's capital was J. Edgar Hoover, head of the FBI. Hoover wooed other editors but always described McGill as "a close friend" of the bureau and kept him on their special mailing list. The fact that the two were fellow Masons was another bond. In 1953 McGill bragged to *U.S. News and World Report* editor, David Lawrence, that for years he supplied the FBI with information. He devoted an entire column in late 1956 to Hoover's book, *The FBI Story*. He lashed out at critics of the bureau "who accuse it of gestapo tactics." Hoover, wrote McGill, had done so well during his thirty-two year tenure that the FBI was quite trustworthy. When McGill witnessed Hoover's efforts to ruin Martin Luther King Jr., he decided this faith was misplaced.[28]

In Washington he picked the brains of James Reston and other journalists based there. McGill knew Reston from days when both were sportswriters. He was affable and given to old-fashioned courtesies especially when cultivating someone. He was a renowned host, Celtic and Southern traditions of hospitality combined. Even his enemies sometimes discovered they enjoyed him. By the mid-1950s he had friendships around the world.

None was more colorful than that with Carl Sandburg. The two had been spending time together for years. McGill enjoyed Sandburg most at Connemara, the author's home outside Asheville. There they would sit on the front porch, looking across at the mountains in what Sandburg called "an impregnable Quaker silence." McGill wrote many descriptions of Sandburg's work and unique lifestyle, including his herd of purebred goats. *Reader's Digest* published one in their "most unforgettable character" series in April 1954. The seventy-six year old author was delighted, calling the article a "lollapalooza."[29]

Two years later McGill arranged for Sandburg to address an Atlanta writers' club at a reduced fee. His appearance turned out to be no bargain. Sandburg skipped the reception to drink goats' milk and bourbon in the editor's kitchen. On another Atlanta visit Sandburg turned up at young Ralph's school. The principal, knowing serendipity when he saw it, suspended lessons and assembled all the grades to hear the celebrated writer talk and strum his guitar to folk ballads.

Even if the two men had not been compatible, McGill would have cultivated Sandburg because of his Lincoln books and Ralph's lifelong fascination with the Civil War president. Some friends suspected McGill of identifying his own troubles with Lincoln's trials that Sandburg knew better than anyone. Lincoln lived with a difficult wife, lost precious children, suffered from melancholy. From his place in the middle of the political spectrum, Lincoln endured the wrath of both radicals and conservatives. He was McGill's model. As crisis gripped the South a century after Lincoln, McGill pleaded for calm public discourse when the region "was frozen in silence."[30]

Speaking out risked losing everything from friends to livelihood, but McGill convinced himself it was right to continue a mediating role. He intended to explain to both whites and blacks what the other was experiencing in this transition, confident that he might change individual minds. His effort recoiled. White supremacy was growing into a deadly force that, like the new hydrogen bomb, would dwarf his weapons of dialogue and attitudinal change. Even mild suggestions brought scorn and threats to the editor. For a time he jeopardized his position at the newspaper and eventually his family's safety. For a decade he had to monitor the right-wing extremists far more closely than he ever had checked on "the pinkos."

Tarver's axiom that half of Atlanta could not eat breakfast *until* they read McGill and the other half could not eat *once* they read McGill was never truer than on April 9, 1953. The column, headed "One Day It Will Be Monday," stated bluntly that the Supreme Court would likely outlaw segregated public schools. Privately

McGill admitted that the entire Jim Crow apparatus was doomed and good riddance. In print he had yet to be so candid. This particular morning he begged white readers to prepare themselves for the aftermath of "separate but equal" schooling. Envisioning a slow transition, he counseled blacks voluntarily to remain segregated for a time though "no longer sanctioned by law." Neither race could accept this contradictory advice.[31]

Meanwhile in southern urban areas blacks continued to gain strength through their votes. McGill and others wanted Atlanta to serve as a model of change using new voting patterns. In 1953 Atlantans gave Bill Hartsfield another four-year term as mayor. His campaign strategy was to disarm his critics in both races. He stole the white supremacists' thunder with his "city too busy to hate" sloganeering. Then at his request black leaders assembled to air their grievances, particularly no Negro fire fighters. After listening, Hartsfield countered that, for all his faults, he was their best hope.

Even more significant than Hartsfield's resounding victory was Rufus E. Clement's election to Atlanta's Board of Education. Clement was the first black to win elective office in Georgia since Reconstruction. Many whites voted for the mild-mannered president of Atlanta University. The step strengthened boosters' arguments that Atlanta was unique among southern cities. Middle class citizens of both races longed for their city to escape the racial turmoil festering throughout the region. Seeing Clement take his seat on the city school board, McGill gave voice to his old hope "that when the people have the facts they may be trusted to do the right thing."[32]

That fall he decided to take a step that also seemed the right thing—returning to Christianity. Months before, a friend started taking Red to activities at the nearby Episcopal Cathedral of St. Philip, hoping the church would become a stronghold to a woman struggling with so many afflictions. Others sometimes took young Ralph there on Sunday mornings. Ralph knew that his own mother prayed daily that he would re-embrace his religious heritage. After Virginia died in 1939 he was unable to relate to God, and most ministers made him "dance with impotent rage or angry denial of their conclusions." So he took refuge in "stubbornness and humility." But he was too emotional to remain a stoic.[33]

McGill found the faith he abandoned thirty years before in two trips to the Holy Land. In 1950 he returned home "stronger, younger, and surer about the eternal verities," unchurched but no longer spiritually lost. Young Ralph and Mary Elizabeth were more and more involved at St. Philip's. He decided to join them. After taking instruction, the three McGills "were confirmed in the Episcopal faith with the laying on of hands by the bishop." Ralph's circle wondered if his move were more than a show of family unity. Deeper than support for his wife and son, however, was a genuine desire to try to be a Christian.[34]

McGill belonged to a generation that invoked the Bible in public rhetoric, knowing the audience would take his meaning. So even before McGill's confirmation, many readers assumed he was a religious individual. Now at cathedral services this fifty-five year old man began building a superstructure for his youthful faith. The old foundation of fire and brimstone Calvinism was still intact. The Bible had always been his book. He had finally outlasted the personal tragedies that drove him from God. As he watched the cross borne down the aisle and received communion, he found a reality in rituals that may have been just habit for lifelong Episcopalians.

The timing of McGill's step was important. The entire Bible Belt was about to undergo a trial that would test the faith of both races. McGill regularly declared that the problem was, at heart, a moral issue, and the black mass movement came out of churches. Back in the church himself after thirty-five years, he began using Christianity as his framework for the civil rights struggle. This angle unsettled readers to whom he now appealed as fellow Christians, but as *Journal* editor Jack Spalding recalled, "He was an evangelist. . . . He died an Episcopalian, but it seems to me he would have done better as a Church of God member."

Almost immediately McGill did a series of columns condemning segregation and its defenders. *Time* magazine featured the Atlanta editor, noting his shift from "an enlightened but discreet course" to boldness. "The Christian of today," McGill had written, "cannot help but wince . . . at the jarring clash of his creed with discrimination against any person because of color." It was an "impossible contradiction." He asked whites to grasp what it actually meant to live under segregation. Legislators in Georgia and other Deep South states vowing to end public education rather than desegregate were, he said, as wrong as the secessionists had been before the Civil War.[35]

The columns and *Time*'s coverage brought mountains of mail to the *Constitution*. Atlanta's black leaders thanked McGill for his courage. William Holmes Borders, pastor of the Wheat Street Baptist Church, added special words of gratitude for McGill's unfailing support of his congregation. The most moving letter came from a New York man whose grandparents had been slaves in Atlanta. He had never wanted to visit the segregated city, but now "I am heartened into believing that it will not be long before my son will be accepted in your community as a man."[36]

McGill made sure that Tarver, now the general manager of ANInc, got samples of the favorable response to show his boss, George Biggers. It did McGill a world of good to write these forthright columns. Yet he knew that Biggers would not tolerate such work. Wright Bryan, McGill's counterpart at the *Journal*, had just resigned. Rumors circulated that Biggers had run him off. McGill concluded that an owner of a newspaper might write what he pleased, considering his advertisers of course. He on the other hand was just an employee of ANInc, and a man with heavy family burdens. What would become of Mary Elizabeth and young Ralph if he lost his job?[37]

Like so many other moderates, McGill decided at this juncture to be a survivor rather than a martyr to the civil rights cause. In the 1980s a young black leader commented that the editor was very "expedient with his liberalism." Given Biggers, McGill felt he was risking a great deal. Lillian Smith had no use for men like McGill or the SRC's Harold Fleming, whom she quoted as saying, "the difference between a moderate and a liberal was that a moderate had a wife and children." They were hindrances to an otherwise feasible desegregation. McGill loathed Smith's unrealistic hopes as much as he hated being labeled "liberal." Aubrey Williams told him in late 1953 he might just as well resign himself to his label and quit hoping that tactics like his anti-Communist blasts would protect him.[38]

Mary Elizabeth became quite ill again in the spring of 1954. In June 1953 she had had a long hospital stay. An allergic reaction to both sulphur and penicillin slowed her recovery. Doctors told McGill surgery for her large kidney stones must wait until she grew stronger. He did stop work for two weeks, but she was too weak to travel to one of their favorite vacation spots. Now worries about her health clouded an otherwise felicitous event.

The Nashville-based publisher, Abingdon Press, produced a collection of McGill columns. The title, *The Fleas Come with the Dog*, honored Uncle Cade Worley who lived nearly a century in Georgia's Blue Ridge mountains. Worley liked to say that the bigger the dog, the bigger the fleas. McGill thought this fit America at midcentury. Abingdon celebrated with a huge party in Ralph's honor at their downtown Cokesbury bookstore. Guests included Tennessee friends from college and newspaper days. Merrill Moore could not attend but wrote, echoing the sentiments of many others who remembered "Mac" as a happy young man. "More and more," he reflected, "the poet in you comes out."[39]

After more than thirty years, poetical impulses shaped his best writing. An Abingdon editor working on *Fleas* wrote, "You have a way of reaching out and dragging the reader deep into the subject with a hook." McGill's favorite hooks were ordinary human experiences like sharing good food with family, confiding in a friend, straining muscle and nerve to win a game or finish a chore, watching for nature's changing seasons. President Eisenhower liked *Fleas* very much. He sent not one but two letters of praise, reminding the editor that he was "one of your fans from away back." McGill had become the writer he was supposed to be.[40]

McGill was in London in May 1954 when the U.S. Supreme Court ruled against segregated public schools in *Brown v. Board of Education*. The London bureau chief for UPI, Eugene Patterson, pondered news of the decision briefly then started searching for McGill. Patterson, a native of Adel, Georgia, had met the Atlanta editor five years earlier. McGill gave him no comment that May evening in London, however. Only after the editor returned to Atlanta and reflected a bit did he discuss *Brown*, reiterating earlier claims that U.S. laws must be obeyed.

When the second *Brown* decision in May 1955 advised school districts to desegregate "with all deliberate speed," McGill wrote each justice of the Supreme Court. He thanked them for acknowledging that "in the final analysis this problem of desegregation had to be solved at the local level." Justice Felix Frankfurter responded that "the ultimate enforcing authority behind law is informed public opinion" and urged the editor to fight segregation. McGill wanted the editorial page of the *Constitution* to do just that, but he could never convert Bill Fields who ran the news departments. As a result, the *Constitution* exhibited a split personality regarding the civil rights movement. Even so, it was one of the few southern newspapers to support the *Brown* decision.[41]

By 1955 McGill could envision a South after de jure segregation and was promoting his new gestalt for race relations. This plus his unyielding support of the Supreme Court made the editor a prime target of white extremists' counterattack. Since however, no new pattern in race relations was possible without their acquiescence, he tried sympathizing with "the segs." In countless letters McGill denied that he "was happy over the Supreme Court decision" or advocated integration. His enemies were wrong about him, he said. He was not a southerner who "betrayed his people." On the other hand he regularly wrote pieces designed to enrage those now declaring with one voice, "Never." In print he dared his enemies to attack or kill him. He even flirted with a kind of martyrdom. Little wonder that some praised his moral courage, while others deplored his expediency.[42]

Mary Elizabeth and young Ralph were the ones who really suffered during this time. He refused to get an unlisted number. Crank calls and telephoned threats became routine at 3399 Piedmont Road. The McGills always owned dogs. Now Ralph named one "Rastus," a nickname that hatemongers gave him. He trained the puppy to bark loudly at the word, "speak." When an angry caller asked for Rastus, he said, "You want to speak to Rastus?" He held the telephone down, and the little dog yipped away. Red McGill later claimed that he would run "an especially hard-hitting column" just before departing for a trip, leaving her to cope with the reaction.[43]

After over a quarter of a century Mary Elizabeth knew that Ralph's absences would only increase. She could no more cure his wanderlust than he could stop her from holding forth in full voice. More often than not, she was setting someone straight about her husband's worth to the paper and the region. As Ralph's reputation grew, so did the rumors that he had a wife who drank too much and could not keep up with him intellectually. Red's friends knew she could handle gossip but worried that this harassing by white supremacists would aggravate her complicated health problems which now included bouts of pneumonia.[44]

Reflecting their parents' hatred, children began to taunt Ralph Jr. at school. They asked, "How come you're a Communist?" Or declared that he, like his father, was a "nigger-lover." McGill took pains to explain the feelings of these schoolmates. It was difficult, however. Young Ralph did not have many friends. He hardly needed this new stigma among his peers. His father tried to compensate for school troubles and his own absences by taking young Ralph with him whenever possible. It was a way to spend more time with the boy. McGill also wanted his son to see well known figures, to shake hands with them, and to associate him with historic events.

When McGill brought guests home or gave a small dinner party, young Ralph stayed up to listen in on the conversation. Preparing fancy food was his mother's forte—with Julia's expert assistance. McGill enjoyed cooking and eating as much as ever. Their guests had meals that surpassed most Atlanta restaurant fare. Red still took food to the *Constitution* when the staff had to work late. If McGill missed his bus, she and Ralph Jr. drove downtown to get him.[45]

His refusal ever to become a driver affected Mary Elizabeth more than anyone else. Someone at the paper was always willing to chauffeur the boss out of town to speaking engagements or events he wanted to cover. However, his wife drove Ralph on more of these occasions than people realized. Despite all the rumors about her alcoholism, Mary Elizabeth McGill never had an auto accident. She handled all the family's Atlanta errands and took the wheel for many a vacation trip. These lasted longer than necessary, young Ralph recalled, because his father had her stop at every historical marker. McGill wrote fondly about "the lady who drives me," but he placed another strain on her.[46]

McGill drew much sustenance from his "family" at the paper. They felt free to jibe "Pappy" about his growing fame, pour out their troubles to him, play jokes on him. He, in turn, lingered over lunch regaling them with stories from his past and commiserating about the present state of the world. Their "warmest memories of the man" flowed from Saturday sessions at Max Muldawer's delicatessen. McGill thumbed his "tattered old paperbook of poems" until he found the one he chose "to read aloud with husky-voiced, croaking eloquence, or listen to, eyes closed, lips moving silently to the familiar words." Those gathered around the red-checked table may not have realized that their boss was reliving Nashville of his twenties. Reminiscing in the autumn of 1954, he admitted being "somewhat halfbaked" and "quite naive" during the Twenties. Like the camaraderie at Max's, memories of those carefree years buoyed his troubled spirit.[47]

In 1956 McGill gained what Harold Martin described as "the closest thing to a soul-brother McGill had in the business." Gene Patterson had impressed Biggers during a business trip to England that year. He brought the UPI bureau chief home as associate editor of the *Journal*. In late 1957 Tarver promoted him to executive editor of both papers and vice president of ANInc. Eventually Patterson succeeded McGill as editor of the *Constitution*.

The two men met in December 1948 while Gene covered the aftermath of a south Georgia lynching that brought McGill to testify before a local grand jury. With Tarver along as a guard, the editor reiterated his urgings that they punish the lynch mob and free Negro residents of Lyons from fearing such atrocities. Though justice was not served in the Lyons lynching, McGill gained an admirer. Patterson recalled: "I loved the man the first day I met him. I was fascinated with him, with the great range of his mind, the depth of his understanding, the utter charity in his heart. . . ."[48]

McGill kept brooding over whites' response to desegregation. "Massive resistance," southern states' attempt to mount legal barriers to federal rulings, was spreading fast by 1956. All his efforts could not dissuade either the resort to violence. The brutal murder of fourteen year old Emmett Till in Mississippi the preceding summer and defiant acquittal of the guilty perpetrators horrified McGill. Raging mobs almost killed Autherine Lucy during her hopeless attempt to integrate the University of Alabama in February.

Late that year columnist Drew Pearson warned Ralph that he too was in danger. According to Pearson's informant, the newly-revived Georgia KKK had paid someone $2,500 to kill him. Pearson's tip came as no surprise to McGill. His torrent of hate mail and the sources of his police reporter, Keeler McCartney, confirmed the Klan's hostility. Ridicule remained his weapon of choice against them. For instance he offered a witty salute to the Lumbee Indians of southeastern North Carolina when these "the 100-per-cent Americans" chased home "the pretenders to Americanism" of the KKK. Despite his tongue-in-cheek, the editor feared the growing thirst for violence.[49]

Nonetheless, McGill emphasized as he had since 1943 that progress was possible if outside forces kept out and local officials acted responsibly. He cited the way Atlanta had recently complied with federal court order to integrate city golf courses. In April 1956 he wrote a friend that two local corporations, Lockheed and Scripto, were hiring Negroes for skilled jobs. Blacks also held many clerical positions in government offices around town. That same month he told readers of *Atlantic* magazine that he did "not feel Pollyannish in believing that there is more good than evil in the people of the South. . . ." He called his article "The Angry South," however, and was obliged to get special permission from Biggers at the paper before submitting it to Edward Weeks.[50]

Ralph McGill's grandfather, David Newton McGill, whose
Tennessee River valley farms was McGill's "homeplace."
Photo courtesy of Virginia Bigelow.

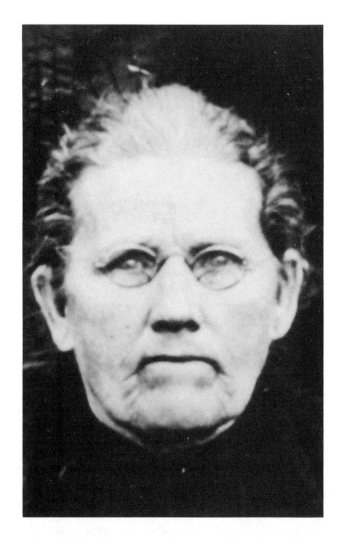

McGill's beloved grandmother, Mary Elizabeth
Wallace McGill, know to all as "Mammy."
Photo courtesy of Virginia Bigelow.

McGill's mother, Mary Lou Skillern McGill, born in 1877 and her family's source of strength for nearly ninety years. Photo courtesy of Virginia Bigelow.

McGill in infancy, the only surviving son of Ben and Mary Lou McGill. Photo courtesy of Virginia Bigelow.

McGill's father, Benjamin Franklin McGill, who moved to Chattanooga in 1904 to give his children opportunities. Photo courtesy of Virginia Bigelow.

Chattanooga, McGill said, is "in a spectacular, beautiful, unique, and abrupt conjunction of mountains and deep valleys." Photo courtesy of Chattanooga-Hamilton County Bicentennial Library.

Downton Chattanooga's Market Street in 1906 when McGill began to explore the growing New South city. Photo courtesy of Chattanooga-Hamilton County Bicentennial Library.

The house on Chattanooga's Kirby Avenue
where McGill and his three sisters grew up.
Photo courtesy of Virginia Bigelow.

Ralph (second from left) with sister
Bessie (far right) and three
neighborhood playmates. Photo courtesy
of Virginia Bigelow.

McGill in 1916 as a football star at McCallie School, founded by his pastor, Thomas H. McCallie. Photo courtesy of Virginia Bigelow.

The city room of the *Nashville Banner* in the 1920s, with McGill (center) wearing hat while writing sports. Courtesy of Special Collections, Woodruff Library, Emory University, Atlanta GA.

In 1929 McGill joined the staff of the *Atlanta Constitution*, located beside Rich's (department store) at Forsyth and Alabama Streets.

Clark Howell Sr., owner of the *Atlanta Constitution* and its editor from 1897 until his death in 1936. Courtesy of Special Collections, Woodruff Library, Emory University, Atlanta GA.

McGill and Mary Elizabeth, welcomed home from Europe in 1938 and congratulated on his promotion to executive editor. Photo courtesy of *Atlanta Journal-Constitution.*

McGill, Harold Martin (2nd from l.) and Jack Tarver (far r.) visit with friend and columnist Westbrook Pegler ("Peg") in 1943. Courtesy of Special Collections, Woodruff Library, Emory University, Atlanta GA.

McGill's daughter Virginia, whose death from leukemia in 1939 devastated her parents. Photo courtesy of Virginia Bigelow.

Ralph McGill Jr., born in 1945, when his mother was forty and his father was forty-seven. Photo courtesy of Virginia Bigelow.

McGill (3rd from l.) in Paris on a global mission on behalf of freedom of the press in 1945. Special Collections, Woodruff Library, Emory University.

(From l. to r.) James Cox Sr., Clark Howell Jr., George Biggers, McGill, and Wright Bryan discuss merged *Atlanta Journal* and *Atlanta Constitution* in 1950. Special Collections, Woodruff Library, Emory University.

McGill's office in 1958 with Henry Grady's rolltop desk in background. Courtesy of Special Collections, Woodruff Library, Emory University, Atlanta GA.

Mary Elizabeth and Julia James Crawford in the McGill kitchen, processing herbs from the garden. Courtesy of Special Collections, Woodruff Library, Emory University, Atlanta GA.

McGill and Ralph Jr., two proud Marines, in 1965.
Courtesy of Special Collections, Woodruff Library,
Emory University, Atlanta GA.

McGill in Togo during 1963 African tour. Courtesy of
Special Collections, Woodruff Library, Emory University,
Atlanta GA.

Gene Patterson, McGill's successor. Special Collections, Woodruff Library, Emory University, Atlanta GA.

Dr. Mary Lynn Morgan becomes McGill's wife in 1967. Special Collections, Woodruff Library, Emory University.

PART III:

1957-1969

9

"A LITTLE LEFT OF CENTER":
1957-1961

BY 1957, JUST AS HIS OWN CAREER WAS TRANSFORMED, McGILL was forced to reckon with an entirely new phase of the civil rights movement—direct action by Jim Crow's victims. Late the preceding year blacks' successful boycott of Montgomery, Alabama, buses inspired members of their race throughout the South. The boycott's young leader, the Reverend Martin Luther King Jr., would shortly become a worldwide celebrity. The Morehouse College graduate grew up in Atlanta where his father pastored the Ebenezer Baptist Church. For thirty years "Daddy" King had been a force to reckon with in Atlanta's black community, as McGill knew.

Now the younger King planned to duplicate his Montgomery success throughout the South. Directed from Atlanta, the new Southern Christian Leadership Conference would send blacks forth from their churches to mass protests. The SCLC approach of direct action, so different from the courtroom strategy of the NAACP, negated the paternalism of southerners like McGill. It would also intensify white backlash. Just as McGill had worried over black leaders' demands in 1942, now he feared that bloodshed could replace what he saw as postwar progress.

His fears of violence began to come true in January 1957. Whites in Montgomery bombed four churches and the homes of two black ministers while the SCLC was being organized in Atlanta. King and the others hurried home to view the damage while McGill voiced outrage: "Those who are in charge of the South must halt the destruction of churches and property and punish the guilty." Seeing blacks initiate change in the name of Christianity, he became their ally. The South today, he wrote, is "on the wrong side of a moral issue," just as it was a hundred years ago. Some began to describe McGill as "the conscience of the South," a role he would soon be free to play.[1]

Now he was convinced that if he got too far ahead of his readers, he would lose his effectiveness and perhaps even his job. Pressured by the paper's management, he alternated ringing appeals for justice with other ideas that confused readers and infuriated bolder leaders. Time and again he implied that it would take the South as long to alter its racial mores as it had to give up on King Cotton. Privately McGill wanted Jim Crow practices to disappear, but it was hard to tell from his column whether he was still a segregationist or an extreme gradualist. He added to the confusion by distinguishing between desegregation and integration. He admitted the former was bound to happen but said the latter would not. This was a bit of sophistry. McGill was trying to calm fears of miscegenation but only weakened his own position.[2]

The Montgomery bus boycott revealed that blacks would no longer wait for cautious whites to make concessions or the NAACP to take every school district to court. They acted on their own. Even older Atlanta black ministers accustomed to pleading with the mayor seized the initiative. On January 9, 1957, without Hartsfield's knowledge, Daddy King, William Holmes Borders, and others sat in the front of a downtown bus. The bewildered driver returned to the garage rather than risk a riot.

Hartsfield was apoplectic. He and Police Chief Jenkins knew that diehard state officials would seize any excuse to enforce segregation laws in Atlanta. After long discussion the ministers agreed to be arrested during a second bus ride with full media coverage. All parties felt certain that the resulting test case would integrate public transit. While the courts deliberated, however, Atlanta blacks had to continue enduring the hated Jim Crow seating system.[3]

Atlanta's political climate grew stormy during 1957. McGill gave Bill Hartsfield such a fervent endorsement in his bid for a sixth consecutive term as mayor that Hartsfield's main opponent accused the editor of maligning him. Tarver and McGill quickly quenched this fire. Their unqualified support of Hartsfield caused consternation among *Constitution* staffers, however. Early that year reporter Jack Nelson exposed Atlanta police accepting bribes from operators of an illegal lottery. A federal grand jury indicted seven of the policemen. Nelson contended that both Police Chief Jenkins and the mayor were tainted with scandal and did not deserve such editorial enthusiasm. McGill disagreed. He thought they rendered invaluable service to the community. Nelson's expose saddened him but did not sway his dogged loyalty to two old friends.[4]

That summer brought one emotional jolt after another. McGill received an invitation to visit Germany, France and Belgium. He increasingly felt guilty about leaving Mary Elizabeth, so he took her to Florida before his trip. No sooner had they returned to Atlanta than a call came from Ohio. Governor Cox had died. The paper ran pages of tributes to its eighty-seven year old owner. McGill wrote a simple account of visiting the governor at his family farm. In moving terms he conveyed the vitality that impelled Cox's long, fruitful life. Less than three weeks later, he attended the funeral of Walter George. For nearly eighty years the former senator had faced life with a simple dignity that Ralph greatly admired. Thus he began a lengthy, hectic trip with emotions overwrought.[5]

The 1957 European tour produced four weeks of superb columns, carried in many newspapers besides the *Constitution*. They came in airmailed bunches to Grace Lundy who did a bit of editing then rearranged their order. Her skill at making the most of the material McGill mailed home was obvious. When her harassed boss wrote that he was traveling too fast to write well, Lundy replied, "The columns are terrific, and everybody thinks so." She passed along reassurances that at his home "everything is going along fine."[6]

While McGill was abroad, Russia announced firing of an intercontinental ballistic missile. After nearly two centuries of natural security, the U.S. was newly vulnerable. From London the Atlanta editor reported that Soviet Premier Nikita Khrushchev's missiles also cast a pall on disarmament negotiations. McGill was confident that despite infirmities, Eisenhower could lead America and her allies through his second term and this new phase of the Cold War.[7]

Just as the Communist threat worsened, Eisenhower faced the strongest domestic challenge to his leadership. Little Rock, Arkansas, exploded in violent protests as the integration of Central High School got underway in September. Until then Governor Orville Faubus seemed unperturbed about token desegregation. He now stirred up the mobs. McGill was shocked. He would have expected such trickery from a governor in Alabama but not a border state. After consulting with Faubus and giving the governor plenty of time to restore order and do his constitutional duty, Eisenhower sent federalized troops to Little Rock.

In McGill's view the Little Rock crisis reversed the dynamics of the campaign against Jim Crow. The South had forfeited a last chance to put its own house in order. Southerners' defiance of the law of the land had brought federal forces to their soil. He predicted that hereafter Washington would coerce the region through its racial revolution. The fact that the confrontation occurred in a relatively progressive capital city in the Upper South galled McGill. He had expected a different response in Arkansas than in the Deep South states.[8]

Many southerners now predicted a replay of Reconstruction horrors, but McGill saw a parallel to Germany in the 1930s. Fresh from his German tour and recalling 1938, the editor predicted a southern scenario resembling the Nazis' rise to power. Those who were placed well enough to influence or sway public opinion cynically inflamed passions and prejudices. Such elites defied the legal mechanisms of the state or subverted them to their own purposes. They convinced those at the bottom of society that minorities (and their outside allies) were to blame for their troubles. Fairminded moderates grew silent, allowing the hate and wrongdoing to prevail. Rather than see this vision come true, McGill vowed to fight intolerance all the harder and to encourage moderate southerners to stand up to the extremists.[9]

Unexpected changes at the paper in late 1957 freed him to make this effort just when other southern leaders were being "effectively stifled." George Biggers suffered a stroke and retired to Florida. Jack Tarver became president of ANInc. Ralph now had a boss he trusted completely instead of one he considered his worst enemy. Already the saying around town was, "Tarver steadies the soapbox for McGill." For the next decade Ralph's ties to his former associate editor grew. He relied on Tarver's judgment about policy at the paper and personal business. He always departed for distant parts with sentimental farewells, but Tarver got a special bear hug with the plea, "If anything happens to me, see that young Ralph gets an education."[10]

The editor's relationship with the Cox family remained smooth. Jim Cox Jr. replaced his father as chairman of the board of ANInc. Ralph sent to Cox's Miami office a steady stream of reassuring messages that all was well at the *Constitution* despite his reputation as a "race-mixer." He made sure Jim got copies of all his messages from Ike. Cox reversed his father's policy and put McGill in national syndication. The governor always insisted that only the Cox chain and newspapers dealing directly with the *Constitution* could have his daily column. Now the North American Newspaper Alliance sold McGill's work to a growing national market. For the next dozen years his visibility and influence grew, and he was less involved at the paper.[11]

The editor now used every means at his disposal to bring Eisenhower into the civil rights struggle, not just as reluctant upholder of law and order but as a moral leader. Even though Ike was a little more than seven years older than McGill, they were contemporaries of sorts. The two men were reared on the same verities. Through different career paths they had arrived by midlife at similar views of America's role in world affairs though not her domestic policy. Over the past ten years opportunities came for them to exchange ideas in person and in letters. No wonder McGill tried influencing a president whose respect he enjoyed. Throughout his editorial career he sent wires regularly to the White Office. He now added long letters assessing for Eisenhower the forces set against him and suggesting options. McGill also conveyed ideas through Bob Woodruff and Press Secretary Jim Hagerty.

The results were mixed. Eisenhower agreed with one of McGill's suggestions that fall. He would not call all southern governors and their attorneys general to the White House as some urged. Both the President and the editor feared defiant politicians would grandstand and further weaken moderates. McGill was unsuccessful in persuading Ike to "reach over the heads of the politician" and encourage the silent moderates who hated violence and lawlessness more than integration. At this point Ike showed much tolerance for the diehards whom he described in a November 4 letter to McGill as "prisoners of their own prior statements and pronouncements."[12]

Like Eisenhower, McGill was an inveterate letter writer. Sometimes he wrote long epistles to people in town, a habit going back to Nashville days. In the 1957 general election Bill Hartsfield faced an unexpected opponent, Lester Maddox. The local restaurateur waged an openly racist campaign, violating longstanding custom in Atlanta to keep race out of politics. He called the mayor a "tool of the NAACP" and worse. Hartsfield seethed with rage. The mayor had sorely tried Ralph's patience throughout 1957. Now he sent a letter of sharp advice. McGill had been the subject of Maddox tirades for years and was used to his outrageousness. He warned Hartsfield to calm down and "take a few suggestions from your friends."[13]

McGill spent huge amounts of time writing letters of recommendation or asking help for some promising individual. He was grateful for those who had encouraged him or intervened on his behalf. He never hesitated to use his influence to open a door for one struggling as he had done. By the time he died, he had protégés scattered around the world. Many of these were blacks. William Gordon, managing editor of the *Atlanta Daily World*, was eager for new professional opportunities. During the 1950s McGill helped Gordon become a Nieman Fellow at Harvard then to obtain an Ogden Reid Fellowship. Afterwards the Eisenhower administration hired Gordon as public affairs officer for the U.S. Information Agency in Nigeria.

The editor sponsored Grace Hamilton on several occasions. Hamilton grew up in the Atlanta University community. She attended graduate school at Ohio State then returned home as a professor's wife in 1943. For eighteen years she headed Atlanta's Urban League and furnished McGill with material he used to plead for just treatment of Negroes. Leaders of both races prized her political sagacity. In 1958 McGill wrote to Clarence Faust of the Fund for the Advancement of Education, "Mrs. Hamilton really is an exceptional person, and is so regarded by everyone here." To McGill's delight, in 1966 she became the first black woman ever elected to Georgia's legislature.[14]

In March 1958 McGill went off to the Pulitzer jury meetings in New York to sponsor his friend Harry Ashmore, editor of the *Arkansas Gazette*. Ashmore was one of several younger southern newsmen who enjoyed the Atlanta editor as a mentor. Bill Baggs, now editor of the *Miami News*, was another. Sardonic messages, often twitting McGill, passed back and forth among the group. Pranks were *de rigueur* at every gathering. Their support of desegregation bonded McGill with his protégés. For two years Ashmore not only battled "the segs" editorially, but also hosted an army of reporters who worked out of the *Gazette*'s newsroom. Finally Ashmore transferred to a California think tank, the Center for the Study of Democratic Institutions.[15]

Long before Ralph had become convinced that he would never claim a Pulitzer Prize. During their 1945 ASNE tour such ill will grew between him and Dean Carl Ackerman of Columbia University's journalism school that he felt Ackerman would block the award. In 1952, when Chester Bowles thought McGill's India columns were Pulitzer material, McGill told him otherwise: "I have long regarded Carl Ackerman as one of the great phonies in the newspaper business, and have on one occasion so expressed myself to him." Ashmore did receive a 1958 Pulitzer Prize for his work during the Little Rock school crisis. McGill devoted a column praising him for "the clean, decent honest newspaper job" he had done.[16]

His sixtieth birthday that spring gave McGill pause. Fraternity brothers and friends from bachelor days were falling by the wayside. One had his third heart attack and resigned a judgeship. A Nashville visit to be in a godson's wedding reminded him that his own two daughters would now be adults had they lived. Yet young Ralph was just entering his teens. How would the boy get through adolescence now that he was "in old age" and Mary Elizabeth so ill? He dieted down to 215, but eating and drinking binges were hard on his health. Gene Patterson watched him consume a bottle of applejack at a convention then confess, "I feel like I'm going to die." He insisted he was quitting, but in 1959 Ashmore found him passed out in a hotel room and told a friend he looked like "a beached whale."[17]

He did not drink when working, however, and still kept a pace that exhausted younger colleagues. His vitality was fed by a tough constitution and an almost perfect match between man and medium. He now focused on plain, painful truths. In 1958 he refuted one of whites' strongest convictions—that they knew all about blacks. From his own soul searching he knew it was not true: "There was never, in the South, any real continuing communication between the two races. . . . Now and then the more curious would ask a maid, cook or yard man about these things and receive comforting assurances that it was, indeed, true . . . the Negro was happy and contented." It was "preposterous that anybody of whatever color would be satisfied with discrimination, often grievous, in every phase of their lives."

He reiterated the need for a new pattern in race relations. It was not enough, he wrote in April 1958, to dismantle the legal structure of Jim Crow—though that "amounts to a revolution. . . ." "Revolutions must be lived through," he continued, "so that when they do end there will be a status which the people accept." If southerners could replace stereotypes with a sense of common humanity, then a new social matrix might begin to emerge. He had taken his parents' insistence that "all are God's children" to ethical maturity and in December 1958 stated, "One of the most difficult things in this complicated business of race is to see one another as persons, minus all the illusions, assumptions, and images which are involved."[18]

Even as a young sports writer McGill had almost a physiological relationship with readers. They responded as never before. Tarver's surveys revealed that he was both the most positive and the most negative aspect of the *Constitution*. Atlanta's business leaders worried over what McGill might say next. Blacks kept a steady flow of encouraging notes coming to the office and hoped privately that this time McGill would stand firm. White supremacists stepped up their vilification of "the Soddy traitor" and harassment of his family. Deliveries of human excrement came to 3399 Piedmont Road. So did police protection at night.[19]

McGill went to New York City at least four times during 1958. He took satisfaction in dealing with editors of the New York newspapers as equals. He provided them with insights and information about the South. They published his feature articles. His piece on southern moderates in the Sunday *New York Times Magazine* of September 21, 1958, brought gratifying responses. Within a year the *Times* ran two more. One story concerned southern clergy, driven from their churches when they refused to support segregation. McGill gave wrenching details about Rob McNeill, a Presbyterian minister who lost not only his pulpit in Columbus, Georgia, but also his health.[20]

New York afforded McGill an even better mix of business and pleasure than Washington. After attending foundation or board meetings, he could indulge his lifelong love of the theater and the ballet. His favorite workplace in New York was a quiet corner of the Associate Press headquarters in Rockefeller Center. There, an old friend observed, with "an ear cocked for fresh bulletins" he would "commune with his thoughts and write his daily column." McGill admitted that he loved the special "noise that news makes" in the AP wire room. The United Nations complex on Riverside Drive became a favored beat. Talking with delegates of the new African nations and reading letters from Bill Gordon, away on his

Reid Fellowship, McGill burned to see the African continent for himself.[21]

Then an incident at home brought fresh attention to his work. On October 12, 1958, a dynamite blast heavily damaged the Temple, Atlanta's largest synagogue. McGill and the rabbi, Jacob M. Rothschild, knew one another well and shared many enemies. White supremacists were reviving anti-Semitism in the region. The day before the Temple bombing, McGill told his readers, such a group distributed their literature at Atlanta's annual Southeastern Fair. Following the blast, bomb threats came to the *Constitution* and the Rothschild home. Rothschild infuriated "the segs" by denouncing plans to close Georgia schools rather than to desegregate them. McGill had been tagged a "Jew lover" since Gene Talmadge's harangues against "Rosenwald Ralph" in the 1930s. The editor's efforts on behalf of Israel only made matters worse.[22]

The Temple bombing put Atlanta in the spotlight. As news broke, Mayor Hartsfield rushed to the scene. National media covered his strong denunciation of the crime and instant offer of a reward for information about the criminals. President Eisenhower was making several public appearances in New York City that day. He too condemned the bombing and ordered the FBI to help Atlanta police with the case. McGill was not in town. He made a talk in a remote community on the Tennessee border, unaware that Atlanta was in turmoil.

His driver delivered the editor home where Red McGill rushed out with the news. He was to continue downtown to his office, she said, collecting Grace Lundy on the way. Lundy answered her boss's questions in the car as best she could. Once at the paper, McGill spoke briefly with reporters in the city room. Then he went into his office and began to type. Lundy timed him. Twenty-eight minutes later the typesetters had the column that he titled, "A Church, A School." McGill's ability to write rapidly under any circumstances was already legendary. He produced a visceral response to these bombers in record time.[23]

The column, cited in his 1959 Pulitzer Prize award, warned of more violence to come if defiance of the Constitution persisted:

"Hate and lawlessness by those who lead release the yellow rats and encourage the crazed and neurotic. . . ." From Jewish friends and a huge background file on the 1915 Leo Frank lynching, McGill knew that Atlanta's Jewish community feared another such spasm of anti-Semitism in the city. Despite this concern, the editor declared in print what many blacks were saying privately: that none of the recent bombings against blacks generated such outrage, even when Negroes lost their lives. McGill's various columns on the Temple dynamiting brought unprecedented reader response. Grace Lundy could barely log the phone calls, much less note all the messages. Mail and contributions poured into the *Constitution*. McGill passed these along to Rabbi Rothschild but replied to some himself. Experiences in prewar Berlin and Vienna, he wrote one bigot, transformed his thinking even before he toured the death camp at Buchenwald.[24]

McGill was so upset because this crime involved Atlanta, supposedly a model of change. In the year since Little Rock, he had been collecting evidence of the chilling effect that massive resistance had on regional development. He knew most business leaders hated his preachments. Now, however, he pleaded with them to allow token school desegregation so that southern economic progress could continue. "What company will want to come into Georgia," he wrote Bob Woodruff shortly before the bombing, "when its employees and executives can't educate their children?" Atlanta must show that a transition was possible.

First the city had to convince the Georgia legislature to let it comply with a pending desegregation suit. Governor Marvin Griffin and his successor in 1959, Ernest Vandiver, seemed bent on closing Georgia's public schools. The legislature had provided them ample authority to do so, starting in 1953. At times McGill succumbed to pessimism and saw no hope of averting disaster. Yet forces were working for open schools, and he made use of every one.

He argued that the dangerous Cold War rivalry called for academic excellence not padlocked schoolhouses. He reminded readers that the Soviet educational system had given the U.S.S.R.

its lead in the new space race. In early 1959 Atlanta mothers organized HOPE, Help Our Public Education. McGill addressed HOPE and all other groups fighting "the segs" in state government. These were not "integrationists," he wrote in a column, but people who put "their children and their future in a competitive world ahead of personal feelings."[25]

In April 1959 McGill marked thirty years of employment at the *Constitution*, one decade on the sports desk and two decades as an editor. Those in the editorial department who brainstormed with him every morning sneaked a lively anniversary tribute onto the editorial page. Both his strength and his weakness, they said, stemmed from the same trait: "He won't budge even if you shout at him if he thinks he's right." After their daily discussion came the writing. As Celestine Sibley observed, "turning toward his type-writer in the swivel chair which he rides with the sort of itchy restlessness of a farm boy traveling bareback on a mule, he would knock out six or eight editorials and his column with a speed which no member of his staff has ever approached."[26]

The sixty-one year old editor never referred to the anniversary in print but often wrote about his profession that spring. He reflected on the media "madness" of 1925 when the hopeless attempt to rescue Floyd Collins was his "first big story." A dark question gnawed at McGill. Would newspapers like the *Constitution* foster a new pattern in race relations, or would they succumb to madness, "to the great disservice of the South and its generations to come"?

In early May came announcement of his Pulitzer Prize. The *New York Times* singled him out for special praise. McGill was incredulous when word reached his office, having believed for fourteen years that his feud with Carl Ackerman would prevent any of his Pulitzer nominations from succeeding. The flood of congratulatory messages encouraged him to keep struggling. Many contemporaries were leaving their editorial posts. Hodding Carter, who had won a Pulitzer in 1946, shortly retired from his Missis-sippi paper. By contrast, McGill's best efforts lay ahead. [27]

The looming desegregation crisis in the city McGill had loved passionately for thirty years caused him to seek relief in travel. Increased pressures at home usually meant more overindulgence on these trips. Down in south Georgia for a trip scheduled to last all weekend, a very drunk McGill began to insist late Saturday afternoon that he must return to Atlanta to teach his Sunday School class at St. Philip's. Finally his companions gave up trying to persuade him to stay. Off they went to the train station where they attached a baggage tag to the now unconscious editor. "This is Ralph McGill," it read, "Put him off in Atlanta." No one ever knew how, but the next morning Ralph taught Sunday School.[28]

He spent the first two weeks of July in Cuba then joined the press and Vice President Richard M. Nixon's party on the second of three trips to the Soviet Union. For a fortnight he filed some of his best foreign correspondence, including an eyewitness account of the famous Nixon-Khrushchev "kitchen debate."[29]

McGill's personal dealings with Nixon never approximated the relationship he enjoyed with Eisenhower, but he cultivated the Vice President. Nixon followed up each contact with a cordial note. Idealists such as Adlai Stevenson or his boss, Governor Cox, commanded his allegiance, but Ralph relished watching tough, cynical politicians like Nixon operate. He fully expected that in 1960 the splintered Democratic party would be no match for a Republican juggernaut led by Nixon.[30]

Reverend Martin Luther King Jr. unsettled Atlanta when he came home to live early in 1960. He would be co-pastor at Ebenezer Baptist Church with his father but planned to devote more time and energy to the Southern Christian Leadership Conference. In the new decade the SCLC intended to attack every form of segregation and to register all blacks to vote. King was vital to this effort as inspiration and fund raiser. Daddy King was over-joyed and relieved, having feared for his son's life in Alabama. Other Atlanta black leaders did not share his feelings. Some worried that the junior King might disturb their tried-and-true way of gaining concessions from Atlanta's white power structure. Others were plainly jealous of his charisma.

The thirty-year old minister intrigued McGill. After three decades of friendship with Daddy King, the editor recognized that some of Martin's moral courage came from his father. McGill also understood from his own trip to India why young King chose Gandhi as a focus in his work. With his keen reporter's sense, McGill saw how King might use the principles of love and non-violence to transform the struggle for racial justice. The editor knew that out of deference to his father's circle, Martin supposedly would not lead local protest movements. However, McGill did worry about King's effect on events in Atlanta and Georgia where diehards vowed to retain segregation at all costs. He wrote Harry Ashmore that King's return could make matters worse.[31]

In the same letter McGill told Ashmore he was to speak at Cooper Union in New York for the centennial celebration of Lincoln's address there. It was, another friend noted, "really quite an honor for Old Peerless McGill," southerner and Democrat. These labels were not quite right. By 1960 the editor was showing his heritage. Like his father and so many other southern mountain Republicans he knew and admired from Tennessee days, McGill was at heart a Union man. He remained in the ranks of the Democratic party. However, his enemies were correct in accusing him of putting national concerns ahead of southern loyalties. He now advocated federal civil rights laws and federal aid to education. The Civil War, he often wrote, resolved the issue of states' rights, and Lincoln had "placed the union firmly on a necessary foundation of authority."[32]

So on February 12, 1960, McGill came to the same podium as his idol. He pleaded, as Lincoln had, for "an honest national dialogue" on the critical issues. Civil rights figured prominently in McGill's speech, but he placed the issue in a context of larger change: population growth, urbanization, technological challenges. He called for leadership that could "fuse moral considerations with social inventiveness," as Lincoln had attempted. Then as now, he continued, both parties, businessmen, and other political pressure groups were failing to do so, giving extremists the upper hand especially in the South. McGill praised the southern moderates—ostracized, abused, but standing firm for the Constitution.[33]

The widely-publicized Cooper Union address brought even more speaking invitations. Though overscheduled, McGill obliged whenever possible. Rarely did his performance on the platform match that at Cooper Union. Time pressures forced him to use the same material over and over. On some occasions he was too tired to be effective. A friend recalled an occasion when he "would swing from conditions in Scandinavia to the starving millions in India, and then he would look about him desperately, as if wondering where he was, and announce with great vehemence, 'And that's why you have to have a YWCA.'" His raspy voice distracted some listeners who thought he was trying to clear his throat. Hearing her boss talk always reminded Celestine Sibley "of a barn door swinging in a high wind." Yet he came across as a decent man working for human rights.[34]

That spring the movement entered yet another phase with student sit-ins throughout the South at variety store lunch counters and other businesses refusing to feed blacks. Privately McGill found the tactic promising. "Some of the ten-cent stores could handle this without trouble," he wrote a friend, "by allowing them to use the counters. . . ." Others would never relent. When the first Atlanta sit-ins occurred in mid-March, his lead editorial commended the students' behavior but not their timing. The battle for open schools in Georgia was at a critical stage, he wrote, and took priority over integrating lunch counters. Noting the violent reactions to sit-ins elsewhere, he cautioned the students about arousing "agitators bent on disorder." After boosting Atlanta for three decades, McGill hated to see it explode rather than set an example.[35]

However threatening these forces, they were nothing compared with a personal trial that began in February 1960. Dr. Joe Wilber admitted Mary Elizabeth McGill to the hospital once again. This episode, he explained to her anxious husband, was different. A lifetime of stones, inflammation, and scarring had damaged her one whole kidney too much. Now loss of kidney function sent her blood pressure dangerously high. Ralph confided to Harold Martin who was away on assignment for the *Saturday Evening Post,* "She will never really be well again." Dr. Wilber hoped to control Red's blood pressure with a new medication but told McGill that treatment of her malignant hypertension might fail. Looking towards the suffering and death that would mark the end of their long life together, McGill decided not to talk to her about this dark reality.

The drugs worked. Mary Elizabeth improved enough to leave the hospital and, after further convalescence, to resume some activities. Her three great loves—Ralph, their son, and her church—kept Red McGill alive long after others would have succumbed to such afflictions. Terrible side effects of the drugs included weakness and fainting spells. She fell down often. She wisecracked to those rushing to help, "People will say, 'There's Mary Elizabeth drunk again.'" For two more years she staved off the fatal effects of uremia. She was determined to see her husband reap well-deserved honors and her boy launched from the nest.[36]

Between his mother's precarious health and father's frequent absences, young Ralph had a rough adolescence. He clung to Julia. "She's always been there," he later told Harold Martin and "brought me up as much as Mother." At fifteen he was taller than his father and weighed 175 pounds. McGill was delighted to inform Bob Woodruff that in football "the coaches tell me he has a hard nose and isn't afraid to bore in and take his share of punishment." "Ralpho" also resembled his parent academically—creative writing awards but uneven grades. He started dating early with one steady girl friend after another.[37]

On May 4 McGill notified Eisenhower and Nixon that he was about to assume a new position—that of publisher. He assured both men, "I am not retiring to an ivory tower" and will write as much as always. Actually it was Clark Howell, turning sixty-six, who was retiring from the *Constitution.* Tarver moved Gene Patterson from being executive editor of both papers to editor of the *Constitution.* McGill was no longer obliged to work daily with the editorial staff and certainly not those managing the paper.

Word around the *Constitution* shop was that McGill's promotion was aimed at alleviating his fears of retirement (and oblivion). As publisher he would not be subject to ANInc's rule of leaving at age sixty-five. The rumors were close to the truth. McGill was forever "proving" he could work as hard as in his youth. He and his friends joked about his elevation to publisher. "I don't know anything about publishing," he told his old Nashville roommate, Brainard Cheney, "and I am just going to keep on doing my column and delegating the details." As newspaper publishers go, wrote Ashmore, "You've got the build, but, unlike Tarver, there just ain't enough son of a bitch in you. . . ." This void was regrettable because tensions built at the paper throughout the 1960s.[38]

After McGill's promotion to publisher his writing seemed more forthright. He did less dissembling. Privately he had been contemptuous of segregation for years. Now he held it up to ridicule in public. Blacks appreciated his willingness to speak out at the very time when many other whites were pressured into silence about race relations. He infuriated "the segs" by making light of their "mongrelization" fears and insisting that desegregation would affect only public dealings. On May 14 his column stated flatly that all businesses should abandon Jim Crow and that most southerners preferred desegregation to turmoil.[39]

Three days later 3,000 Atlanta University students marched to commemorate the *Brown* decision. Police Chief Jenkins led them away from a state capitol crowded with "the segs" to William Holmes Borders's church where Rev. King Jr. called them an inspiration to the entire world. In national media McGill also praised the student protestors for allowing "the moral feature of the whole problem to find expression." "The sit-ins," he observed in a major speech, "telescoped time and courts. . . . it soon became impossible to defend a situation where persons of both races could stand side by side to purchase intimate items of underwear, for example, but were barred . . . from being side by side while buying a sandwich or a cup of coffee."[40]

Despite new job security, McGill manifested a restlessness worse than any since 1937. Partly he was putting distance between himself and looming changes in his family. Whenever possible, he visited friends of his youth. He was often in Washington, New York, or at a distant speaking engagement. In June he toured several NATO countries. The fact that it was a presidential election year gave him an excuse for more travel. He arranged his California convention coverage to include a visit with Harry Ashmore's family. It was a refreshing stopover: "Nobody rang up and called me an S.O.B.; nobody telephoned my home and threatened to kidnap my boy or blow up my house."[41]

Vice-President Nixon seemed bound to win the presidency, an event McGill equated with "the coming of Attila the Hun." Senator Jack Kennedy's riches and ruthless tactics during the Democratic primaries unsettled him. Once Kennedy won the Democratic nomination, McGill followed him onto the campaign trail. He was incredulous that a Roman Catholic might actually win the presidency. He also worried that the forty-three year old candidate's effect on audiences seemed more like that of a Hollywood star or a sports idol from the 1920s than someone in the American political tradition. Kennedy struck McGill as driven, unwilling to wait for the prize despite his youth. On October 17, however, the *Constitution* endorsed Kennedy.[42]

Two days later the Atlanta sit-ins took a dramatic turn. Rich's was now the students' principal target, and Martin Luther King Jr. was among those arrested for "trespassing" at the store. For months King's desire to mediate between generations in Atlanta's black community warred with his support for the students. Finally he joined them. The students' vow of "jail not bail" had a strange irony in King's case. A judge ruled King had violated an earlier probation, denied bail and gave him a four months' sentence. King's attorney appealed, but in the dead of night police secretly transferred him from the DeKalb county jail to a remote south Georgia prison.

The King family's fearful ordeal became a political windfall for Kennedy. Outrage and offers of help from the candidate and his brother Bobby put relentless pressure on Georgia authorities. King walked free. Republican Daddy King and countless other blacks voted for JFK. The Kennedys' interference infuriated white southerners, but McGill addressed a stinging column to them. You alone, he wrote, are responsible for transforming "a relatively obscure minister" into "an international symbol" of courage and moral force. Are you angry at Bobby Kennedy's telephone call? Look instead to injustice and legal discrimination in Georgia. "Without them there would have been no call."[43]

McGill knew that a good offense is often the best defense. By 1960 he had defended desegregation as the law of the land for six years. Now the sit-in movement was breaking existing laws and, many said, violating the sanctity of private property. McGill felt obliged, as did King, to justify this "lawlessness" on grounds of higher principles. Otherwise the student demonstrators would be on the same level as "the segs." His old friend, Dick Rich, who had ordered King's arrest, would never understand.[44]

The election was a cliffhanger. In the predawn hours McGill felt confident enough of JFK's win to lead the *Constitution* gang up Forsyth Street towards Henry Grady's statue on Marietta Street. There he fired Grady's miniature cannon just as Papa Howell had signaled FDR's victory in 1932. It was Ralph's way of keeping faith with his two idols, both of whom he had now surpassed. The old Marine forgot to calculate the little cannon's recoil. Nursing skinned shins and singed eyebrows, he returned to the office to compose a congratulatory message for Kennedy and consolation wire for Nixon. Republicans gained throughout the region and almost carried Atlanta, McGill told the loser whose failure still perplexed him.[45]

A federal court ordered Atlanta to begin desegregation of its schools in September 1961. Countless Atlantans hoped the Georgia legislature would accept the findings of its own special commission and replace massive resistance with local option laws. Others worked to destroy these hopes. On December 11, 1960, night riders dynamited a black elementary school in a formerly white area not far from McGill's home. He stopped at his office before departing for a Detroit speech and wrote a column, blaming "those in established positions who curse the court" rather than the bombers. He anticipated more "needless suffering, violence and ugly lawlessness," but the civil rights movement would win.[46]

To the surprise of all Georgians, their university system desegregated before Atlanta schools. A federal court ordered the admission of two black students when the January term began on the Athens campus. Courts turned down requests for further delays. Hamilton Holmes and Charlayne Hunter went to class, and that evening fifty women students welcomed Hunter to their dormitory. The following night an angry mob surrounded the dorm. Even though the riot was led by outsiders, university officials suspended Hunter and Holmes as threats to law and order. The suspensions did not hold up in court. In a few days it became obvious that the university was not going to remain segregated or even to be closed according to massive resistance laws. Beneath the surface of a melodrama McGill detected changes in public opinion. He took heart.[47]

Preparing to leave for Kennedy's inauguration, McGill gave in to his son's pleas and brought home a guitar. He attached a note, "Dear Ralpho. Please be seated and read this carefully. I want you to have the character to put this away until you have finished with exams Friday." McGill knew that parenting would soon be his responsibility alone. Teachers assured him that the boy was capable of doing outstanding work, yet Ralpho's preference for girls and guitars over homework confounded him. Soon his son would turn sixteen and start wandering farther than ever, particularly if upset about his mother's condition.

Ralph Jr. was already struggling with the realities of a sick mother and famous but unpopular father—both older than his friends' parents. McGill never missed a chance to bring his son in contact with notables. He believed this offset Ralpho's predicament of being "the only child of somewhat aging parents, who are probably a little too emotional about him. . . ." Mary Elizabeth's bad spells and hospital stays affected him deeply. He never understood why she seemed to keep her illnesses from his father as if not to interfere with his career. Also troubling was the matter of "two lost daughters," to whom his father referred more and more in letters and conversations. McGill imagined that had Elizabeth and Virginia lived, they would have families of their own by now. Ralph Jr. not only had to measure up to his dad's achievements but to these fantasies.[48]

10

"BLACK WING OF A GHOSTLY BIRD": 1961-1964

AS A JOURNALIST WHO ARTICULATED NEW POSSIBILITIES IN RACE relations, McGill filled a need and became a national celebrity. The Hall Syndicate took over his column and placed it in fifty-five newspapers with more to come. In January 1961 came word that Harvard would award McGill an honorary degree during commencement festivities in June. He was also invited to address assembled alumni of Harvard's Law School that week. In February he spent a week at Yale University as a Chubb Fellow. Faculty and students warmed to this tireless man. Such academic contacts salved his wound that Vanderbilt seemed to have forgotten his very existence.[1]

The new Democratic president had not. In early February Kennedy gave Ralph the first of several opportunities to serve his administration. He was to head the panel of a Labor-Management advisory committee studying economic growth and unemployment. Working on the committee vastly improved his grasp of economic questions. However, such appointments plus favorable comments about Kennedy's performance brought McGill a new variety of hate mail. Enemies decried his servitude to "the papal slave in the White House."[2]

Given tensions in the region and his new boldness, attacks were bound to intensify. Harassment of his household became intolerable. In March someone put shots through the McGill's mailbox. With the phone sometimes ringing all night, Ralpho and Mary Elizabeth took refuge at a neighbor's house when McGill was away. After decades of informing his enemies that he was in the telephone book should they wish to complain in person, he got an unlisted number. He had no choice at this juncture but probably missed these telephone encounters. Male friends recalled that, if ladies were not listening, McGill could "drive these people raving crazy" with his "command of invective."[3]

Still, he had no illusions about how many dangerous individuals had joined the ranks of those resisting desegregation. The worst of these sociopaths shocked even a veteran "seg" like Lester Maddox. Maddox, who now headed Georgians Unwilling to Surrender (GUTS), was enraged in March 1961, when downtown merchants agreed to desegregate their eating facilities following Atlanta's token school integration that fall. Maddox owned a restaurant, the Pickrick, that was his headquarters and the love of his life. He denounced Mayor Hartsfield and asked whites to boycott any business where Negroes ate alongside them.

In April the failed Bay of Pigs invasion of Cuba took McGill's mind off Atlanta and sent him flying to interview sources in New York and Washington. McGill insisted that Eisenhower's administration had created such momentum for the plan that Kennedy had little choice but to go along. Ralph blamed the former president for so many troubles that he infuriated Eisenhower and his supporters, including many Georgians. The Cuban fiasco put his old friend Adlai Stevenson, now ambassador to the United Nations, in a bad light. McGill kept praising Stevenson's diplomatic skill and warning against unilateral foreign policy but knew Kennedy was unlikely to work through the U.N..[4]

More and more, McGill made use of Cold War rivalries to plead for educational progress and open schools. In May 1961 he addressed the Birmingham Rotary Club just after vicious attacks on Freedom Riders across Alabama. Communists everywhere "make great capital of our racial violence and discrimination," he said. Even more sobering was his claim that future "national survival" turned on educating Americans to compete in global "economic warfare." Back home he wrote Ashmore that in Birmingham he deliberately presented social issues "in a very pragmatic manner" which these businessmen "could understand, even if they didn't appreciate it."[5]

McGill also sought Ashmore's advice. Edward Weeks, he explained, "is after me to try to expand the two or three articles of mine he has published into . . . a sort of reminiscent, experience book." Ralph said he was undecided. Actually Weeks proposed the book idea in May 1959 when McGill won his Pulitzer Prize. He assigned Peter Davison, an editor with *Atlantic Monthly* Press, to develop the manuscript. The men conferred on the project in Atlanta and Boston. Grace Lundy, who ranked her boss's literary gifts with those of Nobel laureates, was retrieving relevant old columns and material from his subject files. By the time he confided in Ashmore McGill had pieced together long parts of the draft mostly by writing while he traveled. Weeks and the *Atlantic* staff believed they were developing an important book, but McGill, haunted by past failures, thought the project would abort. He could not bring himself to tell even Ashmore the truth about his work.[6]

Laurence Winship, Ralph's other Boston friend from the 1943 trip to Britain, was also planning to enhance the Atlantan's growing fame. Upon learning of the upcoming honorary degree from Harvard, Winship dispatched a *Boston Globe* reporter to Georgia. With Grace Lundy's guidance, he interviewed a full complement of friends and enemies, especially Lester Maddox. He also spent an evening *en famille* at 3399 Piedmont Road. The result was a huge feature article set to run in the *Globe* on the Sunday following Harvard commencement week. In late May the reporter sent his copy to McGill who replied, "You're the greatest whitewash expert since Tom Sawyer."[7]

On Monday, June 12, Ralph and Mary Elizabeth set out on their last trip together. They flew first to New York for an evening at a Broadway show then on Tuesday to Boston where Ed Weeks and his wife entertained the McGills. Wednesday Ralph addressed a luncheon gathering of about 1500 Harvard Law School alumni, graduate school students, faculty, and their guests. He focused on the failure of the legal profession in the South to take a stand affording people "an alternative to the peddlers of defiance." McGill expressed his deepest concerns of recent years in terms of simple eloquence. Unlike the driving power of his better columns, this speech offered thoughtful reflections about what laws really did in America. He spoke even more about the moral opportunities "left open for private action and choice." Then, shifting into a reporter's mode, he gave a vivid account of integrating the University of Georgia, "a turning point in the Deep South pattern of pledged total defiance."[8]

Thursday morning McGill took his place in the procession for Harvard's 310th commencement. At last he stood to hear President Nathan M. Pusey read the citation for his degree, Doctor of Laws. "In a troubled time," it ran, "his steady voice of reason champions a new South." A photograph for the *Harvard Crimson* captured an image of the erect old ex-Marine weeping behind his horn-rimmed glasses. McGill received seventeen honorary degrees and countless awards, but none matched this experience. His response to many of the congratulations was that—given Kennedy's propensity for staffing from his alma mater—he too was now eligible for federal employment. Yet thereafter "he always wore the black and crimson tie and drank his office coffee out of a huge cup bearing the Harvard seal."[9]

On August 30, 1961, Atlanta's long-delayed school integration began. Education officials placed nine Negro students among four formerly white high schools. Acceptance of desegregation at the University of Georgia had broken some barriers to change. Nonetheless, Atlanta took no chances. A civic alliance of massive proportions worked for months preparing the local population. Never-ending messages warned of harm done to the economies of Little Rock, New Orleans, and Alabama by violent resistance to desegregation. No one knew for sure whether the propaganda campaign had succeeded.

Even if civic pride overrode racism among white Atlantans, outsiders might precipitate a riot or worse. Plenty came looking for trouble. George Lincoln Rockwell of the American Nazi Party informed McGill that he had a constitutional right to bring his Storm Troopers to Atlanta. Perhaps. But Chief Herbert Jenkins and his policemen thwarted the desire of all the white supremacy groups to foment violence. The transition was completely peaceful.

Publicity surrounding desegregation gave "the city too busy to hate" the national, even international, exposure its boosters craved. This public relations bonanza was due partly to a media army that descended on Atlanta to cover the story. McGill, Hartsfield, Jenkins and a handful of others made special plans for these visitors. They created a press center in the city council chamber where the Superintendent of Schools and some aides also came. As the first school day unfolded, these officials communicated with the four schools on amplified telephones. The news media heard every word. As McGill later explained to a friend, "We knew that one of the reasons so many rumors came out of other school desegregation moves was the inability of newsmen to know what was going on inside the schools." The city also provided buses so that media personnel could visit the schools for a firsthand look. The wire services and networks carried their reports around the world. President Kennedy began a press conference with high praise for the city and urged other communities to use Atlanta as a model. It was the retiring Hartsfield's last hurrah.[10]

Pride in his city almost overwhelmed McGill. Although he hoped that Atlanta had found "a will to obey the law," he was a lifelong worrier with extra anxieties just now. His relief sometimes swelled into hyperbole. "Few cities," he wrote in late September, "have had the opportunity to make, in so short a span of time, so many answers in behalf of the best ideals of Christian and Western civilization." In calmer moments he explained particulars to his readers. Quoting one of Atlanta's policemen who said, "We couldn't have done it without the chief," McGill described the years Jenkins spent preparing himself and the police force for just such a time. Since seeing the Nazis in 1938 McGill feared that if authorities weakened, mobs would rule. He had had even longer to build confidence in his friend, Herbert Jenkins, and gave the chief all the credit he deserved.[11]

His own influence on public opinion was invariably noted as well. He was not content to rest on a now solid reputation as "the conscience of the South," however. He wanted to justify the Hall

Syndicate's faith in his work and match the best of the syndicated columnists by commenting on national and international as readily as southern issues. That had actually been McGill's mix since he moved out of sports in 1938. What changed in the 1960s was his tone. Maybe it was age or broadening contacts or Harvard's dubbing him doctor. Perhaps losing Red's deflating wit that, he always said, kept him from taking himself too seriously. For whatever reason the writer/persona stopped resembling what he called the "Gee-Whiz" school of sportswriters and began to pontificate.

Ralph felt compelled to cover firsthand the latest international crisis unfolding in Berlin. In early September Dr. Wilber told him Mary Elizabeth seemed stable enough for him to be away two or three weeks. So he set out for his fourth trip to Germany. Before leaving he admonished his son about making a strong start to his senior year of prep school. Ralpho had spent the summer away from Atlanta at an Episcopal camp. He wrote the sixteen year old, "I hope you will come back ready to forego all social life and get down to business." The boy got exactly the same message he gave everyone else about Mary Elizabeth. She was "not too well but is better." With few exceptions McGill was silent about her hopeless condition and asked friends not to mention his wife's health to her.[12]

The weeks in Germany and Paris drained body and soul, bringing on afterwards a serious case of flu. Personal memories of bygone days in Germany were haunting. He remembered when he and Mary Elizabeth saw Hitler in 1938 and wrote little Virginia about their day. Death shadowed his writing. On his second trip to Berlin just after the war, he recalled, the "stench of bodies in the ruins competed with the musty smell of burned out ruins . . . and the sour reek of misery." As McGill viewed the Berlin wall, "an ugly, monstrous looking piece of masonry," he felt the entire city was doomed despite Kennedy's vow to defend it. McGill's letters to friends were even grimmer than columns. In correspondence he predicted "there might be a Soviet Germany by 1970."[13]

Kennedy appreciated McGill's support for his foreign policy

and occasionally invited the Atlantan to official functions, usually involving African leaders. In November McGill received a second presidential appointment. He joined the general advisory committee of the Arms Control and Disarmament Agency where, Harold Martin noted, he got "a look at the inner secret workings of our global nuclear policy." McGill tried to use any access to JFK or his brother, the Attorney-General, to encourage executive action for voting rights and against discrimination in federal contracts.[14]

Edward Weeks continued to exert pressure on McGill to complete his autobiographical study. Grace Lundy easily located much of the topical material her boss needed. He lifted sections from the Chattahoochee River book. However, Ralph alone decided what he wanted to tell about his family and upbringing. Unlike his usual "speed" writing, he produced many versions of these parts before he was satisfied. He never mentioned his younger brother, Carl, even though he was almost four when the child died. His mother seemed more real in the book than his father, but Ben rather than Mary Lou McGill was the subject of moving columns. Recently he had described stalking wild turkeys near the river with his father. On the way back to Mammy's house Ben told Ralph about his own youth. "I thought, as a young boy," McGill recalled, "how wonderful it would have been to have seen the things his eyes saw." In late 1961, while working on this part of the book, he commented that "Each person has his own image of his home and homeland." The old farm beside the river had always been what Ralph saw as home.[15]

Mary Elizabeth was able to remain at home during Christmas but spent the last dozen weeks of her life in Piedmont Hospital. Much of the time her husband sat with her. A clergy friend who visited often thought Ralph seemed "like a little child at the end of the bed. He hurt with every moan from Mary Elizabeth. . . ." Balancing a yellow legal pad on his knees, he wrote his column or worked on the autobiography. Grace Lundy handled everything at the office. Julia Crawford kept the household going as she had for almost thirty-two years.

Mary Elizabeth fought death with the mettle she brought to

life. Time and again she went into a coma only to rally and become conscious, even comfortable, for a spell. Sometimes when McGill called to dictate a column or letter, Grace could hear her kibitz. Ralph Jr. knew the end was near. In February Wesleyan College in Connecticut sent word of his admission. His mother was struggling against all odds to see him graduate from prep school. At least she knew where her son would go to college next fall.[16]

By mid-March kidney function was failing fast. McGill wrote Larry Winship that twice she did "what the doctors and the specialists say they have never seen done before—a person with a high uremia toxicity pull back from a strong decline." After each brush with death she conversed with family and friends. Her husband marveled that her "indomitable will to live . . . is almost fantastic." Doctors, nurses, and visitors knew Mary Elizabeth drew upon spiritual resources as well. The last eight and a half years she had lived within the context of the church. It structured her lifelong do-good impulses and refined her bravado into intent. Its mediating forms of grace, especially the sacrament of communion, enabled her to face suffering her husband could barely witness with the same unabashed spirit that first attracted him.

During their thirty-four year relationship it was obvious to everyone that Red lived to make her man happy. Sometimes her efforts misfired or fate barred her way. Eventually - with Julia's help - she succeeded in creating a home and family to which, she knew, Ralph would always return from wandering the world. Mary Elizabeth died on March 22, 1962, leaving behind a sixty-four year old husband and son about to turn seventeen. Neither had been very comfortable with the other for a long time. On the afternoon of her funeral the pair flew to Miami for a visit with the family of Bill Baggs whom young Ralph liked tremendously. Back home the boy noticed changes in his father's behavior. He was pale and withdrawn, not sleeping.[17]

Guilty feelings always came easily to McGill. Now they colored his grieving. Through condolences he discovered countless acts of kindness Mary Elizabeth showered on friends and strangers. Most messages spoke of her devotion to him. He felt unworthy. He had spent too much time away from Red. He had often wished for a different sort of spouse. He could not protect her from pain that seemed more than warranted for several lifetimes. Now he could only atone by spending more time with Ralpho. Yet out-of-town commitments filled the April and May calendar. Often he flew home just "for the daylight hours" or, on April 25, to host his son's birthday party before catching a little sleep and returning to New York. McGill loved travel almost as much as eating. It is hardly surprising that he fought his grief by "keeping myself busier than usual."[18]

His closest male friends were also invaluable. Ralph Jr. came to regard honorary degrees from Negro colleges and drinking as hallmarks of this "fraternity." The 1962 commencement season brought the usual number of honorary degrees for crusaders against "the segs." Bill Baggs should not worry about being dubbed the McGill of Florida, Ralph told the group. After all, he had been called the Harry Ashmore of Georgia for years and even worse, Harry Golden's Georgia twin. Morehouse College of the Atlanta University complex honored McGill in 1962. Dr. Benjamin Mays's citation thanked the journalist for writing the truth "at the risk of losing social prestige, friends, and even life." The audience responded with an ovation the likes of which Harvard's President Pusey, another honoree, had never seen.[19]

In May Edward Weeks capped two decades of friendship with McGill by sending word that his manuscript had won the $5,000 *Atlantic* nonfiction prize. Anxiety eroded Ralph's joy over the award. To Larry Winship he confessed, "I hope the book doesn't fall on its face." The work, titled *The South and the Southerner*, was peculiarly constructed. Weeks, who touted the book as part autobiography and part history, gave definite instructions about material he wanted to include. Grace Lundy functioned as researcher and editor. Ralph finally was satisfied with sections about the early years but omitted significant aspects of his adult life.

He gave the impression that, as a young reporter, "writing politics was my trade." After recounting his reporting of the Democratic primary campaign according to Major Stahlman's orders in the summer of 1922, he said, "I left Nashville not long thereafter. . . ." In fact he stayed nearly seven years longer and became a popular sports editor. That same chapter included detailed descriptions of travels with Governor Alf Taylor's campaign entourage. There is no disputing McGill's deep affection for "Uncle Alf" and admiration for the Taylor family's politics and way of life. He was correct in saying he "heard [the Taylors] talked about a hundred times before I learned to read." However, Stahlman sent Ralph only with Austin Peay and kept a veteran political reporter on Taylor's campaign.[20]

It is understandable that the now distinguished columnist would pass over a decade and a half on the sports beat. Yet why did McGill not mention a twenty-one year association with the Howell family or include the Talmadges in his analysis of southern demagogues? The usual pressures plus the strain of Mary Elizabeth's illness may have blinded him to such gaps. Any autobiography has important omissions. Those in *The South and the Southerner* were baffling. At long last, however, he had produced a bona fide book.

A month-long stay in Japan that summer revitalized McGill. At first he refused the Asia Foundation's request to conduct seminars at Japanese newspapers and universities. He was keen to see if that nation's postwar recovery matched West Germany's but felt the trip would consume too much of his brief time with Ralpho before college. They insisted he take the boy along. McGill hoped it might bond them and cool young Ralph's hot romance. Between seminars he interviewed dozens of leaders and played tourist.[21]

Finally the McGills decided to join the throngs of Japanese climbing Mt. Fuji during the snowfree months, July and August. After the first day's climb their guide, a former submariner, confessed his fear that the elderly, overweight American newsman might not make it to the Buddhist shrine at the peak. Neither the guide nor the young woman representing Japanese newspapers reckoned on McGill's needs at that time. He knew that Buddhists said climbing Mt. Fuji was a purifying experience, particularly if one saw sunrise from the peak. The physical exertion would affirm that he still had life left to him.

Throughout "the long, drawn-out anguish of Mary Elizabeth's dying," he often imagined that he would soon follow her in death. After all she was seven years younger than he. His son was also going from him with, McGill admitted, signs of being a troubled young man. The agony of the climb purged grief and guilt. The others had to push him the last way, but he stood two miles above the earth "legs trembling, lungs laboring" and faced the sun. As in his 1940 Ichauway experience after Virginia's death and Mary Elizabeth's breakdown, McGill found "a sort of exultation."[22]

Back home and more aggressive, the columnist rained down wrath on Klansmen and other whites defying change across the South. He pushed equally hard his conviction that their defiance must not "obscure the vast amount of progress" being made. In autumn 1962 a solitary black man, James Meredith, entered the University of Mississippi after rioting claimed two lives and injured dozens. McGill took after General Edwin Walker for his role in the Ole Miss violence. He reminded readers that Walker, who "led the federal troops at Little Rock," came to Mississippi "to inflame young college students and hoodlums." Now a civilian, Walker defied "the laws of the country he once served with honor." To McGill's grim satisfaction, he was arrested and charged with insurrection and conspiracy.

Like Eisenhower before him, Kennedy had no choice but forcibly to put down this defiance of federal authority that some called the most serious since 1861. McGill approved Kennedy's steps as he had Ike's during the Little Rock crisis, bringing more censure of "the Soddy traitor." The president, he wrote, was neither acting illegally nor initiating trouble as deceitful southern politicians claimed. The issue of national sovereignty, he added, was settled at the time states ratified the Constitution long before 1861.[23]

Coincidentally, Khrushchev flung his own challenge at Kennedy after Ole Miss just as five years earlier he had rattled Eisenhower following Little Rock. The Cuban missile crisis was far more dangerous than the Soviet sputniks and space race, however. McGill was at the U.N. in October when Kennedy announced that the Soviets were constructing missile launching sites in Cuba. McGill gave the president's tough response his full support. He admitted that if war came, it would be "horrible beyond compare." After the crisis he predicted that Khrushchev, now thwarted, would cause trouble elsewhere, most likely in Southeast Asia.[24]

Even though McGill made a kind of peace with the past and worked feverishly after his wife's death, he endured a tough adjustment. Friends and family knew, and his writings contain hints of the struggle. That fall, he did a long article on Margaret Mitchell. When Red McGill died, the black musician, Graham Jackson, told Ralph that he always saw striking similarities in Mitchell and his wife. The piece was more probing than others he had done through the years. McGill made the comment, "It is difficult, perhaps impossible, to know another human being - be it wife or husband, mother, father, son, daughter, friend, or lover."[25]

In early December Ed Danforth died, releasing a flood of memories. In an odd eulogy McGill praised Danforth's knowledge of sports and proficiency at reporting but withheld his customary warmth and affection for a departed colleague. "As for the man himself," the piece concluded, "let us leave that to his friends. . . ." Almost thirty-four years had passed since Danforth had rescued his good friend, Mac, from frustration and misery in Nashville, but Ralph ignored the happy times they shared before careers diverged and friendship fractured.[26]

During succeeding months he kept a frenetic schedule that may have relieved his psyche but harmed his health. In early 1963 he toured eight African countries for the State Department. Watching masses of people leaving their villages for hopeless urban areas, he recalled blacks pouring into Atlanta during the 1930s with no social services and no jobs for them. Thanks to racial problems in the United States, anti-American sentiments were strong in these former colonial regions. In conversations with individuals like Ghanaian strongman, Kwame Nkrumah, and lectures, press conferences, or small discussion groups, McGill was honest about

American racism but hopeful about progress. Newly established U.S. embassies welcomed his help, but the trip gave homegrown white supremacists new reasons to harass him.[27]

The energy and enthusiasm of this man who turned sixty-five while in Guinea astonished his escorts. Peoples, sights and sounds he had longed to experience always exhilarated McGill. In Accra, Ghana, he and Negro jazz musician Cozy Cole agreed to hold a joint press conference even though they had just met. For three and a half hours the Ghanian press "tossed every question imaginable at them." Though "bone tired," McGill stayed up for Cole's late night show to watch audience reaction. U.S. officials remarked on his patience and skill with hostile or uninformed audiences. He said he was grateful to God not to fall ill during the trip. Later he suspected that such overexertions were taking a toll on his heart. He was too old to change his pattern.[28]

His autobiographical work, *The South and the Southerner*, came out shortly after his return from Africa. Jack Tarver and the Hall Syndicate hosted a huge New York luncheon celebrating the occasion. In the front of the book, Ralph acknowledged the collaboration of Grace Lundy, the support of Weeks and Cox. The dedication was revealing. In 1950 he had inscribed *Israel Revisited* to his mother. Now alongside Mary Elizabeth and young Ralph, he placed the name of Jack Tarver. Beyond the remarkable bond with eighty-five year old Mary Lou McGill, these were his primary relationships.

Appearance of *The South and the Southerner* in bookstores across the country and interviews of the author brought an outpouring of messages from old Tennessee friends. The public might associate McGill mainly with Atlanta and Georgia, but one-third of the book recalled his life in Chattanooga and Nashville. Friends wanted "Mac" to know they too remembered bygone days. Some laughed over youthful pranks or Bohemian posturing in the Twenties. Others shared memories of Mary Elizabeth as a child or, most poignantly, as a young woman radiantly in love. McGill was awash in nostalgia. The messages were gratifying but did not help the widower's struggle to shape a new life for himself.[29]

His son also weighed on his spirit. Ralph Jr., just eighteen, was out of Wesleyan College after one year. He took a summer job in Atlanta but planned to leave again. The dilemma would have confounded even the wisest father. Ralph Sr. anguished. Then they persuaded Vanderbilt to admit Ralpho as a special student. Certain of his son's potential, McGill declared there must be no repeat of the Wesleyan disaster.[30]

At least Atlanta's progress at integration reassured McGill that summer. The city, which hired some black fire fighters in the spring, desegregated its swimming pools under a consent decree. Then widening student demonstrations along with counterprotests wore down some downtown businesses. In late June fifty restaurants were voluntarily integrated. His strongest hopes lay in the power of the ballot, however. Recent Supreme Court decisions killed Georgia's iniquitous county unit system. A fair share of political power would finally come to the state's urban areas where Negro voters wielded influence. What a contrast, he invariably declared, Atlanta made to Birmingham where Bull Connor's use of police dogs and fire hoses against peaceful demonstrators shocked the world.

President Kennedy set a dilemma before Mayor Ivan Allen Jr. by asking him to testify on behalf of a civil rights bill that would desegregate all places open to the public. Both Negroes and whites in Atlanta's power structure urged Allen to refuse. Voluntary integration was working in Atlanta, they argued. Why should the mayor risk defeat in 1965 by supporting federal coercion? The *Constitution* opposed the bill editorially, but McGill knew such laws were inevitable. After Allen testified, McGill told him, "two years from now things will have progressed to show your statement as a moderate one." Even bitter Negro protests against job discrimination in Atlanta that summer did not shake McGill. He always said that blacks would have to fight economic bondage after they defeated Jim Crow.[31]

In 1963, however, most of McGill's readers had not accepted desegregation much less equal employment opportunities. He kept telling them that a revolution was brewing in the U.S., pleading that this reordering not be violent. This was never to be the case in Birmingham. The aggressive police tactics inspired more heinous acts. To his relief, no incidents marred the March on Washington on August 28. Almost a quarter of a million demonstrators for civil rights laws heard Martin Luther King Jr. speak passionately about the American dream of freedom and equality. To McGill, the old Calvinist, King was God's instrument. Both black separatists and white supremacists in the Klan and Nazi party violently resisted social change. With his stirring ideals and peaceful tactics, King seemed destined to stave off extremists of either race.[32]

In mid-September McGill's hopeful scenario was blown apart with the bombing of a Birmingham Negro church during Sunday School. Four girls died in the blast. After losing his own two daughters in 1936 and 1939, McGill could not bear the killing of children. The Birmingham deaths devastated him. He recanted his "moderate" position, condemning himself and others who played for time while terrorists acted. He felt as if moderates in the southern power structure had almost consented to this crime. White churches and synagogues got special criticism.[33]

Actually McGill plunged into the turmoil of late 1963 in a more vulnerable state than anyone realized. That spring and summer his behavior worried his confidants. On the one hand he had energy to travel widely promoting *The South and the Southerner*. The book was a success. After six months sales were edging towards 30,000. Weeks planned a paperback edition for 1964. Yet Ralph felt ill and miserable, staying away from old friends. "I am getting more and more anti-social," he wrote to one, "and showing other signs of senility. . . ." Shadows deepened when two individuals he held dear died suddenly within days. Both Martin Sommers and Archbishop Gerald O'Hara had recently written congratulating him on *The South and the Southerner*. He wrote warm eulogies for each man but was obviously upset.

This dark spell, though similar to the 1946 episode, was related more to grief than to stress. His life seemed over and done with. Those closest to him knew he missed his wife, especially with a son who was having troubles. For thirty-four years Julia Crawford had

seen the McGills through their trials. Now she hardly knew what
to do. She often picked up her boss at the airport. Listening to his
gusty sighs, Julia would say, "You going too hard. You ought to let
up." He only tried harder with unsettling results. Writing became
a burden. "I almost hate the sight of a typewriter," he confided to
a friend. His work suffered. He recycled sections from *The South
and the Southerner*. He was heavyhanded, repeated columns, and
made more errors than usual.[34]

Four days after the Birmingham church murders, McGill spent
an hour and a half talking with Bert Hatch, a thirty-two year old
Episcopal priest and family friend. From the tape of their
conversation Hatch wrote an article for the diocese newspaper.
McGill, who tended towards rash statements during interviews,
was brimming over with anger and sorrow when Hatch started
recording. He blasted Birmingham's leaders but admitted
sympathy with that city's clergy who chose not to jeopardize their
jobs by taking provocative stands. He said he endured similar
dilemmas. It was better to stay on and keep some kind of dialogue
going about race relations than be replaced by "a seg."

When Hatch asked Ralph about his row with Atlanta's bishop
over the Lovett School, Hatch's tape captured the wrath his
colleagues knew so well. Months before McGill resigned in protest
from Lovett's board when they rejected some Negro applicants. He
referred over and over to "the Cathedral leadership" as hypocrites.
He had earlier written the bishop angrily that around town the
canon of the cathedral was being called "a seg." The diocese "sold
for scrap" all thirteen thousand copies of the paper containing
Hatch's article and later ran a "censored" version.[35]

National publicity swelled around McGill's fight with the
church, and friends teased that he would be "excommunicated."
For ten years he had enjoyed a satisfying association with the
Cathedral of St. Philip. He taught a teenage Sunday School class.
Mary Elizabeth made it the center of her activities outside the
home. Young Ralph talked of a career in the church. McGill finally
decided to leave the cathedral for All Saints, a downtown church.
Pained at the change, he never dreamed that from the transfer

would come one of the joys of his life.

McGill was an unconventional church member anyway. The Lovett School controversy revealed how differently religion played about in his psyche than many warming the pews on Sunday mornings. He joked with Ashmore, Baggs, and Tarver about blasé Episcopalians tolerating any comers. He spoke bitingly about youthful days among grim Presbyterians who "sin but never enjoy it." After abjuring Christianity for thirty-five years, he said, I am following "the real honest" faith. He tore into the religious establishment and denied ordinary Bible Belt readers their comfortable conventionalities.[36]

In this instance Christian ministers and laity responded with indignant letters, but legal action followed some of his other attacks. The most worrisome was a $10 million libel suit Major General Edwin Walker filed in autumn 1963. Walker claimed that during the integration of Ole Miss "he really tried to stop the riot at Oxford." McGill's columns depicted Walker as instigating mob violence. Walker sued many other newspapers besides the *Constitution* and its publisher. In fact executives of these papers gathered in New York to discuss the suits with legal counsel for the Associated Press.

Atlanta lawyers representing ANInc were more apprehensive than their New York counterparts. They told Tarver they considered McGill's descriptions of Walker extreme. Also a Georgia jury had just awarded enormous damages to football coach, Wally Butts, in his suit against the *Saturday Evening Post*. McGill thought the verdict was partly spite, "to teach that Yankee magazine a lesson." The same fate could befall him, regularly called a traitor to the South. He had faced earlier libel suits. Coinciding with so many other troubles, however, the Walker action undid him. In late October 1963 he described himself to Larry Winship as "a wounded, weary man."[37]

Yet he kept moving, traveling to Boston, New York, Chicago and scheduling a long California trip. On November 22 he was on board a plane bound for Atlanta. The pilot's voice came on the intercom with stunning news. President Kennedy was dead, assassinated in Dallas. McGill arranged to deplane in Nashville. A taxi rushed him to the newspaper building downtown. An Associated Press reporter watched the breathless and shocked publisher read bulletins from their teletype machine. Then *Tennessean* editor, John Seigenthaler, discovered that McGill was in the building and offered the use of his office.

The column that McGill sent to the *Constitution* that afternoon attributed Kennedy's murder to hatemongers on the right. Revelations about the accused assassin, Lee Harvey Oswald, indicated otherwise. Gene Patterson telephoned Nashville, pleading with McGill to kill the piece. It was with the greatest reluctance that he backed down and wrote a substitute. He did express much of his initial reaction shortly in the *Saturday Evening Post*. Titled, "Hate Knows No Direction," the piece and his columns brought outpouring of reaction. "Before we mourn," he wrote, we must admit "that hate, whether of the extreme left or right, can destroy not merely the chief of state, but the state itself."

For twenty-five years he had followed his calling to fight hate, intolerance, and the violence they spawned. Now his pleadings of a quarter century resonated in a stunned national readership. He cited a decade of murderous acts, adding what most readers knew to be his own experience: "The lives of those persons who sought to stand for law have been disturbed by threats and abuse, by filth shouted over the phone, by prowlers and, now and then, by a shot fired into the house." Praise for the truth of his observations was mingled with renewed threats that he, too, would suffer Kennedy's fate for "trying to ram the damn niggers down our throats."[38]

For the year and a half following President Kennedy's assassination McGill's life was a polarity. He was at his professional peak yet, weighed down with worry and sorrow, in the doldrums psychologically. His reputation and influence were never greater. By 1964 he had fulfilled his destiny, not because he was famous but because he had lived up to the commitment made before Hitler's forces in 1938. Carl Sandburg told him he was one of "the ten richest men in the country." He seemed to exemplify the best of the South to those outside the region. A uniqueness settled upon him, largely because of his writing style. Gene Patterson hit upon it when he described McGill as a "man of fire and poetry."

Unassuming as always, McGill was far better known than he usually admitted. *The South and the Southerner* continued to sell well and attract attention to its author. More than one hundred papers carried his syndicated column regularly; even more bought special series. He had friends and contacts around the globe. He would soon add a special honor, the Presidential Medal of Freedom, to the many awards he had already received. A colleague noted, "He held more honorary degrees (17) than any old football guard in history.[39]

Kennedy's successor, Lyndon Johnson, was a longtime acquaintance and fellow southerner. The aging journalist was as vulnerable as anyone to the famous LBJ "treatment." Unlike many of Johnson's other targets, however, McGill had a strong working relationship with the fifth president he covered. Immediately after assuming office Johnson set the final phase of that relationship. He thanked his "loyal friend" for wiring support from the *Constitution* and added, "I need your help now more than ever." Over the next five years McGill did everything within his power to meet that need.

He began by debunking notions that Johnson was unworthy to succeed Kennedy. McGill knew that the martyred president's circle could scarcely bear to see Lyndon in office. Most resented having him on the 1960 ticket in the first place. How could they now work daily for a man many called "ole Cornpone"? Being a great griever, McGill empathized with Bobby Kennedy, Kenny O'Donnell, and other JFK intimates. Yet Johnson needed the confidence of a shocked population. So McGill provided reassuring word pictures of LBJ's political acumen. With more than thirty years' experience in Washington, he said, Johnson understood how to make government work. After the assassination he had "moved with great vigor, direction, and skill. . . ." McGill predicted Johnson would have a successful presidency.[40]

He believed the darkest shadow over Johnson's prospects was the Vietnam War. On New Year's Day, 1964, McGill laid out the

dilemmas that troubled him and soon would obsess the administration. He said the U.S. should assist South Vietnam only if people
there showed willingness to fight "Communist aggression." If they
refused, the U.S. should leave. But how? In succeeding months
McGill grew more pessimistic about South Vietnam's ability to
resist guerillas from the north. The only U.S. policy options he
could see in the "deteriorating" situation were "all-out war or a
treading of water in a sea of change." Neither was acceptable to
him.[41]

Doubts about his son clouded McGill's mood. What if young
Ralph repeated his own pattern that broke Ben McGill's heart
forty years before? "I hope he finds his feet at Vanderbilt in better
fashion than you and I did," McGill wrote plaintively to an old
roommate. Young Ralph did not and was back working in Atlanta
after one term. His upbringing had been somewhat lonely but
always privileged. He was also undisciplined. How could he stay at
the top through his own efforts? His adoring mother was gone. His
father - never adept at parenting - concentrated his fading vitality
on work. No one came forward with answers to the young man's
questions.[42]

Between McGill's trips that summer to the Republican
convention in San Francisco and the Democrats' assembly in
Atlantic City, the situation in Vietnam changed drastically. Off the
coast of North Vietnam a U.S. destroyer came under attack from
that regime's PT boats. On August 7 Congress passed a resolution
that allowed the President "to take all necessary measures to repel
any armed attack against the forces of the United States and to
prevent further aggression." Ralph was sure the U.S. could not
successfully wage land war in Southeast Asia. Supplying a massive
army there would be a logistical nightmare. Even if American
forces were victorious, how, he asked, could this country occupy
that peninsula permanently? For the remainder of 1964 the
columnist pleaded that the only solution was an international
agreement with the Chinese as signatories.[43]

On September 14, 1964, McGill received his Presidential
Medal of Freedom from Lyndon Johnson in a White House

ceremony. He took along Jack and Margaret Tarver, Reb Gershon, and Grace Lundy as his four guests. Ralph Jr., making his third attempt at higher education at Georgia State, stayed behind in Atlanta. At the State Department reception McGill spoke for all the recipients even though many were more eminent than the Atlantan. He seemed in high spirits at a dinner party that Sander Vanocur gave afterwards. By the end of the evening, however, one of his dark spells came over him. He felt unbearably lonely and went off on his own. Next morning he was suffering from a black eye and a hangover.[44]

11

"NEVER GET TOO WISE TO USE YOUR LEGS": 1964-1967

MCGILL DROVE HIMSELF AS IF HE WERE A CUB REPORTER RATHER than a publisher with failing health. He sorrowed over the much publicized feud between the President and Bobby Kennedy. He believed the U.S. had "never had a more dedicated, harder working" attorney general than Kennedy. Their personal regard had deepened over the years. It was only prudent for the Kennedy brothers to cultivate any influential moderate southerner. The wry exchanges between Ralph and Bobby Kennedy went beyond political expediency, however.

LBJ told Ralph early in 1964 that Kennedy would not be his running mate. Yet into the summer the journalist falsely touted a closeness between the men. At the end of July Johnson announced he wanted a vice presidential candidate outside the cabinet. Outmaneuvered by "ole Cornpone," Kennedy resigned and boldly made a bid for one of New York's senate seats. McGill traveled north to watch him campaign, noting along with other commentators the electrifying effect RFK had on young people.[1]

That fall he gave President Johnson's election campaign every possible assistance. He told southern voters to stick with the Democrats. Otherwise the region would lose the power and patronage of congressional seniority. He advised LBJ how to counter the southern strategy of his opponent, Senator Barry Goldwater. Ralph himself waged a wild campaign against the Republican candidate. Thus Senator Goldwater joined a select group of individuals whom McGill detested and pilloried in print. At this point the *Constitution*'s management curbed the news department's coverage of civil rights, saying they were worried about pending libel suits. Yet no one stopped the *Constitution* publisher's scathing attacks on Goldwater.[2]

McGill had been furious since 1960 when Goldwater began cultivating ultraconservative Republicans and disaffected Democrats in Georgia and nearby states. In 1961 the journalist warned the Kennedy brothers that Goldwater was "making a big play to southern audiences picturing himself as a western Confederate." Defiance of the national government was the senator's clarion call. Segregation and racism were subliminal messages. By 1964 Eisenhower Republicans had lost control of state organizations built so painstakingly. Negroes were no longer welcome. McGill mourned that the "Kluxers, Birch types, suburban country-club freedom fighters" and hatemongers dominated the party of Lincoln. His hopes for a reasonable two-party system in the South seemed lost.[3]

If Johnson won election in November, McGill was confident that progress in civil rights would continue. He strongly endorsed the public accommodations bill that LBJ was pressing on Congress. "The bill does not seek to legislate racial equality," he said, but to make all Americans citizens. He denied that the legislation jeopardized privacy or property rights. "It does not touch the private home, club, or social life," he wrote. "It simply says all persons must be treated alike." McGill noted that black communities, particularly urban ghettos, were impatient over delays in ending discrimination. If this bill died, he warned, they could explode in violence. It was enacted into law, but riots broke out anyway in several inner city locations.

McGill's support of the 1964 Civil Rights law shows the transformation of his thinking. During Truman's presidency, he trusted in local initiative and opposed having Washington force change. Now he admitted being wrong. "Not a single reform in the field of civil rights," he wrote, "has come voluntarily. All of them . . . came only through federal action. It would have been possible years ago to have channeled the forces of change and let them work gradually. But we didn't." He knew how to refute spurious objections to civil rights laws because he had once engaged in such arguments. As he admitted to one reader, "It took me a long time to realize it . . . but the Negro is a citizen."[4]

President Johnson's unprecedented election victory was marred for McGill because a Republican presidential candidate carried Georgia for the first time. Even the President's gracious thanks could not cool the columnist's wrath. Goldwater "ducked, dodged, retreated, and reversed himself more than any candidate in years," fumed McGill. How humiliating for the state to support such a "shallow" man. He chastised Senator Richard B. Russell and other Georgians for failing to fight the Republicans.[5]

At least Atlanta could live up to its slogan, "the city too busy to hate." On October 14 Martin Luther King Jr. won the Nobel peace prize. For weeks afterwards many in the city and elsewhere second guessed the Nobel committee. Yet no other Atlantan had been so honored. Surely a civic response was in order. McGill played his favored role of intermediary. On November 13 he wrote Rabbi Rothschild that a Negro delegation had visited him to discuss having a dinner when the Nobel laureate returned from the ceremony in Norway. He wanted Rothschild and Archbishop Paul J. Hallinan to join him and Benjamin Mays as co-chairmen and sell the idea of a huge interracial banquet.

He explained to a friend, "Atlanta has too good an image, in my opinion, to act in a petty manner." First the FBI sabotaged his hopes. The bureau was then culminating its harassment of King. Offering evidence of his marital infidelities to McGill and Patterson, FBI officials insisted his character was not worth honoring. Then white business leaders voiced their opposition. One banker began calling around town declaring that "we ain't gonna have no dinner for no nigger." The head of Sears in Atlanta heard him out, hung up, and told his secretary. That evening she quoted the banker at a dinner that included "a stringer for the *New York Times*." They ran the story on page one. Suddenly bank deals were jeopardized. Finally Bob Woodruff acted. A gathering at the Piedmont Driving Club learned that "the Boss" and all Coca Cola executives were behind the idea 100 percent. The list of sponsors swelled to almost a hundred. The dinner was held on January 27,

1965.[6]

For months McGill had been experiencing disturbing physical symptoms. He put off seeing Dr. Wilber about these episodes of discomfort, sweating, racing pulse. Then in early December a respiratory infection with heavy cough landed him in the doctor's care and revealed a problem with his heart—atrial fibrillation. Wilber started him on digitalis, took him off coffee, and doctored his cold. A week later the patient returned to report he was feeling much better. Wilber assured his friend the condition was not serious but warranted continuing on digitalis. Privately Wilber wondered if he might already have suffered a "silent" heart attack.

McGill told almost no one about his heart condition. His two guardian angels, Julia Crawford and Grace Lundy, tried to ease things at home and the office. The women also kept Dr. Wilber's phone number at hand and began signaling one another when he was en route to and from the *Constitution*. Becoming a heart patient just as society's disruptions worsened did not auger well for McGill's work. He was eager to extend his coverage as a syndicated columnist and was negotiating about future books. Could an aging, ill newsman successfully analyze the complexities of the 1960s for an ever widening audience?[7]

Reverend King went from the warmth of the Atlanta banquet to the hostile and dangerous setting of Selma, Alabama. His goal was a voter registration drive such as those led by the Student Nonviolent Coordinating Committee (SNCC) since 1960. Under the 1964 Civil Rights law all prospective voters faced the same requirements. Registrars could no longer ask blacks to pass ridiculous tests. The new standard for literacy everywhere was a sixth grade education. Despite SNCC's efforts, Alabama blacks were for the most part still disfranchised and afraid to test the new legislation.

McGill strongly supported King's Selma crusade as he had SNCC's work. For two decades the right to vote had been the heart of McGill's vision of a "New South." His first inspiration for changing race relations came from the "citizenship schools" run by AU and the Atlanta Urban League in the 1930s and 1940s. The ballot was more and more pivotal, he thought. Years of experience on the President's Committee on Labor and Management convinced him that job discrimination and poverty were more resistant than Jim Crow. He anticipated that blacks would be struggling to enter the economic mainstream long after they had integrated public spaces. Voting would be a means of empowerment while Negroes struggled to overcome such disadvantages.

However, McGill had no illusions about what King and his demonstrators faced in Alabama. He wrote a northern editor that the Dallas County sheriff was "really a stereotype right out of Faulkner." The journalist also felt King's authority waning. SNCC's conflicts with him widened. Younger blacks questioned his approach of love and passive resistance. How much more could demonstrators take at the hands of brutal enemies before fighting back? McGill never got over the thrill of being on the scene when a big story broke. Most of the time he went flying off with the *Constitution*'s blessing. The only hindrances were Mary Elizabeth's illnesses. Sometimes even these crises did not keep him home. Now his strong reporter's instincts told him to go to Selma.[8]

Two obstacles stood in his way. One was his own weakened health. Another was a conflict at the newspaper. Management thinking, which came down "from Tarver through his assistants, William H. Fields and William I. Ray," was that the *Constitution* sustained enough financial damage from its editorial support for civil rights. The problem might be offset if the news department did not directly cover the movement. Management's position hardened after "the Meredith incident at Oxford gave rise to the libel suits." The ANInc lawyers, expecting shortly to be in federal court with General Walker, ordered the paper to "keep a very low profile when black and white were confronting each other on the streets." No reporters could go to Selma.

Completely exasperated by the decision, McGill stormed into his old editor's office where he informed Gene Patterson the two of them would defy Tarver and join the Selma marchers. McGill's reaction was all the more irrational since he was sick with worry over the pending libel suits. Why go against the lawyers' advice?

Patterson calmed him down then tried to dissuade him. Relations between Tarver and Patterson were strained. The editor anticipated some disagreement making it impossible for him to continue as successor to McGill, his boyhood idol. On occasion Gene interceded for frustrated reporters with Fields and Ray. He did not make an issue over Selma, however.[9]

McGill, the *Constitution*'s publisher and its claim to fame, actually held the balance of power. He ranted about the humiliation of no civil rights coverage but used neither his position nor prestige against Tarver. Their long and complex relationship would determine the outcome of the festering conflict. By entrusting his financial and professional affairs to Tarver, McGill gained freedom to travel and write about what he observed. More than Major Howell or Governor Cox, Tarver made it possible for McGill to realize his ambitions. Ralph's gratitude and loyalty to him was unbounded. It would have been completely out of character for McGill to fight with Tarver, especially after Jack saved him from retirement, which he dreaded more than anyone realized.

He continued to brood about his son. Ralph Jr. had no more success at Georgia State than at his other two colleges. Ralpho's pattern of attending only classes that especially interested him was exactly how his dad had conducted himself at Vanderbilt four decades earlier. A difference was that McGill was a Marine veteran and five years older than his son was when academic failures hit. They decided that young Ralph would enter the Marine Corps for six months then serve five years in the reserves. He was "overeating badly" when he left for boot camp, but its rigors took fifty-two pounds off his frame.[10]

The last thing the sixty-seven year old expected at this point was to embark on a romance. In the spring of 1965 he met Mary Lynn Morgan at the home of mutual friends. A pedodontist in her mid-forties, Dr. Morgan graduated from Emory Dental School in 1943 and stayed in Atlanta. She never married, filling her life with the children in her practice, Emory professorial duties, and civic activities. She was in the choir and vestry at All Saints Church which McGill now attended. They also belonged to the same gun club. Like most Atlantans, Morgan was familiar with the journalist. By the end of the evening at their friends' home Ralph not only knew Mary Lynn but was eager to see more of her.

They began to meet after work for dinner and on Sunday for brunch following church. Mary Lynn enjoyed these outings and was flattered that this busy, important man showed such interest in her life. From the start however, McGill's feelings ran deep. For years he had longed for a woman to share all his mind and heart. Just a few conversations convinced him Mary Lynn was that person. She was as straightforward as Mary Elizabeth had been but self-possessed and cool. Her chiseled features and blue eyes gave the same impression as photos of young Mary Lou Skillern McGill. How cruel, he realized, to have found exactly what he needed too late. He was old enough to be her father.[11]

He went to Washington as often as possible in spring 1965. Lyndon Johnson was surpassing even McGill's expectations as an effective political leader. First, the columnist rated the president ahead of his martyred predecessor. Kennedy "understood the art of politics," he wrote but was never "an old pro." Johnson was the first politician-president "in our time." Then McGill raised his estimation. The legislative victories that promised to realize Johnson's "Great Society" vision, he declared, surpassed the record of FDR—the political archetype for both men. The Georgia journalist sent a steady flow of messages to the White House, recommending persons for jobs and suggesting ways to reconcile the South to change.[12]

Then McGill himself made a change that embittered his last years and alienated close friends. In May he attended a private Washington dinner where Johnson had heated exchanges with some guests about his Vietnam policy. Ralph was incensed. He fired off a note telling the president this "stupid, low-level thinking" embarrassed him. In fact opinions about America's involvement in the war were dividing rapidly as LBJ changed the U.S. mission there. In March Johnson abandoned his campaign pledge "not to send American boys 9 or 10,000 miles away from home to do what Asian boys should do." The first American combat troops were two Marine battalions, guarding an airbase. Having recently ordered massive daily bombing of North Vietnam, the president had to protect aircraft and crews. However, "American boys" soon assumed a wider role in the conflict. By mid-summer they amounted to eighteen battalions.

Furious at growing criticism of his Vietnam policy, LBJ lavished appreciation on defenders like McGill. The newspaperman insisted that the U.S. wanted to leave South Vietnam and should depart. Here he parted company with administration critics whom he accused of offering no way to withdraw. He wanted the U.S. to fight just long enough to insure a negotiated settlement favorable to South Vietnam and anti-communism. Withdrawal then would be timely and honorable. By the end of 1965, when American forces numbered almost 200,000, he supported the war effort fully.[13]

Why did he change? Constant exposure to Gene Patterson's thinking affected his position. The *Constitution* editor visited South Vietnam in late 1964. Thereafter Patterson believed America should insure that South Vietnam not fall to Communism. Second, the war and Ralph Jr. became linked. In mid-May 1965 McGill traveled to Parris Island to attend his son's graduation from Marine boot camp and see him off to Camp LeJeune. Hopeful that his twenty-year old offspring was finally outgrowing his problems, McGill filled letters with eloquent ideas of what Ralpho might achieve in a career. If he should sacrifice his life in Vietnam instead, then the war must be worth such a terrible price.

Third, McGill began to view the entire issue as an old Marine. For years friends and family laughed whenever his "gung-ho Leatherneck" side reappeared. All knew that after nearly half a century he was still in thrall to the mystique of the Corps. Now Marines were fighting hard in Southeast Asia. His only child probably would soon join them. Loyalty, pride, and dread turned him against those who criticized the war.[14]

McGill would have objected to some antiwar demonstrators even without personal feelings. He first noted youths whom he called "beatnik types" in the civil rights movement. Soon they were forming what the media called a "counterculture." The student radicals and hippies of the 1960s confounded this man who never turned away young people seeking help about schooling or jobs. His openness and streak of naiveté allowed easy rapport with many in their teens and twenties. The counterculture was beyond him. He might have forgiven their clothes and hairstyles but could not condone their method of protest and mocking patriotism.[15]

He lost a valued friend when Adlai Stevenson died suddenly in mid-July 1965. Both men derived sustenance from their correspondence that started during the 1952 campaign. McGill later refused an inquiring biographer's request for his Stevenson letters on grounds they were just "facetious." He was actually protecting cherished mementos. Reflecting on his father's life, Adlai III wrote McGill, "Dad always counted you among his closest friends." They shared the same birthday though Adlai was two years younger than Ralph. As always when death came close, McGill brooded over whether his own life's work was all it should have been and how much time still remained to him.[16]

Such reactions confounded those in his circle amazed at his youthful *joie de vivre*. He took as much delight in pranks as ever. During a 1965 newspaper convention McGill, Ann Landers, and Bill Baggs "assisted" as a Washington dermatologist "operated" on journalist Larry Fanning's face at three a.m. "'Did you hear that McGill took out Larry Fanning's appendix last night?'" someone asked Landers the next day. She was incredulous. "'Oh yes,' was the response, 'Ralph went to medical school, you know.'" Back home, Landers got one of the whimsical messages McGill loved sending her way. At the next convention, he promised, we will give Fanning a complete face lift.[17]

Small wonder that one so full of life would fall in love. For months Ralph's strong sense of propriety overrode his desire to tell Mary Lynn Morgan all she meant to him. Finally he could contain the words no longer. Dr. Morgan responded that she took great pleasure in his company but felt nothing stronger than respect. He assured her they would continue as dinner companions and friends, nothing more. As in everything, once McGill had made up his mind, that was that. Mary Lynn seemed fixed, but so was he. Watching her, being with her, observing her reactions, sharing her thoughts was what he wanted. In time she found in the depths of his devotion something she could not resist.[18]

In the autumn of 1965 came news that assaulted his core. His mother was terminally ill with multiple myeloma. Throughout nearly nine decades of living, Mary Lou McGill was a healthy, vigorous woman. Family life still centered around her house in Chattanooga. For the next ten months the cancer weakened her frame to the point that changing her sheets or bedclothes broke a bone. Her affirming presence throughout Ralph's life was a gift few children possess. He prepared to lose that resource just as his own health began to fail and his son seemed hopelessly lost.[19]

Then a godsend came straight through the gloom settling about him. Mary Lynn Morgan changed her mind about their relationship. She had gone on a long vacation out West. The distance and time away from Atlanta gave her a different perspective on this individual for whom she had thought she felt only respect. When she returned she admitted to herself that it was love. She broke the news to him in terms as blunt as her earlier rejection had been. She added a pledge. If things did not work out as he wished, the fault would be hers not his. The strength he derived from Mary Lynn's commitment to his well being offset for a time all he was losing.[20]

This personal joy did not soften his professional wrath against any and all critics of the Vietnam War. In late 1965 and early 1966 J. William Fulbright chaired televised hearings on Johnson's conduct of the war before the Senate Foreign Relations Committee. The proceedings so incensed LBJ that he broke with his old friend and Senate colleague. McGill followed suit. A cordial Washington contact was lost to the columnist. He claimed that Fulbright's stand against the administration was revenge for not being chosen Secretary of State. In a wire to Dean Rusk, who testified as head of the State Department, McGill congratulated his fellow Georgian for showing Fulbright up as the "petty, vindictive, sick man that he is." He began to impugn the motives of anyone criticizing the war.

Even McGill's closest friends now realized that no dialogue about the subject was possible. A minister who had known and admired him for years wrote expressing disappointment "that you are not playing your usual role of stimulating critic." He was at a loss to understand this "100% defense of administration policy." By return mail the minister received a sharp letter stating that "our national security is critically involved." McGill explained that, unlike his detractors, LBJ was honest and sincere in alternating bombing with peace feelers. McGill did not blame the president for being angry. He accused critics of having no real plan for ending the war yet undercutting efforts at negotiating a settlement. He began comparing Johnson with Lincoln who also endured criticism of his war policy.[21]

Urban ghettos exploded nationwide in the mid-1960s. With a certain satisfaction, McGill could now emphasize that "the agony of change" in race relations was a national not just a regional problem. For nearly twenty years he had suffered with other white southerners whom "the segs" considered traitors. He always denied the charge, insisting that he worked out of love for his homeland and had no intention of leaving. The persecution took its toll. It was a relief to focus outside the South. When he visited the great Northern cities, he went to troubled neighborhoods and talked with residents. He asked his readers to be honest; to look beyond the media images of fire and looting at the frustration of fellow human beings: "Any persons, of whatever color, so long compressed in poverty, crime . . . and an environment of hopelessness will, in time, ignite spontaneously."

He took pains to check on the mood in Atlanta's slums, wanting nothing to mar the city's bright image. He knew that the Summerhill neighborhood was roiling with discontent. In September 1965, after Ivan Allen Jr. won another term as mayor, McGill advised preventive measures. Let's "proceed immediately with one or two superficial moves," he wrote Allen, "such as building a couple of playgrounds in the area." Actually it was already too late for just "superficial moves." Atlanta's highly politicized black community was getting ready to serve notice on the white power structure that the arrangements that had served for over two decades were outmoded.[22]

In the spring of 1966 Atlanta moved a step closer to becoming a national city, and one of Mayor Allen's fondest dreams came true. Major league baseball came to town. The National League Milwaukee Braves transferred to a new stadium built on urban renewal land just south of downtown. Allen worked informally behind the scenes on the deal which he sealed with a handshake. It would be "the last time such a major civic decision could be made by the benevolent oligarchs of the business leadership without broader community input." The National Football League provided an expansion team for Atlanta, making it the first city to acquire both top professional sports at once.

McGill was almost as elated as the mayor. He praised the city for outstripping others in the region, attributing recent progress to Atlanta's ethos. This city, he wrote, has turned its back "on ugly violence and on those who trade in prejudice and hatreds." He reminded readers that it was his predecessor, Henry Grady, who in 1885 started organized baseball in Atlanta and founded the old Southern League. Throughout the season McGill did other baseball columns. The old sports writer was quick to point out that black players like Hank Aaron were now "heroes of white-skinned fans as well." As a boy Ralph read mostly about noble, triumphant heroes and still drew upon that literary tradition. Privately he knew that many black leaders cared nothing about becoming heroes in whites' eyes and even more resented displacement to make way for the stadium. Some were now demanding racial separatism as vehemently as his old bad guys, "the segs."[23]

"Black power," a new dynamic in race relations became obvious to all in June 1966. During a violent march in Mississippi, Stokely Carmichael, who had just taken charge of SNCC, began urging participants to abandon passive resistance and go on the attack. McGill saw it coming. He watched King's approach of non-violence wear thin. In March he wrote the White House that SNCC workers were about to crack under the strain of their efforts. When the angry young Carmichael shouted, "Black power," marchers took up the cry. The legislative phase of the civil rights movement had peaked. Rather than wait further for gradual improvement, Carmichael said, blacks must forcibly seize what they needed.

Black power jeopardized McGill's vision of steady desegregation and economic mainstreaming of Negroes. He sympathized with blacks' frustration but pleaded with them not to become separatists. Throughout the summer he reiterated his belief that in time "a pluralistic society of power and democratic strength" would emerge. Carmichael was the sort of leader McGill had fought since 1938, but he blamed hatemongers of his own race for this ugly offshoot of the movement. Black power, he wrote, is rooted in "slogans of white supremacy, the burning crosses and the bombings and beatings of Negro citizens." SNCC and other groups were just imitating violent whites who had proved to him they were "among the lowest forms of civilized human beings."[24]

Ralph helped arrange for his dying mother's care and spent as much time in Chattanooga as possible. On one visit Mrs. McGill asked Mary Lynn to step closer. "Young lady," she whispered, "I just want you to know that we all love you very much." Her family's kidding never daunted Mary Lou McGill in her open adoration of Ralph. She read his column daily and clipped favorites. Wherever he wandered, Ralph wrote, wired, or phoned to let her know what he was doing. Now her family decided to withdraw life support that was prolonging her agony. At McGill's request, her daughters and grandchildren made their farewells. He kept a solitary vigil. Three days later she died.[25]

Shortly afterwards, Atlanta experienced a riot of sorts. Trouble was limited to Summerhill, the slum adjacent to the new stadium. Police wounded a suspect while attempting to arrest the man. A SNCC sound truck soon appeared on Summerhill streets, urging blacks to revolt. Atlanta was headquarters for SNCC, and Carmichael hoped to make the city a beachhead in his campaign against whites. Even though *Constitution* management did not allow SNCC as a regular beat, neither McGill nor reporters were surprised to hear that Carmichael had attracted a crowd of two thousand. Mayor Allen contacted twenty-five black ministers with whom he had a standing agreement about defusing a riot then went directly to the scene.

No serious injuries or death occurred that hot September afternoon. Police finally used tear gas to disperse the mob. Images of Allen atop a police cruiser pleading for calm through a bull horn went across the country on television's evening news. Once again McGill had grounds for claiming Atlanta was unique. "No other mayor of any city experiencing the trauma of riots has so behaved," he wrote. A prominent Atlantan read the column over breakfast then sent the publisher a note. Allen was praiseworthy, he agreed, but "I remember another very forthright, brave man who stood up almost alone and fought the Ku Klux Klan. . . ." Along with the letter came a new batch of hate mail blaming the Summerhill riot on McGill's having stirred up Atlanta's blacks. His battles with extremists of both races grew uglier.[26]

At age sixty-eight McGill finally went to war. He had never forgotten that he trained but failed to fight for the Great Crusade of 1914-18. Its youthful casualties—including many friends—were enshrined in his memory. World War II came when midlife pressures weighed heavily. His encompassing view of that war befitted a serious editor seeking a national audience. While American forces fought in Korea, his main concern was avoiding nuclear holocaust. Vietnam brought McGill again to the heroic dimension of war. As soon as possible after his mother died, he spent a fortnight in South Vietnam. He had not been out of the U.S. for three and a half years. No other trip abroad had such impact on him. The pilots, soldiers, medics, and sailors there became fixed in his mind as heroes, assisting the South Vietnamese in nation building.

His visit produced more than a month's worth of columns. Aside from a few interviews with top U.S. officials, McGill stayed mostly with combat forces and wrote about the operational side of war. The men who escorted McGill during two tours of the Mekong River delta and three days on a carrier in the South China Sea remarked about his esprit de corps. He might have been one of them instead of an elderly person with a bad heart.

In his enthusiasm, McGill overlooked what became the deciding factor: North Vietnam's ability to wage a prolonged war of attrition. He stressed that this was a different sort of war to which U.S. military forces were adapting successfully. "This is the first army," he wrote, "we have ever had that was encouraged and taught how to work sociologically." His positive accounts of doctoring, reconstructing villages, and digging wells ignored GIs' frustration and anger over how to know who the enemy was. Yet their dilemma of telling friendly villagers from Viet Cong had deadly consequences.[27]

LBJ paid a brief visit to Vietnam in October 1966, not long after McGill left. He sent the president a five-page letter, enclosing columns from his own trip. In a sense it was the reconnaissance of a scout for his commanding officer. Mostly it was an expression of solidarity and sympathy. Opponents of the war, he wrote, did not understand "why Asia and not Europe is a great center of the power struggle. . . ." Nothing made McGill madder than administration critics' claim that Johnson's offers to negotiate with North Vietnam were phony. The critics, he argued, were the real saboteurs of negotiation. They were playing right into the hand of North Vietnamese leaders who would like nothing better than for America to give up and go home.[28]

McGill himself had come home to a bizarre development in Georgia politics. Lester Maddox won the Democratic nomination for governor and promised to defeat arch-conservative Republican Howard H. "Bo" Callaway in the general election. Months earlier McGill had warned Ellis Arnall to adjust his gubernatorial campaigning or fall victim to growing white resentment of civil rights. Sure enough, Arnall lost the primary to Maddox, the rabid segregationist who closed his Atlanta restaurant rather than serve blacks. The *Constitution* endorsed neither Callaway nor Maddox. McGill and other image conscious Georgians were horrified. He wrote President Johnson that picturing his old foe, Lester, as governor "makes you draw back in disbelief." A huge write-in vote robbed both Maddox and Callaway of the necessary majority.

Would the courts or the legislature decide the outcome of the election?

Exactly twenty years before, Gene Talmadge's death following his election as governor afforded Georgia similar notoriety. There were striking parallels between the elder Talmadge and Maddox. Both symbolized defiance of federal authority. Neither felt bound to Democratic party loyalty and freely played the maverick. The favored political posture of each was friend of the poor, forgotten (white) folk. However, Talmadge ruled the state's political apparatus and its government. Maddox understood little about the functioning much less the control of either. Unlike the debacle of 1946, the crisis of 1966 was resolved in an orderly way when the courts allowed the legislature to elect Maddox. McGill started writing columns warning Maddox not to join George Wallace's third party.[29]

Georgia's tangled politics coincided with more parental headaches for McGill. Marine discipline did not carry over into young Ralph's civilian life. In 1966, after giving up on college, he joined the Atlanta office of a national advertising agency as a copy writer and announced that he was marrying his current sweetheart. McGill knew his son was too young and unsettled to make a strong start at marriage but would proceed with or without his blessing. The bride was Adelaide Martin, whom everyone called Lady. McGill became overly protective of the newlyweds, worrying constantly about his son's health.[30]

To McGill's surprise, Harry Ashmore and Bill Baggs turned up in Communist North Vietnam in early January 1967. Under the auspices of a papal initiative, his two friends wanted to enhance the latest peace feelers by meeting Ho Chi Minh. Baggs was the first American newsman to interview Ho in years. The erstwhile negotiators had a State Department briefing before their trip and fully expected afterwards to tell President Johnson North Vietnam's terms for starting peace talks. Johnson refused to see them. McGill was not so standoffish. He flew to Washington and had a reunion of sorts with "Ho Chi Minh's two envoys."

By now he directed as much righteous indignation towards

"peace cultists" as he did at "the segs." He let everyone know he thought Ashmore and Baggs were naive and their scheme "simplistic." Breaking with Baggs was more painful than disagreeing with Ashmore who was years away from the newspaper field and in a think tank with "intellectuals," a McGill dislike. Baggs remained his protégé. He became editor of Cox's *Miami News* shortly after the Governor died. The promotion came at McGill's behest. He tolerated Baggs's pranks and foibles as readily as he forgave Ralph Jr.'s missteps, behaving more like a father than mentor. Then Baggs went too far. To his worship of the Kennedys, he added insulting behavior towards President Johnson.[31]

Never one to be outdone, McGill wrangled an official foreign trip while he was in Washington. He informed Tarver that the invitation came from the highest levels of the State Department, including Dean Rusk. He was to make what "they consider an important mission trip to about five African countries." It had a legitimacy denied the rejected envoys to Hanoi. He assured Tarver the trip would not be as hard on him as the African tour in 1963 had been. He added that this junket would not cost the paper anything. He also made a great point of the trip to the Hall Syndicate. Their marketing strategy was to offer his good pieces from Africa to over two hundred newspapers.[32]

This journey would give McGill and Mary Lynn Morgan one last chance to reconsider their plans to be married. McGill's old fashioned sense of propriety warred with his joy at the prospect of having a woman like Mary Lynn as his wife. She was not only twenty-three years younger than he. She was a youthful forty-six. He worried about being her husband. Conversations with Dr. Joe Wilber reassured him that, despite his heart trouble, they could look forward to some good years.

Forty years earlier McGill had proposed to another vivacious, youthful woman then backed off. Steve, he decided, would end up feeling sorry for him. He hated that prospect. He turned instead to Mary Elizabeth and avoided the problem. Now here he was again wondering if a love affair could become a marriage. In the ensuing decades he had learned much about the gifts of life: the gifts of love, the gifts of success. He had also experienced loss and seen how important it was to take a gift when it came. He approached marriage differently than he had forty years ago. Later Mary Lynn wrote to Steve, that first love, "For him this was something to be worked at, examined, given to." She also was willing to give a great deal. She broke longstanding patterns to care for him, to conserve his strength.

So in late February he flew off to Africa, knowing that never again would he experience a solitary homecoming. The worse part of being a widower, he told Celestine Sibley, was "coming home from a trip and getting to the airport and having nobody to call. All these years I've called home and said, 'I'm back.' Now there's nobody there to hear . . . or to care." Sibley did not realize the significance he placed on homecomings. Ever since he was a child and could walk up on the porch of the house on Kirby Avenue and shout, "I'm home," or come back to Atlanta from a trip and find that Mary Elizabeth and Julia had everything ready for him, these were pivotal moments.[33]

For the most part McGill's African stops in 1967 were new to him, slaking his thirst to see as much of the world as possible. Ghana was the only repeat of his 1963 itinerary. He constantly pondered how the Cold War would be played out on the entire continent. He was a gratifying enrollee in the State Department's efforts to counter anti-Americanism. Everyone marveled at his energy, his willingness to undertake a heavy schedule, and his zest for a sixty-nine year old. Few realized that opportunities to show that he could still do a reporter's legwork revitalized him. All of this was at the expense of his health, however. It was more and more difficult for him to do his columns, make appearances scheduled for him by the State Department and get any sleep at all. He prided himself on handling the ordeal. He made as many friends as he had in 1963, promising to come back and see all of them again.[34]

McGill got home a little faster than he planned. No longer under the auspices of the State Department, he went into Rhodesia and intended to go on to South Africa. At the last minute that government denied a visa. He was confined to a lounge in the Johannesburg airport. This denial created international publicity. His supporters thought South Africa succeeded only in increasing his fame.

Once out of Africa, McGill talked about the people he met in Rhodesia. They reminded me, he said, of "people in the South just before the Civil War." Just as he had chastised southerners for decades about being on the wrong side of history, he described these Rhodesians as being "in a cul-de-sac of history. They may go on for years in a state of mental and economic siege." By this time he hoped that the worst was over in his homeland. The South's siege mentality was fragmenting, but he saw no hope in southern Africa.[35]

12

"ONE MORE RIVER TO CROSS": 1967-1969

MCGILL'S FINAL MONTHS WERE TURBULENT DESPITE A HAPPY second marriage. On April 20, a beautiful spring day, he and Mary Lynn were wed at All Saints Church. McGill's worries over what people would think of this step were misplaced. Gene Patterson summed up reaction in a column about the wedding. The *Constitution*, he stated, was a "distinctly personal newspaper." The *Constitution* family realized that their boss was "not meant to be alone." Patterson described Ralph's Welsh strain of melancholy and recent signs of loneliness. He concluded, "Those of us who live around him have been very pleased to see the old sunshine to break upon that clouded brow of late. This makes life easier for all of us."

A huge crowd of well wishers saw them on their way to a honeymoon in New England. There they spent some time with McGill's old friends, also Mary Lynn's brother, Mac Morgan, and his wife, Helen, then went on to a publishers' banquet in New York. By the time they returned to Atlanta, he was quite ill. On April 28 Dr. Wilber got a call to come to the house. He found there a very sick patient with an irregular pulse, viral pneumonia and the beginnings of congestive heart failure. He had made two foreign trips back to back in a period of four to five months. A less determined individual probably would have landed in the hospital, but he had refused to rest. He resumed fiery correspondence about the Vietnam War with old friends. When he married, he was on the edge of exhaustion and susceptible to rapid worsening of his heart trouble.[1]

Still weak, McGill was cheered when the Pulitzer board awarded Gene Patterson a prize in May 1967. As he told LBJ, "I take great pride in the fact that I helped rescue him from the administrative side and got him over to the editorial side." The Pulitzer board especially noted Patterson's criticism of the Georgia legislature's refusal to seat Julian Bond in January 1966. Bond was not the first black to win election under recent voting reforms. Leroy Johnson integrated the state senate in 1963. Legislators barred Bond on grounds that his antiwar remarks violated the country's draft laws. The Supreme Court rejected their specious claim and ruled they violated Bond's First Amendment right of free speech.

Patterson's defense of Bond showed his editorial strengths and how he differed from his predecessor. No one was more fiercely prowar than Patterson. Yet he did not let this conviction override constitutional realities. He utterly condemned the legislators. McGill, ever the mediator, only suggested they had made a martyr of young Bond. McGill had praised Bond's leadership in the Atlanta student sit-ins. Now Martin King, Bond, and other blacks he admired were turning against the government's Vietnam policy. Would he portray them as heroes if they were unpatriotic, even disloyal? Shortly after Gene won his Pulitzer, McGill admitted in a column, "We are in a period complex, emotional, and difficult when common sense, understanding, and patience are required of us."[2]

In late June Dr. Wilber felt obliged to consult Emory cardiologist Bruce Logue about McGill's condition. Dr. Logue confirmed Wilber's guess of an earlier silent heart attack and suggested a month's course of medication for the arrhythmia. Despite these problems McGill made one strenuous journey after another that summer. Sometimes he had a speaking commitment that meant much to him. Mostly he traveled to see firsthand the unrest and violence overtaking the country. Mary Lynn worried that such strain might shorten their life together but realized his wanderlust was worse than ever. She kept their local engagements to a minimum and treasured every bit of time they spent at home alone.[3]

Throughout the summer of 1967 urban riots exploded in city

after city. Atlanta experienced three days of confrontation between Dixie Hills residents and police in June. Anger, recrimination, and fear of the radicalized SNCC rattled white and black leaders. However, the single fatality and thirty-three arrests paled beside the dozens of deaths and destruction elsewhere. McGill wondered if many inner city youths would heed urban guerillas' calls for revolution. He urged readers to recognize and correct underlying conditions in these ghettos. Such pleas mostly netted indignant law-and-order letters, but he did not budge. It was cheaper, he insisted, to remove the causes of rioting than to clean up the devastation. His harshest words were for those he labeled "political looters." These exploiters stood to gain far more than those pilfering goods from the ruins.[4]

In late July came word of Carl Sandburg's death at his home, Connemara. McGill typed a column of remembrance and journeyed to Flat Rock, North Carolina, where he joined the family for a private service. Sandburg's most valuable gift over years of friendship was a bit of wisdom about loneliness. From childhood Ralph suffered spells of sadness. Knowing he was deeply loved did not ward off the ache. Twenty years older and possessed of a much calmer disposition, Sandburg advised, "One of the most important things a man can learn is how to be alone." Using resources from nature, books, and music, one could be alone without fear or loneliness. Ralph took this to heart, especially during five years as a widower. Two days after the funeral Sandburg's daughter mailed McGill the green eye shade her father wore while writing, his penknife, and a picture of the two men on the porch at Connemara. In the photo a much younger McGill studied Sandburg's face as if to claim some of its strength for himself.[5]

In early August former *Constitution* reporter, M. L. St. John, presented McGill to a local audience. Atlantans, he said, seemed divided between worship and loathing of his old boss. He asked both extremes simply to think of McGill as "a crusader with an understanding heart." That heart was faltering. Dr. Logue thought an electric shock might restore normal rhythm. McGill readily agreed. When Logue succeeded on the first try, his patient exulted.

He wanted to accept LBJ's recent invitation to oversee upcoming elections in South Vietnam with other newspapermen. Logue refused. So McGill sent word to the White House that, while his heart rhythm was now perfect, he must rest for two weeks. Tarver cautioned him but reported to friends, "you know as well as I the futility of arguing with a McGill emotion once unleashed."[6]

A day and a half later the atrial fibrillation returned. Logue tried shocks twice more without success then discharged McGill. Although he missed the Vietnam trip, his doctors let him attend a follow-up White House gathering in September. Johnson, now in political peril because of his war policy, greeted his Atlanta ally warmly. Back home McGill wrote the beleaguered president that except for the "erratic beat," his health was great. As if to prove this, he intensified attacks on administration critics. Tens of thousands of protesters marched on the Pentagon in late October. Two days later Ralph and his wife arrived in Washington for a ten day stay. He visited the protest site, talked with journalists, and lambasted those who were not only unpatriotic but obscene. The couple went to the White House for what Mary Lynn assumed would be a few minutes' visit with the chief executive. Instead the McGills got several hours worth of the famous "LBJ treatment."[7]

The conflicts worsened. Harry Ashmore wrote a piece accusing the president of double-dealing over peace negotiations and requested that the *Constitution* run his amplifying letter. The paper refused. McGill hated choosing between "one of the three or four old friends whose friendship you cherish above all others" and LBJ. McGill did acknowledge that the war jeopardized domestic reforms. However, he would never admit what many other journalists concluded by late 1967—that the South Vietnamese government was hopeless and that the U.S. war machine had not even fazed North Vietnam. The U.S. must fight on, he said. They must deny the Communists victory in a war of "national liberation" and keep faith with the thirteen thousand Americans slain in battle.[8]

For three decades his job seemed granted and protected by Providence. Then in late 1967 two episodes of taunting shattered this confidence. First a young reporter for *Newsweek*, angered by his positions on the war and Black Power, wrote suggesting that he did not know what he was saying and should quit. McGill's reply was defiant, but he sent a troubled letter to the fellow's boss. He often went overboard to help younger journalists and enjoyed the respect of many following him in the profession. What if, instead of this deference, he were increasingly to be ridiculed as a "has been"?

Following close on this exchange came caustic words from Jack Tarver suggesting retirement. For decades the two men had twitted one other, so bystanders passed off Tarver's remarks. That evening, moreover, Jack was smarting from an earlier showdown with Martin Luther King Sr. Through Operation Breadbasket King's ministerial group pressured businesses patronized by blacks to employ them. In Tarver's judgment ANInc. had helped far more blacks than most Atlanta corporations. Even if Daddy King had agreed, hearing Tarver utter the word, "nigra," would have set off the formidable preacher. Before walking out of the meeting Daddy King forced Tarver to pronounce "nee-grow" satisfactorily and threatened to picket the paper unless he hired more blacks. Better retire now, Tarver later told McGill, and avoid the embarrassment of crossing picket lines of his Negro friends and supporters. Ralph was distraught.[9]

Next year the *Constitution* would mark its centennial. McGill was already planning ways to publicize and commemorate this milestone. He began to worry that he might no longer head up the celebration. Even the joyful prospect of his first grandchild did not offset fears that his career was ending. Since in his case life and work were one, how could he survive? He initiated new outside writing projects. He could not reasonably expect to deliver such manuscripts, but the plans were insurance against loss of occupation. No matter that in the minds of most, McGill *was* the *Constitution*.

He showed uncharacteristic concern about how posterity would view his work. A Kentucky graduate student writing a thesis about McGill's career got letters of protest from his subject. Normally McGill would not have pursued revising a thesis that few would ever see. Now he offered to pay for retyping with the desired corrections. He confided to Gene Patterson that he had been rereading old columns with regret. Patterson countered that McGill had been "extremely bold" under the circumstances, but these assurances did not comfort the *Constitution*'s publisher. General Edwin Walker's multimillion dollar lawsuits against him and the paper tormented him. Until both were settled out of court in April 1968, he feared that the public believed Walker's false accusations about his columns.[10]

Though embattled, he clung in print to his cherished vision of progress. The ideal seemed incongruous amid the upheavals Americans endured in 1968. White backlash and black power threatened recent advances in American race relations. However, McGill continued to act as a mediating force between extremists of all races. He acknowledged that "the violence is not a good thing" but asked readers to remember how much conditions had improved since 1945. He welcomed the voices crying, "black is beautiful" as strongly as he had condemned those shouting, "black power." He commended the new emphasis on African heritage in the black community. He urged that all U.S. students learn about the culture and politics of the continent he had already visited twice and intended to see again.[11]

His comments about the Vietnam War showed none of this moderation. He branded the public demonstrations against the war as "a form of narcissism." He attacked any and all of President Johnson's critics, deploring their "calumny." He labeled the so-called doves as hypocrites and political opportunists, denying that North Vietnam wanted peace negotiations. When soldiers wrote asking him if the stakes were as high as he claimed, McGill advised them to focus on their oath of loyalty rather than the complexities of Southeast Asia. He had abhorred disloyalty since boyhood. That reaction drove him closer to Lyndon Johnson and away from old friends whom he now called "enemies." The President responded with grateful messages and invitations to the White House.[12]

McGill was on the road constantly in 1968, making the final months of his career a reprise of sportswriting days. His heart

disease grew worse during February. Yet in late March he journeyed to Mexico City for signing of a nuclear non-proliferation
treaty. After five years advising the U.S. Arms Control and Disarmament Agency, he wished to witness a small bit of progress.
Instead he witnessed the downfall of a presidency. In a televised
speech, which McGill watched at the American Embassy in Mexico
City, Johnson announced he would not seek reelection in November and would pursue a negotiated end to the war. Sitting in the
room was Vice-President Hubert H. Humphrey, leader of the
treaty delegation and an old McGill friend. Would Humphrey join
those already contending for the Democratic presidential nomination?

McGill plunged to work with the eagerness of a cub on his first
big story. He began composing a column while waiting his turn for
a phone. Suddenly he got an incoming call, jumping him ahead of
the other frantic journalists. Grace Lundy was on the line from
Atlanta, ready to take dictation then rush the piece to the composing room. Once home, McGill sent the staff an exultant memo. He
was grateful that their "magnificent issue" chronicling Johnson's
withdrawal included his column dictated from Mexico. "God
knows how she heard it," he marveled, given the terrible telephone
connection. Grace made this effort succeed just as she had
countless others throughout nearly sixteen years. She always knew
where he was, what background material he had studied, and how
he wrote. Even when she could barely hear him, Grace would take
his dictated thoughts, and the resulting column would be just
right.[13]

Two days after McGill returned from Mexico, someone killed
Martin King in Memphis. His wrathful columns resembled those
on earlier occasions when racial hatred spawned violence and
death. However, King's murder affected McGill in ways he did not
express in print. Coinciding with Lyndon Johnson's downfall, the
tragedy seemed not only to close a period of civic progress but also
to portend darkness, chaos.

Richard Nixon, seeking the presidency again, asked McGill to
arrange a visit with King's widow when he arrived for the funeral

set for April 9. McGill obliged even though he had wondered in a recent column how the Republicans could "stomach the coarse, vulgar personality of Nixon." Then, while Atlanta coped with 100,000 visiting mourners and celebrities, he departed for a week's engagements in the northeast. Some of the cities he visited were battle zones because King's murder triggered the worst rioting in recent times.[14]

Mingled with these troubles were times of personal joy. Welcoming his grandson into the world was such a moment. In autumn 1967 Ralph Jr. and his wife, Lady, transferred from Atlanta to Richmond where he wrote copy for an advertising agency. McGill continued to fuss over the couple, despite a hectic schedule. Marriages of both father and son had eased the uneasy relationship between them. On April 23, in New York on business, Jack Tarver opened a telegram, "We are off to Richmond. Lady in labor." Tarver recalled his own tense vigil at Mary Elizabeth's delivery and wire to the absent father in Fiji.

Ralph Emerson McGill III, was his grandfather's delight. The family decided to call the baby Trip and planned an Atlanta christening in mid-June. In his column McGill recounted for Ralph Jr., his race homeward in April 1945. Twenty-three years later he was still guilty over missing his son's birth. Shortly after Trip's arrival McGill wrote in a revealing column on parenthood that the best gift a parent could offer a child was to "be available." Given his obsessive work pattern, it is unlikely he could ever have been that sort of father to Ralph Jr.[15]

When Trip was a few days old, he received a letter from another doting grandfather, Lyndon Johnson. The President wanted the baby to know about McGill's long struggle "for human dignity." Despite many "scars from those fights," Johnson continued, "he has the satisfaction of knowing that he has helped many people, here and abroad, understand what our country is all about." McGill was closer to Lyndon Johnson than any of the five presidents he covered. Across the years he spent more time in Eisenhower's company but never really bonded with the man. He saw Johnson as a great leader whose sacrifice left McGill more bitter than ever about the Vietnam War.[16]

He did not dwell long on LBJ's fate, however, but set his sights on the presidential campaign. With Johnson out, Vice President Humphrey had to decide whether to run. As McGill expected, he did enter but without Johnson's endorsement. McGill had long admired Humphrey and tried to put a gloss on his friend's plight. McGill told readers that LBJ was probably thinking of 1938 when presidential efforts to influence voters backfired. Yet no farfetched history lesson could remove from Humphrey the taint of a discredited administration. More galling to McGill was the fact that, once Johnson's opponents succeeded, Senator Robert Kennedy joined the race. Despite strong personal regard for the senator, McGill could not stomach this blatant opportunism.[17]

The candidacy of George Wallace troubled him most. Twenty years before, a third party movement had skewed presidential politics in the South. Unlike 1948, Wallace's diatribes against recent reforms had national appeal. McGill feared that Wallace would get enough votes in 1968 to deny victory to either major candidate. He knew what fears and resentments drew voters to the feisty former governor of Alabama. For thirty years he had worked hardest to reach this category of reader. When Wallace beguiled audiences by promising a return to segregation, the columnist relentlessly exposed his deceit. McGill never gave up arguing that ending segregation meant progress for both races.[18]

Reporting on the 1968 campaign and other crises improved McGill's writing but sealed his fate. Direct experience always led to his best writing. These events were too close personally. They drained his very life force. With the assassination of Senator Robert Kennedy in early June he felt the forces of darkness to be overpowering. His files were crammed with decades worth of hate mail and literature. He reviewed them and concluded, "America is sick—sick with its haters . . . sick with its cowards . . . sick with its do-nothing 'good people.' "

He forgot Bob Kennedy's expediency, celebrating only his commitment to justice. Listening to Ted Kennedy eulogize his slain brother in St. Patrick's Cathedral, McGill marveled at the "style and guts" of this family. Back in Atlanta he received a letter from Kennedy thanking him for being "a good and valued friend to all of us." It was especially true of Bob. Throughout the murdered senator's years as Attorney-General, Ralph tried to help with the snares of desegregation. He either contacted Kennedy directly or sent messages through his old friend, John Seigenthaler, while the Nashville editor was Kennedy's aide.[19]

As the *Constitution*'s centennial year climaxed in June 1968, McGill showed that he had lost none of his flair for public relations. During his early years in Atlanta he soaked up the newspaper's lore. He knew the tale that President Andrew Johnson suggested the *Constitution*'s name when founder, Carey W. Styles, called at the White House. Thus McGill's tag line was "the only newspaper in the long history of the nation to be named by a President of the United States." At his behest, another President Johnson honored its "one hundred years of exceptional public service." The effusive presidential letter to "Dear Ralph" ran beside the *Constitution* publisher's centennial column.[20]

McGill slighted the Howell family's contribution to the newspaper in favor of the old Governor and Jim Cox. Perhaps in memory he linked Papa Howell with Major Stahlman and Jimmy Stahlman as obstructing his ambition. Clark Howell Jr. deserved better. He not only promoted Ralph from sports in 1938 but also stood up to his critics for a dozen years. McGill acknowledged Howell's support in a *Saturday Review* piece about the *Constitution*. In his centennial column he mentioned neither Clark Sr. nor Clark Jr., while lavishing praise on their successors. It took more courage for Major Howell, broke and beleaguered with competition from Cox's *Journal*, to publish McGill's early notions about racial fairness than anyone seemed to recall.

In July Pan Am began direct airline service to Moscow, and McGill was on the inaugural flight. It was his third visit to the Soviet Union and last foreign trip. He devoted a week's worth of columns to the experience. He tramped around with the other VIPs, but his mind was not on the sights and diversions. It ranged back to previous impressions. During these stops on his 1945 odyssey he endured blizzards and at Stalingrad witnessed "the desolation of the artifacts of war."

In 1959 he had returned to the U.S.S.R. as part of Vice President Nixon's entourage, astonished at the rebuilding of a devastated country. He recalled Nixon's 1960 claim that his "kitchen debate" with Khrushchev, which McGill witnessed closehand, proved he would be a President tough on the enemy. McGill reiterated his judgment that the debate was inconsequential. Far more significant were Ike's misgivings about Nixon. McGill made this dig, knowing that the Republicans would shortly convene to give Nixon his second nomination for the presidency.[21]

The only drawback to the "very exhausting but rewarding" Soviet trip and other junkets was being away from his wife. Throughout their twenty-two month marriage McGill relished sending happy status reports to his sister-in-law in Boston. "I am sad when separations come," he lamented upon returning from Moscow. Qualms about their age difference evaporated as Mary Lynn became his ideal wife. He could lavish affection on her, be as romantic as he liked. All the while, the woman he sometimes called, "the Paragon," brought an undreamed of order to his domestic life. She was the first person since Coach Dan McGugin who got him to stick to a health regimen. Best of all, she assuaged his melancholy streak. In her bright company he just did not dwell on sad thoughts. His biggest regret was that their lives had not been joined sooner.[22]

Covering the Republican convention in early August, McGill abandoned all hope for a genuine two party system in the South. The ranks of delegates assembled in Miami were purged of blacks. If this "lily white convention" were not galling enough, McGill found Strom Thurmond of South Carolina, former Democrat then Dixiecrat, dictating election strategy to Nixon. Thurmond advised countering George Wallace's appeal by choosing a running mate whom McGill called "a bigot." Irate, McGill produced a memorable lead: "Old Massa Nixon was worried about the fields of white down in dear old Dixie. There was this boll weevil sort of fellow George Wallace who seemed already to have eaten up much of the cotton states' vote crop, and so it was that old Massa Nixon called in some help to have his crop sprayed with the old reliable Dixie insecticide labeled, 'states rights and segregation'. . . ."

His trip to the carefully orchestrated Republican show was irksome, but attending the Democrats' debacle in Chicago days later was devastating. The convention had originally been timed for President Johnson's sixtieth birthday. Now LBJ could not even risk attending. McGill knew that radical activists might make good on their pledge to lead 100,000 protesters into the streets. Before their violent encounters with Chicago police escalated, he took an afternoon walk to see for himself what sort of individuals were camping in Lincoln Park. Talking with many convinced him that a "hard-core group" of "real revolutionists" were manipulating youngsters whom he thought "were just fine." After the bloody rioting died down, McGill found enough blame to go around. The police and their National Guard reinforcements overreacted, he wrote, but what provocation they had endured![23]

As Gene Patterson wrote when McGill remarried, the *Constitution* staff was like a family. In any family, internal tensions occasionally swell into destructive conflict. That occurred at the newspaper in September 1968, and Patterson resigned as editor. He followed his twenty-two year old protégé, B. J. Phillips, out the door. Her column for the September 11 first edition riled Jack Tarver. Tarver had understood that editors of both papers were not going to attack a Georgia Power rate increase. Phillips did. Tarver made an angry phone call to Patterson but did not kill the piece that appeared in subsequent editions. However, Phillips believed Tarver's call threatened her integrity as an editorial writer. She quit. Both Patterson and Phillips took positions at the *Washington Post*, he as managing editor.[24]

McGill knew that Patterson's differences with Tarver might compel the editor to move. He had even considered possible replacements. During the summer, when Gene confided that he found the situation intolerable, McGill begged him to reconsider leaving. Now no pleas would stop him. Patterson's resignation brought longstanding conflicts between the news staff and ANInc management into the open. The gap between editorial force and newsroom weakness was more than some reporters could bear. Several disillusioned ones had already left. Even if Jack Tarver had not been president of ANInc, his biting wit and abrupt manner would have cast him as the heavy. Ensuing national publicity leaked by demoralized staffers mocked McGill's centennial paeans.

Media versions pictured McGill either as powerless or far removed, but he was neither. Both Tarver and Patterson, a half dozen years apart in age, could have been sons. They manifested different aspects of McGill's complex personality. Working with Gene brought out his idealistic streak. As he told readers, they shared "the intangible but important values of life" and could "talk with one another in the full meaning of that word." Yet McGill could be as tough and ambitious as people reckoned Tarver was. Enduring fifteen bad years at the *Constitution* together so bonded these two survivors that three generations of Tarvers considered McGill family.[25]

One part of McGill's personality that baffled Tarver and others was his habit of "looking upon himself as a man of meager resources." When Jack tried to tell him otherwise, McGill's response was always, "I don't want to know." However, Tarver had been just as willing to arrange McGill's financial security as he had to "steady his soapbox." What with his salary, syndicate income, and "a company stock-option arrangement that at the time of his death was worth over a million dollars," McGill had no right to play poor.

He continued to do so in part because he always wanted to identify with the vulnerable, the victims, the oppressed rather than those powerful and wealthy. Back in April a woman wrote complaining that privilege shielded him from the woes that integration visited upon her. He replied that he did understand. He did "not even own an automobile" and his house was "a small one in a declining neighborhood." In fact McGill resided in the heart of Buckhead within hollering distance of some Atlanta "Big Mules" but wished this reader to think otherwise.[26]

His analysis of the 1968 political campaign focused on the

South. The Republicans' 1964 victory in Georgia still infuriated him. So he took some consolation in knowing that most of Wallace's Georgia votes would come at the Republicans' expense. It gave him perverse pleasure to chronicle Governor Lester Maddox's confused political moves. However, he regularly scanned the horizon for a new sort of leader. Partisan realities persist, he wrote, but there are "not two politically different ways of solving the paradox of urban growth and decay, of human neglect revealed in the problem of the minorities of the poor, the untrained, the uneducated." He knew that recent political attempts to solve these had ended and that he would not live past the upcoming reactionary phase to greet a new season of reform.

McGill's last attempts to change the minds of his readers confounded many. In late 1968 and early 1969 he attacked use of the Confederate battle flag and the song, "Dixie," especially by desegregated schools. He thought both represented oppression and racism to black students. Even some of his fans took exception when his plea for sensitivity deteriorated into snide comments about southern heritage. McGill's mountain background always set him apart from whites who clung to tradition. He boasted of the fact, and his enemies agreed, raging that he was no true southerner. The columns and correspondence about Dixie and the flag had a new edge. It was as if by obliterating symbols of the Old South, he could finally become a midwife to a New South.[27]

Not if his enemies could help it. While McGill regretted that progress was halting, its opponents feared matters had gone too far already to reverse. Blacks were employed in positions that once would have been unthinkable. School desegregation inched along. Most whites seemed unfazed when Negroes got the same service as they did in restaurants, stores, and other public places. The white supremacists fought on. Plotting and carrying out acts of violence such as assassinating King were extreme forms of reaction. An easier way to vent their fears and frustrations was to threaten and attack individuals like McGill.

So it is not surprising that, with a legal framework of racial justice in place, his hate mail was unabated. In a late 1968 column he described a death threat from the Ku Klux Klan. He blamed his recent spate of messages on the election campaign. "The vicious, often vulgar, filthy mail," he wrote," is like a fever chart. It goes up when emotions are aroused. . . ." More likely the letters stemmed from his own scathing comments about a new KKK squad killing in the name of the Almighty. This particular death threat began fervently, "God Damn Your Soul."[28]

McGill was just as unpopular with the New Left as with extremists on the Right. Starting in spring 1968, Atlantans had a lively alternative to their conventional newspapers. *The Great Speckled Bird* lambasted any and all of the city's Establishment. McGill was a favorite target. Not content with calling him a "senile red baiter," *The Bird* pronounced him dead. Its writers most deplored his support for recent U.S. foreign policy, especially the Vietnam War. As owner of part of the media, they claimed, he could spread "the Big Lie" and unfairly attack dissent. An interviewer asked McGill about *The Great Speckled Bird*'s views of him. He gave a characteristic response. He began, "all of the so-called underground press has a place." *The Bird* must be allowed to continue "making a protest" even though they were "absolutely wrong in their charges."[29]

McGill often confounded his enemies with surprising gestures. Lester Maddox was his most active foe. Gene Talmadge's rallies always included a set piece. His men yelled, "Tell 'em about old Ralph McGill, Gene," cuing Talmadge for a frenzied attack. However, Maddox produced posters, artifacts, writings—anything to vilify the newsman. When Maddox was running for governor, police arrested his son for some robberies. Supporters urged Maddox to enhance his law and order stance by disowning the young man. McGill wrote Maddox, begging him to stand by his son. Early next Saturday morning Lester was waiting at the *Constitution* for McGill whom, he knew, often worked when nobody was around. Gene Patterson arrived in time to witness Maddox's emotional thanks and the bear hug he received.[30]

After the election of Nixon, McGill spent much time speculating in private and in print about America's political future.

Franklin Roosevelt's New Deal coalition no longer seemed viable to him. Present day union bosses and agribusiness men bore little resemblance to their counterparts of the 1930s when he swapped sportswriting for political commentary. McGill begged Democrats to build on their support in urban areas and cultivate youthful voters. He did not believe they could beat the GOP in the suburbs but could woo young people. He gave Nixon one caveat over and over: manage desegregation from Washington. If as rumored, the new administration returned control to state and local officials, bigotry would prevail. He scorned those "who say progress comes only when men's hearts change," contending that only federal law could "accomplish reform." For years he had argued just the opposite.[31]

A Christmas visit to Richmond provided precious time with his eight-month-old grandson. A happy baby, Trip squealed with delight riding on his grandfather's shoulders and pulling his hair. Mary Lynn, who had eased into her unexpected role as a grand-mother, enjoyed calmer parts of the routine like rocking the child to sleep. They took Trip along on a visit to the Virginia capital's art museum. McGill even found a Japanese landscape scene that included Mt. Fuji and whispered to the wide-eyed baby in his arms about an unforgettable climb that ended his mourning for Mary Elizabeth six years before.[32]

As the year that many were calling an apocalypse drew to a close, McGill felt a relief deeper than these family joys. Year-long fears of a forced retirement abated. Gene Patterson unwittingly released some of that tension when he left the newspaper. The new arrangement with Reg Murphy simply "editor of the editorial page" suited Tarver better. He railed less at the hypersensitive publisher who could now confidently plan the celebration of his fortieth anniversary with the *Constitution*. The Paris peace talks and Bill Baggs's worsening health ended acrimonious exchanges about Vietnam. When an interviewer noted that he would soon reach age seventy-one (exceeding not only business retirement rules but also the Biblical allotment of "three score and ten"), McGill pooh-poohed both. "I'm feeling good and working hard," he declared, "and I'm not nearly finished with what I hope to get done."[33]

As if to prove this to himself, he joined a small army of the press in Memphis where Martin Luther King's accused assassin would stand trial next spring. Celestine Sibley, whom the *Constitution* chose to cover the trial, also went for security clearance and other preliminaries. Sibley had worked with and observed McGill since 1941 but saw her boss in a new light—as "a working reporter." She followed him all over Memphis from the room where James Earl Ray supposedly fired on King to a park honoring a jazz musician. Sibley assumed McGill was getting background. She did not know that forty-six years ago he filed his first big stories from Memphis as Senator K. D. McKellar's reelection bid climaxed in July 1922. The handful of columns McGill wrote on this trip were brimming with interest. The old police reporter was obviously anticipating Ray's trial.[34]

On December 29 Bill Baggs reentered a Miami hospital. Little more than a week later he was dead at age forty-six. McGill's behavior at the funeral of his protégé worried friends. He wrote Baggs's son, Craig, a long letter after the boy returned to boarding school. In explaining more about Baggs's medical history to Craig, McGill digressed to describe his own grief at the loss of two daughters and Mary Elizabeth. He promised the boy that time would "dull some of the feeling of loss and resentment." He refrained from telling Craig of his long travail with these very two emotions.[35]

Shortly before traveling to Nixon's inauguration, McGill typed a fiercely loyal message to President Johnson. He consoled the man facing an ignominious retirement with assurances that history would vindicate him. "You have stuck with me in good days and bad," Johnson replied. A word of thanks seemed inadequate for such loyalty. Despite misgivings about the incoming administration, McGill covered the festivities with almost as much enthusiasm as his first inaugural in 1937. Besides writing several columns, he did some feature stories that the staff abridged before running them. Back in Atlanta he pinned a plaintive memo to the city room bulletin board. "At any rate," it concluded, "as I learned over forty years ago—it is hell to be cut."[36]

Unlike some other editors and nationally syndicated columnists, McGill grounded his work in observing people rather than in
abstract ideas. His seventeen years in sports probably shaped this
approach as much as personality. Also he never wavered in his
insistence that travel was essential to his success. He may have
been excusing his restless temperament, escaping family problems,
or just telling the truth. His travels did produce memorable copy
but also led to exhaustion and illness. Toward the end he might
have helped many readers by staying home and doing more
reflective work. No one, however, could have persuaded him of this
possibility.

On the afternoon of February 3, 1969, McGill went to Atlanta's Booker T. Washington High School. A class that was
studying his work asked him to speak. Visiting schools was a
favorite pasttime, so he was in good spirits. Someone brought
along a tape recorder. For over two hours black students and
teachers overflowed the auditorium, listening to a white newsman
ramble then answer questions. McGill began by reviewing his own
life. In two days he would celebrate his seventy-first birthday, he
said, so he was "thinking back to beginnings." He mentioned the
old homeplace on the river, the misery of Soddy's mines but
mostly reflected on how hard Ben McGill struggled to give his
children the best education possible.

His life's work figured prominently in the afternoon. He gave
listeners a version of Vanderbilt that glossed over failures to
prepare for a career either in medicine or law. He never mentioned
being a writer from childhood or how he struggled to find the best
use of his talent. He said the Nashville newspaper job was merely
a way to earn a living when he gave up on school. They wondered
how he managed to keep up with events then produce so much
commentary about them. McGill joked at first then in an offhand
remark gave the key to his career: "I can write almost anytime." He
described how he relished reading books and newspapers to gain
the necessary background. Fulfillment shined in the tape recording.
At one point he declared, "I don't know what else I would rather

have done."[37]

Back at the *Constitution* McGill took a long nap in his office then visited with staffers while waiting for Mary Lynn to pick him up. Reg Murphy, still settling into McGill's old role, wanted to ask him how travel generated material for the editorial page. Later he pulled out his wedding photograph, reminiscing about the happy day. Finally he descended to Forsyth Street and went off to a joint birthday celebration at the home of a black music teacher, John Lawhorn. Lawhorn's son would turn twelve the same day that McGill was seventy-one. The year before McGill publicized Lawhorn's method of using music to improve all the learning skills of youngsters. He helped Lawhorn obtain a grant to finance work with Atlanta's black children.

After dinner McGill was discussing ideas for enlarging the project when he suddenly stopped speaking. By Ralph's expression, Mary Lynn knew the dreaded crisis had come. He rose, asked to go home, then collapsed. Mary Lynn began resuscitation while Phyllis Lawhorn summoned Joe Wilber and an ambulance. Nothing Dr. Wilber or Mary Lynn could do brought either pulse or heartbeat. They raced to the nearest hospital. McGill was Wilber's patient for a decade. The physician marveled at the range of his interests and capacity for friendship. It went hard with him that evening to see all his doctoring fail. Even before Wilber came to speak with her, Mary Lynn abandoned her hopes that Ralph would revive. Nothing remained but to go home and begin final arrangements.[38]

Grace Lundy set aside her own sorrow to guarantee that all went well, especially at the *Constitution*. She was watching the late news when Jack Tarver telephoned word. Stopping only briefly to see Mary Lynn, Grace drove to the office. She stayed most of the night. What six hours ago was a convivial gathering place around "Pappy" became a national news site. The staff would never forget Grace's strength as they struggled to put the paper together and fended off interviewers. After the paper hit Atlanta's streets, Grace followed the habit of her beloved boss and pinned a memo to the city room bulletin board. "You are beautiful people," it concluded.

They actually felt as one staffer said, "like we were in a damned crazy dream." Reg Murphy wrote the lead story and editorial. Murphy had assumed he could rely on McGill's guidance and support as his predecessor, Gene Patterson, had done. Now the stunned editor composed the first reviews of his mentor's life and work. Celestine Sibley drew the assignment of doing stories related to the funeral. The student editor of Vanderbilt's *Hustler*, who had traveled from Nashville for the service, talked with Sibley. She revealed that their files contained no prepared obituary of McGill. "He was the only man in the world," she observed, "I thought would never die."[39]

McGill would have relished Sibley's masterful weaving of information and recollection. The sorrow of down and out Atlantans who habitually "had mooched" from him came across as strongly as that of statesmen around the world. Sibley knew that hatred of McGill ranged from the rich Buckhead subscriber who paid his delivery boy extra money to cut McGill's photo out of the *Constitution* each morning to the KKK leader furious that the newsman died without suffering. However, she reaffirmed Jack Tarver's claim that those he got to know "couldn't help warming up to him."

One of McGill's enemies did more than rejoice at his removal. A bomb threat came as mourners filled All Saints Church long before the service. Atlanta police and Secret Service agents decided they had time to search and need not evacuate the crowd. They found no explosives. On schedule Rector Frank Ross led the casket down the aisle, his mind reeling that some individual tried a final, futile assault on the newspaperman. As always on such occasions, some within the packed pews wondered about life after death. The fact that McGill, whose writing elicited powerful reactions, would continue to affect attitudes and actions was one answer to this perennial question at funerals.

Sibley described the scene as the procession traveled from downtown to West View Cemetery. Along the route and at the grave site blacks of all ages from school children to frail, elderly citizens paid their respects. A black Boy Scout troop from a storefront mission came to the cemetery. Standing in uniform, they formed an honor guard of sorts for one "who had fought for their rights long before they were born." On what would have been his seventy-first birthday he was laid to rest with Mary Elizabeth and their two little daughters.[40]

McGill died full of ambition and plans, but the heyday of such newspapermen was ending. Thanks to his toughness and some luck, he had already outlasted most contemporaries in southern journalism. Coverage of the civil rights movement showed how television would soon supplant the influence of newspapers whose readers clipped and reread editorial columns. Any social revolution, however, has varying roles, and for a few years McGill played his as "conscience of the South."

From his youth when Tennesseans flaunted Prohibition laws, he believed that legal reforms would fail unless public attitudes changed along with them. When he won the Pulitzer Prize in 1959, he told an interviewer he felt "frustrated and sad that in a lifetime I've been able to change so little with so many words." Yet Dr. Benjamin Mays, longtime president of Morehouse College, conducted a revealing poll: "Without exception Ralph McGill was named by the respondents as having done more than any other writer to get Atlanta and the South to accept federal decrees and congressional legislation in the interest of justice and democracy in a sane and reasonable manner."

McGill also lived long enough to attempt an even larger role. During much of his editorial career he was forced to play southern apologist. This, along with his pragmatism and inconsistency, earned him the enmity of many doctrinaire liberals. A few days before he died, he explained to a Nevada editor why his syndicated column was in such demand. The South, he wrote, has become just the "focal point" of a "national story of racism, civil rights, and politics." Thus he ended his career and his life as "conscience" to a national readership. The best of his work is still relevant a generation later.[41]

NOTES

1. David R. Goldfield, *Promised Land: The South Since 1945* (ArlingtonHeights, IL: Harlan Davidson, 1987), 81. Hereafter cited as *Promised Land.*

2. Numan V. Bartley, *The New South, 1945-1980* (Baton Rouge: Louisiana State University Press, 1995), 71-73, 166, 234.

Chapter 1:
Republican From East "Tenn-o-see": 1898-1917

1. McGill family records. The Ralph E. McGill papers in Special Collections, Woodruff Library, Emory University, Atlanta, Georgia, form the basis of this book. References are to that source unless otherwise indicated. The following abbreviations appear in all the notes:

Ralph E. McGill	REM
Harold H. Martin papers, Emory University	HM papers
Atlanta Constitution	AC
Nashville Banner	NB

2. Ralph McGill, *The South and the Southerner* (Boston: Little Brown & Co., 1963), 38, 33-34. Hereafter cited as *S&S*; family records.

3. *S&S*, 52; *AC*, 1 December 1946; *AC*, 12 January 1956.

4. *AC*, 27 June 1966; family records; *S&S*, 34; Gilbert E. Govan and James W. Livingood, *The Chattanooga Country, 1540-1962*, rev. ed. (Chapel Hill: University of North Carolina Press, 1963), 351-391. Hereafter cited as *Chattanooga Country.*

5. *S&S*, 33; Folder 4, Box 25, HM papers.

6. *S&S*, 50-52, 30.

7. *Chattanooga Times*, 1 June 1947; REM to John M. McGill, 9 March 1954, Box 9; *AC*, 18 May 1964; family records; see also Jim Stokeley and Jeff D. Johnson, eds. *An Encyclopedia of East Tennessee* (Oak Ridge: Children's Museum of Oak Ridge, 1981).

8. Ralph McGill, "My First Boss," *Atlantic*, February 1959, 69; Barry Bingham to HM, 24 November 1969, Box 28, HM papers; *S&S*, 38.

9. Grace Lundy to Edward Weeks, 12 February 1969, quoting REM manuscript, Box 26.

10. *AC*, 18 December 1949; Celestine Sibley, "They Don't Scare McGill," *Saturday Evening Post*, 27 December 1958, 51. Hereafter cited as "Scare McGill."

11. *S&S*, 38; Lucille McGill Staley interviews; *AC*, 3 December 1945; *S&S*, 58.

12. Folder 4, Box 25, HM papers; *S&S*, 36-38; Folder 4, Box 27; family records.

13. Box 23, HM papers.

14. Folder 4, Box 25, HM papers; *AC*, 6 February 1969, next door neighbor quoting Mary Lou McGill; according to family records sisters' birth dates are: Bessie, 7 February 1904, Lucille, 11 June 1906, and Sarah, 17 November 1915.

15. *S&S*, 49; examples of nostalgia in *AC*, 5 February 1951, 11 October 1951; see also *AC* 5 November 1946; Lucille McGill Staley interviews.

16. *S&S*, 52; see also *AC*, 1 December 1946, 19 November 1957, and Grace Lundy to Edward Weeks, 12 February 1969, quoting REM manuscript, Box 26.

17. Folder 4, Box 25, HM papers; Lucille McGill Staley interviews.

18. *S&S*, 49; Lucille McGill Staley interviews; see also *AC*, 6 May 1952, 2 November 1954.

19. *Chattanooga Country*, 331-332; Lucille McGill Staley interviews; Gene Patterson interview; *S&S*, 44; *AC*, 1 September 1947, 3 June 1949, 1 February 1952.

20. *AC*, 13 January, 12 February, 17 February 1948; *S&S*, 34; *AC*, 16 March 1964; Lucille McGill Staley interviews.

21. *NB*, 21 January 1927; *NB*, 17 February 1928.

22. Charles Peacock diary in Box 23, HM papers; Lucille McGill Staley interviews; *NB*, 26 September 1928.

23. *S&S*, 40-42; *Chattanooga Country*, 211-251.

24. *S&S*, 42, 43; *AC*, 9 March 1959; Mary Lou McGill to REM, n.d., Box 1; *Chattanooga Country*, 185-189, 241.

25. *AC*, 30 August 1956; *S&S*, 53-54.

26. *S&S*, 38; *Chattanooga Country*, 404; *AC*, 3 November 1954; *S&S*, 103-104; see also Gordon B. McKinney, *Southern Mountain Republicans, 1865-1900: Politics and the Appalachian Community* (Chapel Hill: University of North Carolina Press, 1988).

27. *Chattanooga Country*, 373; *S&S*, 33; *S&S*, 40.

28. *AC*, 27 June 1966; *S&S*, 38-40; Lucille McGill Staley interviews.

29. *McCallie Pennant*, 1913-1917, in family records; Folder 19, Box 1; *S&S*, 39.

30. *AC*, 8 November 1949; Lucille McGill Staley interviews; Charles Peacock diary in Box 25, HM papers.

31. Lewis Cox to Cal Logue quoted in Ralph McGill, *Ralph McGill: Editor and Publisher*, 2 vols, ed. Calvin M. Logue (Durham: Moore Publishing Co., 1969), 1:30, Hereafter cited as *Editor & Publ*; clipping in Scrapbook 2; *S&S*, 55.

32. *S&S*, 54-55; see also Reb Gershon-Cal Logue interview, audiocassette in Box 102, reprinted in Ralph McGill, *Southern Encounters: Southerners of Note in Ralph McGill's South*, ed. Calvin M. Logue (Macon: Mercer University Press, 1983), 295-315. Hereafter cited as Gershon interview, *Southern Encounters*.

33. *AC*, 8 November 1949.

34. 1915 diary in Box 95; Harold H. Martin, *Ralph McGill, Reporter* (Boston: Little Brown & Co., 1973), 13. Hereafter cited as *Reporter*. This biographer had unrestricted access to McGill's papers and accumulated many documents on his

own. His book has no footnotes. Often I located Martin's documentation either in his or McGill's manuscripts and cited that. References to *Reporter* occur only when Martin himself is the source or when documentation was lost; scrapbooks 2 & 3; see also *NB*, 28 December 1925, 11 November 1926, 15 January 1927.

35. 1915 diary in Box 95; *S&S*, 56; see also Grady McWhiney, *Cracker Culture: Celtic Ways in the Old South* (Tuscaloosa: University of Alabama Press, 1988).

36. Photos in Scrapbooks 2 & 3; *S&S*, 34.

37. *Diagnostic and Statistical Manual of Mental Disorders* (Washington, D.C.: American Psychiatric Association, 1994), 345-350; interviews with Virginia Staley Bigelow and Dr. Joseph A. Wilber.

38. Clipping in Scrapbook 3; *AC*, 6 August 1947; Lucille McGill Staley interviews; see also *AC*, 2 November 1963.

39. Grace Lundy to Edward Weeks, 12 February 1969, quoting REM manuscript, Box 26; *McCallie Pennant*, 1913-1917, in family records; McCallie School transcript; *AC*, 18 February 1947.

40. *AC*, 2 August 1967; Lucille McGill Staley interviews; *S&S*, 104, 102.

41. Clipping in Scrapbook 3; *S&S*, 58; *NB*, 23 September 1927, 7 March 1928.

CHAPTER 2:
VANDERBILT LINEMAN AND LEATHERNECK: 1917-1921

1. REM to Coleman A. Harwell, 24 February 1959, (including manuscript), Box 34; *AC*, 14 April 1950.

2. Paul K. Conkin, *Gone With the Ivy: A Biography of Vanderbilt University* (Knoxville: University of Tennessee Press, 1985), 208-211; 229; 232-233. Hereafter cited as *Gone With Ivy*; Edwin Mims, *A History of Vanderbilt University* (Nashville: Vanderbilt University Press, 1946), 330. Hereafter cited as *Vanderbilt*.

3. *S&S*, 72-73; Dan E. McGugin to Ed Danforth, April 1929, Scrapbook 4; *Vanderbilt Hustler*, 1917, clipping in Scrapbook 3.

4. Vanderbilt, 282-283; *AC*, 23 September 1963; *NB*, 26 August 1923; *NB*, 30 January 1926; *AC*, 4 December 1948; *AC*, 15 November 1950.

5. *AC*, 3 June 1949, 2 November 1963; Russel Nye, *The Unembarrassed Muse: the Popular Arts in America* (New York: Dial Press, 1970), 72-75.

6. *S&S*, 74; see also *AC*, 14 April 1950, 28 August 1962.

7. *Gone With Ivy*, 219; momentos in Scrapbook 3; Lucille McGill Staley interviews; see also *AC*, 13 January 1948, 22 January 1952.

8. Dan F. McGugin to Ed Danforth, April 1929, Box 3.

9. *S&S*, 70; Lucille McGill Staley interviews; *AC*, 8 December 1956; Vanderbilt University transcript.

10. *Gone With Ivy*, 189-190, 232; Don Doyle, *Nashville*, 2 vols. (Knoxville: University of Tennessee Press, 1985), 2:6. Hereafter cited as *Nashville*; *AC*, 22 January 1952; *S&S*, 72; see also REM to Helen Wright 12 June 1959, Box 9.

11. REM to Cal Logue, 29 November 1966, Box 16; invitation in Scrapbook 3; *Vanderbilt Hustler*, 29 May 1918, in Special Collections, Heard Library, Vanderbilt University, Nashville, Tennessee.

12. Photos in Scrapbook 3; *S&S*, 74; *AC*, 11 December 1958; more background in *Gone With Ivy*, 305.

13. *Nashville*, 2:42, 44, 68; REM to Charles Moss, 26 February 1957, (including manuscript), Box 34; "Western Front" article clipping in Scrapbook 3.

14. *Nashville*, 2:21, 27; *Vanderbilt*, 257; *AC*, 30 June 1951, 1 May 1964.

15. David D. Lee, *Tennessee In Turmoil: Politics in the Volunteer State, 1920-1932* (Memphis: Memphis State University Press, 1979), 12-13. Hereafter cited as *Tennessee In Turmoil*; *AC*, 13 August 1955; more on Stahlman-Lea feud in Ralph McGill, "Pulitzer Memorial Address," Columbia University, 29 May 1959, reprinted in *Editor & Publ*, 2:140-148. Hereafter cited as "Pulitzer," *Editor & Publ*; more on history of *Banner* in *NB*, 5 April and 1 July 1925.

16. Dan E. McGugin to REM, n.d. [1918], Scrapbook 3.

17. Gershon interview, *Southern Encounters*, 296 ; *AC*, 24 October 1968; *AC*, 4 September 1947.

18. *NB*, 27 June 1928.

19. Dr. A. M. Patterson notes, Brainard Cheney notes, Virginia Schubert notes, all in Box 28, HM papers; *Reporter*, 74.

20. Lucille McGill Staley interviews; Ralph McGill, "My First Boss," *Atlantic*, February 1959, 70, 68, a self-serving version written when McGill was often mocked as a "Jim Crow liberal."

21. *Gone With Ivy*, 243; Vanderbilt University transcript; *Gone With Ivy*, 307-308; *Vanderbilt*, 285-286, 288; *NB*, 15 November 1928; see also *NB*, 27 November 1927.

22. *Vanderbilt*, 262-263; *NB*, 14 October 1925; clippings in Scrapbook 3; *NB*, 14 October 1925; *AC*, 25 April 1948; Brainard Cheney notes in Box 28, HM papers.

23. *S&S*, 75, 77; *AC*, 5 April 1939; *Gone With Ivy*, 320.

24. *NB*, 14 October 1925; *Gone With Ivy*, 135; *NB*, 1 July 1925; *S&S*, 76; *AC*, 30 July 1956.

25. *S&S*, 75.

26. Lucille McGill Staley interviews; Folder 19, Box 61; clipping in Scrapbook 3.

27. *NB*, 14 April 1928.

28. Vanderbilt University transcript; REM to Cal Logue, 29 November 1966, Box 16; Brainard Cheney notes, Box 28, HM papers.

29. *S&S*, 91; REM to Charles Moss, 26 February 1957, [including manuscript], Box 34; more on Morton in *NB*, 3 March 1929.

30. *S&S*, 91; see also *Tennessee in Turmoil*, 12, 13; *AC*, 8 August 1948; Mary B. Scheib to REM, 10 July 1963, Box 12.

31. REM to Coleman A. Harwell, 24 February 1959, [including manuscript], Box 34; *S&S*, 86-87.

32. REM to Charles Moss, 26 February 1957, [including manuscript], Box 34.

33. Ibid.

34. Ibid.

35. *AC*, 11 December 1946.

36. Stories in Scrapbook 3; see also W. H. Fawcett to REM, 12 May 1922, Box 3.

37. Vanderbilt University transcript; REM to Cal Logue 29 November 1966, Box 16.

38. Lucille McGill Staley interviews.

39. John D. Barrow notes in Box 28, HM papers; REM to Ben McGill, 5 February 1919, Box 2; momentos in Scrapbook 3 include 1920 Harding-Coolidge election badge.

40. Ralph McGill, "Four Teachers Remembered Best," *Vanderbilt Alumnus*, March 1952, reprinted in *Southern Encounters*, 98. Hereafter cited as "Four Teachers"; Dr. A. M. Patterson notes in Box 23, HM papers.

41. *Reporter*, 21; *AC*, 25 April 1948.

42. Clipping from *Chattanooga News*, 25 April 1921, Folder 1, Box 98, gives story of prank and expulsion; see also Dr. A. M. Patterson notes in Box 23, HM papers; *Editor & Publ*, 1:40, quoting interview McGill gave *Nashville Tennessean Magazine*, 5 November 1961.

43. Ralph McGill, Lecture at Emory & Henry, 29 March 1968, *Editor & Publ* 2:470.

44. *NB*, 20 July 1924.

CHAPTER 3:
SPORTS "BALLYHOO": 1921-1929

1. Ralph McGill, "Booker T. Washington High School Speech," 3 February 1969, in *Editor & Publ*, 2:500. Hereafter cited as "Washington H.S."; *NB*, 30 June 1924.

2. *NB*, 26 August, 9 September, 25 October, 4 December 1923; *AC*, 4 September 1949; REM to Owen Conrad, 21 August 1958, Box 7; photos in Scrapbook 3.

3. *Tennessee In Turmoil*, 13; articles appeared in *Banner* between 18 June and 4 August 1922; *NB*, 29 July 1922; *S&S*, 93-94, 99.

4. Articles appeared in *Banner* between 17 October and 6 November 1922; *Tennessee in Turmoil*, 22-36.

5. *NB*, 10 January, 15 January 1923; *NB*, 19 September, 8 October, 13 October, 14 October, 15 October 1922.

6. Frederick Lewis Allen, *Only Yesterday: An Informal History of the Nineteen Twenties* (New York: Bantam Books, 1946), 186-190, describes "golden age of sports."

7. *Banner* sold radio sets as a promotion and sponsored radio programs. See *NB*, 7 November 1926 and 5 December 1927.

8. *NB*, 4 December 1923.

9. *NB*, 15 October 1922; *NB*, 12 October 1926.

10. *NB*, 7 November 1926.

11. *NB*, 3 July, 18 July 1923; *NB*, 30 March 1925.

12. *NB*, 7 December 1928; *NB*, 5 September 1925.

13. *NB*, 17 April, 23 April, 24 April 1927.

14. *NB*, 20 April 1924.

15. *NB*, 1 April 1927; *NB*, 30 July 1923; *NB*, 16 April 1924.

16. *NB*, 16 August 1924.

17. John D. Barrow notes in Box 28, HM papers; *NB*, 14 October 1923.

18. REM to Cal Logue, 29 November 1966, Box 16; *NB*, 14 June 1926; Brainard Cheney notes in Box 28, HM papers; *NB*, 19 December 1927.

19. Brainard Cheney notes in Box 28, HM papers; *NB*, 5 February 1926; *NB*, 20 September 1926; *NB*, 12 October 1926; *NB*, 10 February 1927.

20. Articles appeared in *Banner* between 13 and 18 February 1925; *NB*, 18 February 1925; see also *AC*, 22 January 1951, 28 March 1959.

21. *NB*, 13 July 1925; *Tennessee In Turmoil*, 57-58; *AC*, 22 November 1968.

22. *NB*, 31 July 1925.

23. *NB*, 6 August 1925.

24. *NB*, 29 November 1925; Brainard Cheney notes in Box 28, HM papers.

25. Syndication announced in *NB*, 20 August 1925; other clippings about "Gink" popularity in family records; see also *NB*, 8 February and 5 July 1924, 29 June 1925 for fine samples; *Banner* ran a contest for readers to submit "Gink" pieces in *NB*, 30 November 1928.

26. *NB*, 17 November 1927.

27. *NB*, 17 August 1928.

28. *NB*, 6 December 1925.

29. *NB*, 12 October 1926; *NB*, 14 September, 30 October 1923; *NB*, 18 August, 22 September 1926.

30. *NB*, 18 December 1927; Some love letters from REM to Louise Stevens in Folders 1-6, Box 104; more on their romance in Brainard Cheney notes, Box 28, HM papers.

31. *NB*, 22 August 1927.

32. *S&S*, 107; *NB*, 5 October 1927.

33. *NB*, 20 May 1927.

34. Articles appeared in *Banner* 26-30 December 1927 and 2-3 January 1928.

35. *NB*, 18 January 1928.

36. *NB*, 13 January 1928; *NB*, 5 February 1927; *NB*, 6 February 1928.

37. *NB*, 14 April 1928; see also *AC*, 12 December 1956 and 1 July 1963.

38. Articles appeared in *Banner* between 30 June and 2 August 1928; *NB*, 28 July 1928.

39. Dr. Joe Wilber interview; obituary in *AC*, 22 March 1962; Cora H. Smiley to REM, 23 September 1965, Box 15.

40. Gershon interview, *Southern Encounters*, 312; Betty Danforth notes in Box 24, HM papers; Mary Benson Scheib to REM, 5 April 1962, Box 1; see also Mary Daniel Whitney to REM, 22 July 1963, Box 12 and Helen Moore to REM, 23 July 1967, Box 23, HM papers.

41. *NB*, 20 December 1928; *NB*, 1 January 1929; *NB*, 2 January 1929.

42. *NB*, 12 January 1929; *NB*, 13 January 1929; *NB*, 14 January 1929.

43. Articles appeared in *Banner* between 14 January and 22 February 1929; Clipping in Scrapbook 6; *NB*, 31 March 1929.

44. *NB*, 1 February, 5 February, 22 February, 24 February 1929; REM to Louise Stevens, 5 February 1929, Box 104.

45. REM to Louise Stevens, 19 April 1929, Box 104; *Reporter*, 27; REM to Louise Stevens, 17 August 1928, Box 104; REM to Louise Stevens, 5 February 1929, Box 104.

46. REM to Louise Stevens, 5 February 1929, Box 104; REM to Louise Stevens, 19 April 1929, Box 104; Betty Danforth notes in Box 24, HM papers.

47. *NB*, 31 March 1929; clipping of Keeler's column in *Atlanta Journal*, 15 August 1928, in Scrapbook 3.

48. REM to Louise Stevens, 19 April 1929, Box 104; McGill described his arrival in Atlanta in "It's Constitutional," *Newsweek*, 13 April 1959, 102.

CHAPTER 4:
ATLANTA AND HARD TIMES: 1929-1936

1. File on Clark Howell in ANInc reference room; see also Raymond B. Nixon, *Henry W. Grady: Spokesman of the New South* (New York: Alfred A Knopf, 1943) and Dennis J. Pfenning, "Evan and Clark Howell of the *Atlanta Constitution: The Partnership, 1889-1897*" (Ph.D. dissertation, University of Georgia, 1975). Hereafter cited as Pfenning, "Howell."

2. Clarence N. Stone, *Regime Politics: Governing Atlanta, 1946-1988* (Lawrence: University Press of Kansas, 1989), 14-21. Hereafter cited as *Regime Politics*; Barrett Howell interviews; The first "Forward Atlanta" campaign began in 1926.

3. File on Clark Howell in ANInc reference room; Wallace B. Eberhard, "Clark Howell and the *Atlanta Constitution*," *Journalism Quarterly* 60 (Spring 1983): 118-122.

4. In *AC*, 3 April 1929, Ed Danforth's personal column, "Mawnin'," described McGill's first day on the job.; Clifford M. Kuhn, Harlan E. Joye, and E. Bernard West, *Living Atlanta: An Oral History of the City, 1914-1948* (Athens: University of Georgia Press, 1990), 326. Hereafter cited as *Living Atlanta*; Herbert Jenkins interview transcript for "Dawn's Early Light," Box 111.

5. Don Marquis to William Cole, 16 August 1930, Box 10, Julian L. Harris papers, Emory University.

6. *AC*, 15 April 1929; Norman Shavin and Bruce Galphin, *Atlanta: Triumph of A People* (Atlanta: Capricorn, 1982), 226-228. Hereafter cited as *Atlanta: Triumph*; *AC*, 4 April 1929.

7. REM to Louise Stevens, 19 April 1929, Box 104.

8. Lucille McGill Staley interviews; Mary Benson Scheib to REM, 5 April 1962, Box 1.

9. Engagement story in *AC*, 17 August 1929; Betty Danforth notes in Box 24, HM papers; *AC*, 5 September 1929; many wedding clippings in Scrapbook 4.

10. Reese Cleghorn, "McGill," *Georgia*, January 1973, 29.

11. *AC*, 1 September, 3, 7, 9, 10 October 1929; more on Mehre in Kenneth Coleman and Charles S. Gurr, eds., *Dictionary of Georgia Biography*, 2 vols. (Athens: University of Georgia Press, 1983), 2:702. Hereafter cited as *Georgia Biography*.

12. *AC*, 13 October 1929; *AC*, 30 October 1929.

13. *AC*, 8 January 1930; *S&S*, 145-158; REM to Tom Chubb, 14 June 1937, Box 104.

14. *AC*, 9 January 1930.

15. *AC*, 20 July 1930; *Living Atlanta*, 158.

16. Ann Wells Ellis, "The Commission on Interracial Cooperation, 1919-1944: Its Activities and Results," (Ph.D. dissertation, Georgia State University, 1975). Hereafter cited as "Interracial Cooperation"; more on Raper in *Georgia Biography*, 2:824-25; REM to Louise Stevens, 5 February 1929, Box 104.

17. "Four Teachers," *Southern Encounters*, 96; Lucille McGill Staley interviews.

18. *AC*, 3 July 1930; *AC*, 10 July 1930; *AC*, 13 July 1930; *AC*, 14 July 1930; for McGill's awe of Jones se *AC*, 12 June 1942 and *AC*, 9eFebruary 1944; more on Jones in *Georgia Biography*, 1:554-556.

19. *AC*, 16 October 1930; *AC*, 18 October 1930; *Living Atlanta*, 89, 202, 204, 205.

20. *Nashville*, 2:6; see also Paul K. Conkin, *The Southern Agrarians* (Knoxville: University of Tennessee Press, 1988).

21. *AC*, 12 February 1931.

22. Institute of Citizenship Scrapbook 1, 1931, Cullen Gosnell papers, Emory University; In *Editor & Publ*, 2:504 McGill says he attended night classes for several years. See also Francis Marion Smith, "A Study of Ralph McGill's Early Life and of His Editorial Treatment of Three Southern Problems," (Master's thesis, Emory University, 1953), 16, where McGill told Smith he hired tutors to fill gaps in his background. Hereafter cited as "Three Southern Problems." On several occasions McGill mentioned attending continuing education classes at Emory. Nothing corroborates these claims.

23. Arthur Raper-Daniel Singal interview transcript, Box 39, Arthur Raper papers, Southern Historical Collection, University of North Carolina at Chapel Hill; Arthur F. Raper, *The Tragedy of Lynching* (Chapel Hill: University of North Carolina Press, 1933); John Egerton, *Speak Now Against the Day: The Generation Before the Civil Rights Movement in the South* (New York: Alfred A. Knopf, 1994), 49, 56. Hereafter cited as *Speak Now Against the Day*.

24. Walter White to Julian L. Harris, 12 January 1934, Box 10, Julian Harris papers, Emory University; more on regionalism developing during the 1930s in Michael O'Brien, *The Idea of the American South, 1920-1941* (Baltimore: The Johns Hopkins University Press, 1979).

25. Louis T. Griffith and John E. Talmadge, *Georgia Journalism, 1763-1950* (Athens: University of Georgia Press, 1951), 340; *AC*, 6 March 1931; *AC*, 1, 2, 4, 5 July 1931; all Stribling material in Scrapbook 5.

26. Clipping in Scrapbook 5; *Reporter*, 32.

27. *AC*, 15 July 1931; congratulatory messages in Scrapbook 4.

28. *Living Atlanta*, 180, 182, 325-326; *AC*, 4 February 1932.

29. *Living Atlanta*, 326; Herbert Jenkins interview transcript for "Dawn's Early Light," Box 111.

30. *AC*, 2 November 1934; *AC*, 3 November 1934.

31. 17 August 1933; background on Mary Elizabeth McGill from Dr. Joe Wilber interview; Lucille McGill Staley interviews; Gershon interview, *Southern Encounters*; Ralph McGill Jr., interview transcript for "Dawn's Early Light," Box 111; Celestine Sibley interview transcript for "Dawn's Early Light," Box 111; C. Ralph Stephens, *The Correspondence of Flannery O'Connor and the Brainard Cheneys* (Jackson: University Press of Mississippi, 1986), 150.

32. Virginia Schubert notes in Box 28, HM papers; various notes in Boxes 25 and 26A, HM papers; *Reporter*, 74; William Emerson interview transcript for "Dawn's Early Light," 11, Box 110.

33. *Reporter*, 31. Other memories of hard times at *Constitution* in REM to C. Kersey Smith, 16 January 1961, Box 10; REM to Ralph McGill Jr., 20 March 1968, Box 2; Barrett Howell interviews; Folder 1, Box 11, Julian Harris papers, Emory University; *Living Atlanta*, 200.

34. *AC*, 3 January 1932; *AC*, 3 July 1932; See files in pre-presidential papers, Franklin D. Roosevelt Library, Hyde Park, New York, where correspondence with Howell begins in 1928. Presidential papers include even more evidence of their longstanding relationship; *AC*, 9 November 1932.

35. *AC*, 24, 25, 27 November 1932; *AC*, 18 June 1933.

36. *AC*, 24 November 1934; *AC*, 25 November 1934; Lucille McGill Staley interviews.

37. Articles appeared in *Constitution* between 1 and 10 August 1933; Sumner Welles to REM, 8 December 1933, Box 3; Sumner Welles to Clark Howell Sr., 26 August 1933, Box 3; clippings of syndicated artices in Scrapbook 5; thirty-five years later McGill gave a different and very bitter version of Cuban trip in REM to Joe Cumming, 25 November 1968, Box 62.

38. *S&S*, 167; Gershon interview, *Southern Encounters*, 314.

39. *AC*, 8 February 1934; file on Clark Howell in ANInc reference room; Barrett Howell interviews.

40. William Anderson, *The Wild Man From Sugar Creek: the Political Career of Eugene Talmadge* (Baton Rouge: Louisiana State University Press, 1975), 116-117, 133-135. Hereafter cited as *Wild Man*.

41, REM to Tom Chubb, 17 January 1935, Box 104; Lucille McGill Staley interviews; bound volumes of *Red Barrel* at Atlanta History Center reveal how often McGill sold pieces to Coca Cola; 1935 contacts described in REM to Ralph McGill Jr., 26 February 1968, Box 2; correspondence between REM and Robert W. Woodruff as early as 1936, Box 83, Woodruff papers, Emory University.

42. REM to Tom Chubb, 2 April 1935, Box 104.

43. Lucille McGill Staley interviews; *Reporter*, 49.

44. *Reporter*, 51; early columns about Chubb, *AC*, 22 February 1933, 2 February 1934, 7 February 1934.

45. *AC*, 20 January, 21 January 1936.

46. REM to Tom Chubb, 10 June 1936, Box 104; *Reporter*, 52.

47. Lucille McGill Staley interviews.

48. *Wild Man*, 158.

49. *AC*, 23 June 1936; *AC*, 27 June 1936.

50. *AC*, 7 August 1936; *AC*, 9 August 1936.

51. *Wild Man*, 161.

52. *AC*, 18 August 1936; *Wild Man*, 164.

53. Margaret Mitchell to REM, 30 November 1936, Box 3; REM to Westbrook Pegler, 9 May 1963, Box 135, Pegler papers, Herbert Hoover Library; Lucille McGill Staley interviews; Darden A. Pyron, *Southern Daughter: The Life of Margaret Mitchell* (New York: Oxford University Press, 1991), 142-143, 151-152. Hereafter cited as *Southern Daughter*.

54. Ralph McGill, "Little Woman, Big Book: the Mysterious Margaret Mitchell," *Show*, October 1962, reprinted in *Southern Encounters*, 47; *New York Times*, 4 October 1936, sec. 2, p. 3; REM to Tom Chubb, 13 October 1936, Box 104..

55. *Reporter*, 53-54; obituary clipped for Clark Howell file in ANInc reference room; *AC*, 2 September 1934.

56. Harold Martin, "Notes on Ralph McGill," Box 28, HM papers; Martin repeated this story in Reese Cleghorn, "McGill," *Georgia*, January 1973, 27.

CHAPTER 5:
"THE MOST IMPORTANT DAY OF MY LIFE": 1937-1940

1. *AC*, 19 January 1937; *AC*, 20 January 1937.

2. *AC*, 21 January, 22 January, 9 February, 12 February 1937; Jack Temple Kirby, *Rural Worlds Lost: the American South, 1920-1960* (Baton Rouge: Louisiana State University Press, 1987), 64-65. Hereafter cited as *Rural Worlds Lost*; "Interracial Cooperation," 315, 322-323.

3. Arthur Raper described Alexander's interest in McGill in an interview with Morton Sosna, transcript in Box 39, Raper papers, UNC; Edwin R. Embree and Julian Waxman, *Investment in People: the Story of the Julius Rosenwald Fund* (New York: Harper's, 1949).

4. McGill described application process in "Three Southern Problems," 40; REM to Tom Chubb, 9 March 1937, Box 104; Gershon interview, *Southern Encounters*, 302; "Interracial Cooperation," 322-323; Mark Ethridge to Edward Weeks, 29 July 1969, Box 28, HM papers.

5. *AC*, 30 March 1937; REM to Tom Chubb, 21 April 1937, Box 104; Jack Tarver interviews.

6. REM to Tom Chubb, 21 April 1937, Box 104; *AC* 3 May 1937; "Three Southern Problems," 40; award recalled in *AC*, 9 June 1948.

7. REM to Tom Chubb, 14 June 1937, Box 104; Lucille McGill Staley interviews.

8. *AC*, 1 May, 7 May, 10 May 1937; McGill's travels for Emory in Box 7, Gosnell papers, Emory; REM to Tom Chubb, 14 June 1937, Box 104.

9. REM to McGill family, 10 December 1937, in family records; see Ralph McGill and Thomas C. David, *Two Georgians Explore Scandinavia* (Atlanta: State Department of Education, 1938), Box 44; article series for *Nashville Banner*, 19 March-2 April 1938, Box 31; some clippings of many Scandinavian article series appearing February, March, April, May 1938 in *Constitution* in Scrapbook 4; "Three Southern Problems," 40; "Washington H. S.," *Editor & Publ*, 2:501.

10. REM to Virginia McGill, 20 February 1938, in family records; *AC*, 9 March 1938, ran a huge story followed by series late in March.

11. "Three Southern Problems," 43; REM to Robert W. Woodruff, 23 March 1938, in Woodruff papers, Emory.

12. *AC*, 25 March 1938.

13. Mary Elizabeth McGill to McGill family, 31 March 1938, in family records; Gershon interview, *Southern Encounters*, 303; clipping from article series in *Chattanooga Times*, 12 June 1938, Scrapbook 4; more on Hitler in series for *Constitution*, 23-28 March 1938.

14. Typical mentions of "Damascus Road experience," in Ralph McGill, "Southwestern Journalism Forum Speech," 1 May 1953, *Editor & Publ*, 2:34 and "Elijah Parish Lovejoy Convocation Address," *Editor & Publ*, 2:185; memory of "oath" in *AC*, 22 July 1942.

15. "Three Southern Problems," 42; Clark Howell Jr., to REM, 24 March 1938, Box 3.

16. REM to Robert W. Woodruff, 23 March 1938, Box 32, Woodruff papers, Emory.

17. Clipping from *Chattanooga Times*, 12 June 1938, Scrapbook 4; *AC*, 27 March 1938.

18. *AC*, 17 June 1938; *Reporter*, 69.

19. *Reporter*, 69.

20. *AC*, 17 June 1938.

21. "Radio Program Concerning the South," Ralph McGill, *No Place to Hide: The South and Human Rights*, ed. Calvin M. Logue, 2 vols. (Macon: Mercer University Press, 1984), 2:566. Hereafter cited as *No Place*; *AC*, 18 January 1936.

22. Harold Martin's "Notes on McGill," Box 28, HM papers; mocking of sportswriters recalled in Charles Whipple, "Ralph McGill: Conscience of the South," *Boston Globe*, 18 June 1961; Betty Danforth notes, Box 24, HM papers; Jack Tarver interviews.

23. Ann Waldron, *Hodding Carter: The Reconstruction of a Racist* (Chapel Hill: Algonquin Books, 1993), 84-86.

24. James C. Cobb, "Not Gone But Forgotten: Eugene Talmadge and the 1938 Purge Campaign," *Georgia Historical Quarterly* 59 (Summer 1975): 197-209.

25. By now Jimmy Stahlman hated the New Deal and would soon despise McGill. See *Speak Now Against the Day*, 465; *AC*, 8 August 1938; FDR to James A. Farley, 26 November 1938, in Franklin D. Roosevelt, *FDR: His Personal Letters*, 4 vols. (New York: Duell, Sloan and Pearce, 1950), 4:830.

26. *AC*, 19, 20 August 1938 and *AC*, 3, 5 February 1939 are examples of flip flops; Jack Tarver interview.

27. Two attempts to blend McGill unsuccessfully into a collectivity of "liberal" Southern journalists are Dorothy C. Kinsella, "Southern Apologists: A Liberal Image," (Ph.D. dissertation, University of St. Louis, 1971) and John T. Kneebone, *Southern Liberal Journalists and the Issue of Race, 1920-1944* (Chapel Hill: University of North Carolina Press, 1985); Thomas A. Krueger, *And Promises To Keep: the Southern Conference for Human Welfare, 1938-1948* (Nashville: Vanderbilt University Press, 1967), 22. Hereafter cited as *Promises*; see also Linda Reed, *Simple Decency and Common Sense: the Southern Conference Movement, 1938-1963* (Bloomington: Indiana University Press, 1991); REM to Roy Harris, 29 June 1954 and REM to Roy Harris 12 July 1954, Box 5; *AC*, 28 November 1946, McGill claimed he was prouder of this slogan than anything he ever wrote.

28. *AC*, 14 August 1938; Reb Gershon to REM, 2 February 1939, Box 14, Josephine Wilkins papers, Emory; more on McGill and the CFFM in J.C. Wardlaw to REM, 20 February 1939, Box 14, Wilkins papers; H.L. Barker to REM 27 April 1939, Box 14, Wilkins papers; REM to Robert Stiles, 9 May 1939, Box 15, Wilkins papers; Robert Stiles to REM 10 November 1939, Box 16, Wilkins papers.

29. For background see Clement C. Moseley, "Invisible Empire: A History of the Ku Klux Klan in Twentieth Century Georgia, 1915-1965," (Ph.D. dissertation, University of Georgia, 1980). Hereafter cited as "Invisible Empire"; *S&S*, 135-137; *AC*, 17 January 1939.

30. "Invisible Empire," 124; *S&S*, 137; *Living Atlanta*, 314.

31. *Reporter*, 75; Barrett Howell interviews.

32. For more on their relationship see REM to Robert W. Woodruff, 22 December 1938; REM to Robert W. Woodruff (wire), 7 February 1939; REM to Robert W. Woodruff, 20 March 1939, all in Box 83, Woodruff papers, Emory; McGill recalled how philanthropy evolved in REM to Robert W. Woodruff, 22 January 1966, Box 39, Woodruff papers; see also Frederick Allen, *Secret Formula* (New York: Harper Business, 1994); Harold H. Martin, *William Berry Hartsfield* (Athens: University of Georgia Press, 1978), 59-60. Hereafter cited as *Hartsfield*.

33. REM to Tom Chubb, 20 July 1939, Box 104; Lucille McGill Staley interviews; *Reporter*, 72.

34. REM to Helen Moore Cole, 25 July 1967, Box 17; Lucille McGill Staley interviews; REM to Tom Chubb, 11 November 1939 and REM to Tom Chubb, 4 December 1939, Box 104.

35. Anne Edwards, *Road to Tara* (New Haven: Ticknor and Fields, 1983), 282; more on Mitchell's problems with the premiere in *Southern Daughter*, 376-378.

36. *AC*, 22 November 1939; Lucille McGill Staley interviews; obituary in *AC*, 20 December 1939.

37. James M. Cox, *Journey Through My Years* (New York: Simon & Schuster, 1946), 388, 403, 392.

38. REM to Tom Chubb, 21 March 1940, Box 104; Lucille McGill Staley interviews; *Reporter*, 73.

39. REM to Robert W. Woodruff, 8 February 1940, Box 83, Woodruff papers, Emory; *Wild Man*, 186-190.

40. *AC*, 1 February 1940; REM to Robert W. Woodruff, 5 March 1940, Box 83, Woodruff papers, Emory.

41. *Living Atlanta*, 319; *AC*, 5-8 February 1939.

42. *AC*, 10 March, 12 March, 31 March, 1 April 1940; Keeler McCartney material in Folder 4, Box 3 and Folder 4, Box 60; early columns on Kuhn in *AC*, 2 June, 29 November 1939.

43. *Wild Man*, 186-189; predictions of Talmadge win in *AC*, 4 February 1939, 12 July 1940, 18 August 1940.

44. *AC*, 20 April 1940, 21 April 1940, 2 August 1939, 2 August 1940; "arrogant" comment in *AC*, 11 September 1940; "new awareness" in *AC*, 3 July 1940.

45. Although McGill discarded files regularly, he kept some early data on region. See Folder 18, Folder 22, Box 67; Folder 7, Folderx13, Bo 68; Folder 6, Box 45; Arthur Raper-Daniel Singal interview transcript, Box 39, Raper papers, UNC; *Promises*, 59.

46. *S&S*, 190; *AC*, 4 March, 13 July 1940.

47. Lucy R. Mason to Emil Rieve, 9 May 1940, Box 2, Lucy Randolph Mason papers, Perkins Library, Duke University; Lucy R. Mason to Paul Kellogg, 24 April 1940, Box 1, Mason papers.

48. *AC*, 9 May 1959; McGill used fond reminiscence of Mason as a colorful introduction to his discussion of labor in *S&S*, 190-193. She would have taken exception because their relationship turned bitter after a few years. See Lucy R. Mason to Hugh A. Brim, 18 April 1950, Box 7, Mason papers, Duke; *Speak Now Against the Day*, 136, wrongly credits McGill with turning the *Constitution* "more aggressive editorially" in the late 1930s.

49. REM to Ralph McGill Jr., 30 April 1968, Box 2; *Reporter*, 75; Doris Lockerman interviews; Jack Tarver interviews.

CHAPTER 6:
HENRY GRADY'S HEIR: 1940-1945

1. *AC*, 16 September 1940; *AC*, 13 September 1940; *AC*, 16 September 1940; *AC*, 11 September 1940; see Frederick Allen, *Atlanta Rising: The Invention of An International City, 1946-1996* (Atlanta: Longstreet Press, 1996), 42-43, 47, for speculation about the two. Hereafter cited as *Atlanta Rising*.

2. FDR's third term, *AC*, 20 April, 13 July, 24 August 1940; preparedness, *AC*, 3 June, 4 June, 16 August, 12 September 1940; Willkie, *AC*, 19 August 1940.

3. *AC*, 15 July 1941; see also Sue Bailes, "Eugene Talmadge and the Board of Regents Controversy," *Georgia Historical Quarterly* 53 (December 1969): 409-423; James F. Cook, "The Eugene Talmadge-Walter Cocking Controversy," *Phylon* 35 (June 1974): 181-192.

4. *Wild Man*, 198.

5. Ralph McGill, "It Has Happened Here," *Survey Graphic*, 30 (September 1941), reprinted in *No Place*, 1:70, 78, 74.

6. *AC*, 6 June 1939; 21 November 1939; 17 September 1941; 3 December 1941; no legal rights, *AC*, 6 August 1940; praise, *AC*, 4 February 1940, 20 April 1942; fullest statement of stand against prejudice and for segregation, *AC*, 7 March 1942; sharp criticism of McGill's paternalism in Myles Horton interview transcript for "Dawn's Early Light," Box 111 but a revealing alternative view in Ivan Allen Jr. with Paul Hemphill, *Mayor: Notes on the Sixties* (New York: Simon & Schuster, 1971), 10, "'Liberal' is a relative word, and a liberal on the race issue in the South during the forties was someone—and I don't think this is overstating it too much—who felt vaguely uncomfortable over the mistreatment of people with black skin." Hereafter cited as *Mayor*.

7. Obituaries in *AC*, 7 August 1940 and family records; Lucille McGill Staley interviews; Mary Lou McGill to REM, n.d., Folder 9, Box 2.

8. REM to Tom Chubb, 21 March 1940, Box 104; REM to Tom Chubb, 8 April 1941, Box 104; Mary Elizabeth McGill to McGill family, 31 March 1938, in family records; *Reporter*, 79-80.

9. Dr. Joe Wilber interview; Lucille McGill Staley interviews.

10. Gershon interview, *Southern Encounters*, 312; *Reporter*, 77-78.

11. *AC*, 31 March 1942.

12. *AC*, 23 April 1942; some correspondence in Box 28, HM papers; see also audiotape, Box 102 and Ruthanna Boris interview transcript for "Dawn's Early Light," Box 110.

13. *AC*, 21-22, 24-30 May 1942.

14. *Wild Man*, 200; *AC*, 19 June 1942.

15. *AC*, 2 September 1942; *AC*, 7 September 1942; REM to Westbook Pegler, 15 January 1943, Box 134, Pegler papers, Hoover Library.

16. *AC*, 17 September 1942; Barrett Howell interviews; for media view of promotion see "Strong Constitution," *Time*, 14 September 1942, 46; *Speak Now*

Against the Day, 248-252, summarizes the stance of other Southern newspapers at this time.

17. Barrett Howell, Celestine Sibley, Jack Tarver, and Dixon Preston interviews; Sibley aptly contrasted *Journal* and *Constitution* in Celestine Sibley, *Peachtree Street USA* (Garden City: Doubleday, 1963), 162-64 and *AC*, 16 June 1993.

18. *AC*, 1 September 1942.

19. *Living Atlanta*, 138.

20. Durham Conference Statement reprinted in *New South*, 19 (January 1964): 3-10.

21. McGill's pessimism dated from Talmadge's attack on the university. See REM to Edward Weeks, 14 December 1961, Box 27; for example, *Speak Now Against the Day*, 257, contrasts McGill with fellow editor Virginius Dabney.

22. *AC*, 24 October 1942; *AC*, 7 March, 24 June 1942; *AC*, 3 December 1941, 24 October 1942, 24 June 1943; *AC*, 20 November 1942; *AC*, 18 December 1942.

23. Margaret Rose Gladney, ed. *How Am I To Be Heard? Letters of Lillian Smith* (Chapel Hill: University of North Carolina Press, 1993), 65, 64.

24. *AC*, 30 March 1943; transcript of broadcast in Folder 19, Box 44.

25. *AC*, 13 February 1943; *AC*, 29 March 1942, 7 February 1943; *AC*, 24 October 1942; *AC*, 18 December 1942.

26. Josephine Wilkins gave an account of the Atlanta Conference and Collaboration Committee in *New South*, 19 (January 1964): 22-26; Patricia Sullivan, *Days of Hope: Race and Democracy in the New Deal Era* (Chapel Hill: University of North Carolina Press, 1996), 165. Hereafter cited as *Days of Hope*.

27. David Knopf to REM, 1 December 1947, Box 39; REM to David Knopf, 6 January 1948, Box 39.

28. *AC*, 8-15 June 1943.

29. *AC*, 20 June 1943; see also *AC*, 20, 25, 28 July 1943.

30. REM to Edward Weeks, 17 January 1966, Box 15; Notebooks, Box 23, HM papers.

31. *AC*, 21 November 1943; for more on the McGill-Tarver bond see Ralph McGill, "Jack Tarver: A Newspaper Man's Newspaper Man," *The Mercerian*, September 1967, reprinted in *Southern Encounters*, 105-109; REM to James M. Cox Jr., 15 November 1957, Box 51; REM to Sissy Tarver Jason, 2 October 1968, Box 20; REM to Brainard Cheney 13 November 1963, Box 6, Cheney papers, Vanderbilt.

32. Grace Hamilton and John Griffin interview transcripts for "Dawn's Early Light," Box 110; *AC*, 21 September 1943.

33. *AC*, 1 February, 8 February, 10 February, 16 February, 27 February, 22 March 1943; *AC*, 12 September 1944.

34. Ralph McGill, "Southern Exposure," *Vogue*, 1 January 1942, 44, 81, 84; *AC*, 6 February 1944; *AC*, 3 March 1944; *AC*, 5 March 1944; *Speak Now Against the Day*, 320, is a perceptive summary of the hopeful mood.

35. *AC*, 17 February 1944; REM to Sol Markoff, 11 February 1958, Box 7.

36. *AC*, 10 March 1944.

37. Jack Tarver interviews; REM to Tom Chubb 31 October 1945, Box 104.

38. *AC*, 21 January 1945; records of ASNE trip in Folders 6, 7, Box 78.

39. Dr. Joe Wilber interview.

40. REM to Tom Chubb, 8 May 1945, Box 104.

41. *Reporter*, 99; *AC*, 16 March 1951; *AC*, 18 February 1945.

42. *AC*, 7 May 1945; REM to Mary Lou McGill, 15 March 1945, in family records.

43. *AC*, 1 May 1945; Ralph McGill, "Free News and Russia," *Atlantic*, April 1946, 76-79.

44. *AC*, 3-5, 9-10, 14-15, 17 May 1945; *AC*, 13 July 1951.

45. *AC*, 4 February, 27 February, 23 June 1944; *AC*, 1 September 1944.

46. *AC*, 14 April, 1 May 1945.

47. REM to Tom Chubb, 8 May 1945, Box 104; REM to Mary Lou McGill 15 March 1945, in family records.

48. For fears and concern see REM to Mary Elizabeth McGill, 14 January 1945; REM to Mary Elizabeth McGill, 3 February 1945; REM to Mary Elizabeth McGill, 19 February 1945, Box 1.

49. Jack Tarver interviews; REM to Tom Chubb, 6 January 1953, Box 104.

50. REM to Harry S. Truman, 3 May 1945 (wire), President's Personal File, White House Central Files, Harry S. Truman Library, Independence, Missouri; *AC*, 12 August, 13 August 1945.

51. *Reporter*, 109-111; State Department clipping in Scrapbook 6; Ralph McGill Jr.-Harold Martin interview audiocassette, Box 102.

CHAPTER 7:
"THE SOUTH IS IN A DILEMMA": 1946-1949

1. *Reporter*, 111.

2. William Benton, Assistant Secretary of State to American Chiefs of Mission in Europe and the Near East (memo), 16 January 1946, Box 3.

3. *AC*, 26 February 1946; *AC*, 17 March 1946.

4. *AC*, 11 March 1946; *AC*, 24 March 1946; *AC*, 4 May 1946.

5. Harry Ashmore interview transcript for "Dawn's Early Light" and Harold Fleming interview transcript for "Dawn's Early Light," Box 110; *Speak Now Against the Day*, 334, reiterates McGill's role.

6. Summary of Arnall's accomplishments in Numan V. Bartley, *The Creation of Modern Georgia* (Athens: University of Georgia Press, 1983), 183-187. Hereafter cited as *Modern Georgia*; *AC*, 21 May 1945.

7. *Modern Georgia*, 185; *Wild Man*, 217; *Days of Hope*, 203, describes 1946 Georgia as "one of the most promising arenas for liberal political action in the South," but McGill's pessimistic view was far more accurate.

8. *Modern Georgia*, 186-187; *Wild Man*, 219; William L. Belvin, "The Georgia Gubernatorial Primary of 1946," *Georgia Historical Quarterly* 5 (Spring 1971): 38. Hereafter cited as "Gubernatorial Primary"; *AC*, 5 May, 7 May, 31 May, 5 July 1946.

9. *Living Atlanta*, 341; Herbert Jenkins interview transcript for "Dawn's Early Light," Box 111.

10. *Living Atlanta*, 333-337; Harold H. Martin, *Atlanta and Environs: A Chronicle of Its People and Events* 3 vols. (Athens: University of Georgia Press, 1987): 3:133. Hereafter cited as Martin, *Atlanta*; Lorraine N. Spritzer, *The Belle of Ashby Street*, (Athens: University of Georgia Press, 1982) tells Mankin's story.

11. "Gubernatorial Primary," 39, 44-45, 40-41.

12. *AC*, 15 May 1946; *AC*, 26 May 1946.

13. Ralph McGill," Free News and Russia," *Atlantic*, April 1946, 76; Martin Sommers of the *Saturday Evening Post* helped McGill become a successful magazine writer. See REM to Ralph McGill Jr., 14 January 1969, and REM to Ralph McGill Jr., 23 January 1969, Box 2; *AC*, 24 June 1948; *Speak Now Against the Day*, 257, discusses the problem of labeling McGill and others, concluding that "the terms remain frustratingly imprecise and ambiguous."

14. *AC*, 15 July 1946; *AC*, 17 July 1946.

15. *Reporter*, 117-118; see also Celestine Sibley, "Ralph McGill, Newspaper Reporter," Ralph McGill Lecture Series, University of Georgia, 14 February 1991. Hereafter cited as Sibley, "Ralph McGill."

16. *AC*, 29 July; *AC* 3 August 1946.

17. REM to Ruthanna Boris, 31 August 1946, Box 28, HM papers; REM to Robert W. Woodruff, 29 October 1946, Box 39, Woodruff papers, Emory; *Reporter*, 240.

18. *AC*, 20 October 1946.

19. Reb Gershon interview in Carolyn Ann Marvin, "Running on the Fence," (Master's thesis, University of Texas, 1974), 115. Hereafter cited as "On the Fence"; Harold Fleming interview transcript for "Dawn's Early Light," Box 110; *AC*, 10 November, 13 November, 11 December, 15 December 1946; Keeler McCartney got McGill information on Columbians from Atlanta police. See Folder 4, Box 3.

20. *AC*, 8 December 1946.

21. *AC*, 20 December 1946; *AC*, 22 December 1946.

22. Ralph McGill, "How It Happened Down In Georgia," *New Republic*, January 1947, reprinted in *No Place*, 1:90; *AC*, 5 January, 16 January, 17 January, 26 January 1947.

23. Data from trip in Folder 1, Box 80; *AC*, 2 March 1947; examples of new position in *AC*, 8 August, 20 September, 27 September 1947; REM to Arthur H. Vandenberg, 6 January 1947 (wire), Box 3; REM to Dean Acheson, 20 January 1948, Box 3; George C. Marshall to REM, 26 January 1948, Box 3; *AC*, 27 January, 19 March, 2 April, 22 July 1948.

24. REM, Chairman of Committee For United States Information Abroad, to Charles Ross, 6 January 1948, with enclosed letter to Arthur H. Vandenberg *et.al.* 5 January 1948, General File, White House Central Files, Truman Library; *AC*, 29 September 1949.

25. *Speak Now Against the Day*, 167; *Days of Hope*, 154-55, 240; *AC*, 3 November 1947; *AC*, 30 September 1947.

26.Clark Foreman to Robert L. Foreman, 15 January 1948, Box 3; Aubrey Williams to REM 23 September 1947, Box 3; *AC*, 30 January 1948; REM to Aubrey Williams, 17 October 1947, Box 3; *Days of Hope*, 246 and *Speak Now Against the Day*, 446 give two more versions of the incident.

27.*AC*, 15 November 1947; more on this remarkable man in James W. English, *The Prophet of Wheat Street: the Story of William Holmes Borders, A Man Who Refused to Fail* (Elgin, Ill: David C. Cook, 1973).

28. Barrett Howell interview; *AC*, 29 December 1947; "Constitution Amended," *Time*, 5 January 1948, 48; *AC*, 1 March 1948.

29. *AC*, 16 December 1947; Martin, *Atlanta*, 3:37; *Reporter*, 121.

30. *Reporter*, 130; Ralph McGill, "The 'Constitution' Story," *Saturday Review*, 8 June 1968, 69; *AC*, 24 June 1948; *AC*, 27 February 1948; *AC*, 3 January 1947; *Speak Now Against the Day*, 466, explains that separate and equal was a common plea at this time.

31. *AC*, 3 January 1947; see also *AC*, 4 January and 22 January 1948; *AC*, 24 June 1948.

32. One example is REM to E. A. Rogers, 4 November 1947, Box 66; *AC*, 22 January, 9 February, 19 June, 16 September, 10 December 1948.

33. *AC*, 26 February, 10 March 1949; McGill wrote to 3 Real Estate Commissioners and to Governor Talmadge 23 February 1949, Box 4. He also wrote a pamphlet, "The Housing Challenge," published by the Atlanta Housing Authority in May 1948, reprinted in *No Place*, 1:108-117; Ralph McGill, "She'll Talk Later," *Harper's*, October 1947, 365-369; Merle Miller to REM, 18 February 1948, Box 39.

34. *AC*, 16 September 1948; *AC*, 18 July 1948; *AC*, 1 March 1948; report of CBS radio broadcast, *AC*, 23 February 1948, *AC*, 22 January 1948.

35. *AC*, 1 March 1948; Gary M. Pomerantz, *Where Peachtree Meets Sweet Auburn: the Saga of Two Families and the Making of Atlanta* (New York: Scribner, 1996), 207-208; Jack Tarver interview; Gershon interview, *Southern Encounters*, 308.

36. Grace Hamilton interview transcript for "Dawn's Early Light," Box 110; Will Alexander to REM, 2 March 1948, Box 3; *AC*, 5 March 1948.

37. *AC*, 18 July 1948.

38. Dixon Preston interviews; *McCallie Alumni Journal*, July 1948, 3, 9; *McCallie Alumni Journal*, October 1948, 8; *AC*, 8 November 1949.

39. REM to Robert F. Hills, 26 February 1949, Box 4; memo for Robert W. Woodruff, 1 March 1951, Box 39, Woodruff papers, Emory; Ralph McGill Jr.-Harold Martin interview audiocassette, Box 102.

40. Lucille McGill Staley interviews; Mary Lou McGill to REM, n.d., Box 2; Dr. Joe Wilber interview.

41. *AC*, 13 February 1948; Jack Tarver interviews.

42. Lucy R. Mason to Hugh A. Brim, 18 April 1950, Box 7, Mason papers, Duke; *AC*, 13 August, 28 September 1948; *AC*, 24 November 1949; Gershon interview, *Southern Encounters*, 313; *Reporter*, 106, ix; Harold Fleming interview transcript for "Dawn's Early Light," Box 110; Ralph McGill Jr., interview transcript for "Dawn's Early Light," Box 111.

43. REM to Ralph McGill Jr., 14 January 1969, Box 2; much correspondence with *Saturday Evening Post* in Folder 9, Box 40 and Folder 17, Box 67; river book correspondence in Box 4 and in Folder 2, Box 29.

44. Ralph McGill, "Will the South Ditch Truman?," *Saturday Evening Post*, 22 May 1948, reprinted in *No Place*: 1:96-107; *AC*, 16 September 1948.

45. *AC*, 20 January, 3 March, 13 April, 16 July, 2 October 1948; REM to Donald S. Dawson, 15 September 1948, (wire), Official File, White House Central Files, Truman Library.

46. Matthew M. Warren to Edward Weeks, 29 August 1969, Box 108, recalls vigil on election night; *AC*, 3 November 1948; *AC*, 4 November 1948; REM to Harry S. Truman, 3 November 1948 (wire), President's Personal File, White House Central Files, Truman Library; *AC*, 21 January, 22 January 1949.

47. West's background in Anthony P. Dunbar, *Against the Grain: Southern Radicals and Prophets, 1929-1959.* (Charlottesville: University of Virginia Press, 1981); *AC*, 18 June, 27 June, 7 July, 5 August, 13 August, 28 September 1948; Lucy Mason was furious about McGill's Red baiting but admitted that West was at least a "Fellow Traveler" in Mason to Hugh A. Brim, 18 April 1950, Box 7, Mason papers, Duke; *Speak Now Against the Day*, 290, concluded that West "defied characterization" other than as a radical Christian; *AC*, 14 June, 16 June, 16 October 1949.

48. *AC*, 7 September, 10 September 1949; *Living Atlanta*, 341-344; *Regime Politics*, 29-30; Ralph McGill," Civil Rights For the Negro," *Atlantic*, November 1949, reprinted in *No Place*, 1:134-140.

CHAPTER 8:
"FLEAS COME WITH THE DOG": 1950-1956

1. Barrett Howell interviews; *AC*, 20 March 1949.

2. *AC*, 20 February, 26 February, 10 March 1949; *AC*, 12 April, 17 April 1949; *AC*, 10 September 1949; REM to Walter C. Johnson, 6 July 1949, Box 4.

3. Allen A. Long, "A Study of the *Atlanta Constitution* Before and After Its Consolidation," (Master's thesis, Emory University, 1952), 32-38. Hereafter cited as "Consolidation"; Jack Tarver interviews; Barrett Howell interviews.

4. *AC*, 1 June 1950; *Reporter*, 122.

5. "Merging the Elephants," *Time*, 27 March 1950, 47-49; "Synthesis in Atlanta," *Newsweek*, 27 March 1950; 59; Jonathan Daniels to Edward Weeks, 11 July 1969, Box 108; Jack Tarver interviews.

6. Millard B. Grimes, *The Last Linotype: The Story of Georgia and Its Newspapers Since World War II* (Macon: Mercer University Press, 1985), 80. Hereafter cited as *Linotype*; *Reporter*, 123.

7. REM to staff, 5 June 1950, quoted in "Consolidation," 56; Jack Tarver interviews; *Reporter*, 134; *Linotype*, 82; James M. Cox to REM, 18 January 1951, Box 51; file on Biggers in ANInc reference room; "Scare McGill," 52.

8. *Reporter*, 134; Gershon interview, *Southern Encounters*, 307; *AC*, 4 November 1947; *Reporter*, 120-121; Jack Tarver interview transcript for "Dawn's Early Light," Box 111; *AC*, 3 October 1948.

9. REM to Clark Howell, n.d. but shortly after merger, Box 4; "Consolidation," 48-49, 58; REM to James M. Cox Jr., 27 June 1950, Box 51.

10. REM to Mrs. Hervey Allen, 6 April 1950, Box 4; Ralph McGill, *Israel Revisited*, (Atlanta: Tupper & Love, 1950). Hereafter cited as *Israel Revisited*; correspondence about Chattahoochee book in Folder 2, Box 29.

11. REM to Mrs. Hervey Allen, 6 April 1950, Box 4; Ralph McGill, "George Armistead Smathers: Can He Purge Senator Pepper?," *Saturday Evening Post*, 22 April 1950, reprinted in *Southern Encounters*, 231-242; REM to Martin Sommers, 8 May 1950, Box 4.

12. *AC*, 29 September 1950; *AC*, 9 January 1951.

13. *AC*, 21 September 1950; *AC*, 20 February, 7 June, 9 June 1950.

14. *AC*, 14 December 1950.

15. *AC*, 14 July 1950, 19 May 1951; FBI files on McGill in Box 109; boasting about cooperation with FBI in REM to David Lawrence, 23 June 1953, Box 5.

16. Martin, *Atlanta*, 3:169-170; *Hartsfield*, 87; REM to William Howland, 29 June 1951, Box 4; hate mail in Folders 1 and 2, Box 57.

17. Dixon Preston interviews; *Reporter*, 208; "Scare McGill," 51; "Consolidation," 89.

18. *Linotype*, 80-81; Jack Tarver interviews; Barrett Howell interviews.

19. *Reporter*, 134-135; Jack Tarver interview transcript for "Dawn's Early Light," Box 111; REM to Ralph McGill Jr., 30 April 1968, Box 2; REM-Cal Logue interview, 29 December 1965, reprinted in *Editor & Publ*, 2:82.

20. All India columns, which ran between early December 1951 and early January 1952, are in Folder 2, Box 44; materials from trip in Folder 8, Box 80; *AC*, 21 November 1951; Chester Bowles to Harry S. Truman, 26 December 1951, President's Personal File, White House Central Files, Truman Library; REM to Chester Bowles, 13 February 1952, Box 5.

21. *AC*, 28 June, 3 July, 28 August, 29 August 1950; *AC*, 16 April, 20 September, 28 December 1950; *AC*, 25 April 1950; *AC*, 11 February 1950; *AC*, 7 January, 21 April 1950.

22. Dr. Joe Wilber interview; Lucille McGill Staley interviews; REM to Tom Chubb, 6 January 1953, Box 104; *AC*, 21 November 1951.

23. Jack Tarver interviews; REM to Barry Bingham, 29 September 1952, Box 5; REM to H. L. Williamson, 24 October 1952, Box 5; *Reporter*, 139.

24. Adlai E. Stevenson to REM, 10 November 1952, Box 5; REM to Adlai E. Stevenson, 19 November 1952, Box 5; Adlai E. Stevenson to REM, 1 December 1953, Box 5; Adlai E. Stevenson to REM, 11 May 1954, Box 5; Adlai E. Stevenson to REM, 5 November 1954, Box 5; Adlai E. Stevenson to REM, 20 February 1956, Box 6; REM to Adlai E. Stevenson, 21 March 1956, Box 6; Adlai E. Stevenson to REM 15 June 1956, Box 6; Adlai E. Stevenson to REM, 9 December 1958 and Adlai E. Stevenson, 13 December 1958, Box 7.

25. REM to Ralph Hayes, 13 November 1952, Box 5; REM to Dwight D. Eisenhower, 20 September 1957, Box 6; REM to Dwight D. Eisenhower, 21 August 1958, Box 7; REM to Dwight D. Eisenhower, 23 February 1959, Box 7; *AC*, 12 November 1953, 21 November 1953, 19 March 1954; *AC*, 16 June 1954, 4 November 1954.

26. REM to Bicknell Eubank, 16 January 1953, Box 5; Gerald O'Hara to REM, 17 November 1942, Box 5.

27. Grace Lundy Tackett interview transcript for "Dawn's Early Light," Box 111; examples of Lundy's reports during 1957 trip to Germany in Box 6.

28. REM to Bill Baggs, 7 October 1953, Box 5; see FBI reports on McGill in Box 109; REM to David Lawrence, 23 June 1953, Box 5; *AC*, 15 December 1956; REM to J. Edgar Hoover, 11 May 1953, Box 5; REM to J. Edgar Hoover, 9 October 1953, Box 5; REM to J. Edgar Hoover, 19 March 1954; Box 5, J. Edgar Hoover to REM, 26 March 1954, Box 5; J. Edgar Hoover to REM, 14 May 1954, Box 5; "Scare McGill," 51.

29. Carl Sandburg to REM, 14 March 1954, Box 23; Ralph McGill, "The Most Unforgettable Character I've Met," *Reader's Digest*, May 1954, 109-113, quoted in *Southern Encounters*, 35-40; Carl Sandburg to REM, 26 April 1954, Box 23.

30. Carl Sandburg to Atlanta Writers Club, 15 October 1956, Box 6; Ralph McGill Jr., interview; *Reporter*, 165; Gene Patterson quoted in Howell Raines, *My Soul Is Rested: Movement Days in the Deep South Remembered* (New York: G. Putnam's Sons, 1977), 368. Hereafter cited as *Soul Is Rested*.

31. *AC*, 2 and 11 December 1953; REM to Keeler McCartney, 1 May 1956 (memo), Box 6; Boxes 56 and 57 contain information on hate groups that McGill reminisced about in *AC*, 19 August 1961; exchanges with archenemy Roy Harris during summer 1954 in Folder 13, Box 5; *AC*, 9 April 1953.

32. *Hartsfield*, 100-101; Martin, *Atlanta*, 3:195-196; Richard Bardolph, *The Negro Vanguard* (New York: Rinehart & Co., 1959), 274; *AC*, 5 June 1953.

33. Celestine Sibley interview; Lucille McGill Staley interviews; *AC*, 18 February 1947; *Reporter*, 146.

34. *Israel Revisited*, 2,1; *Reporter*, 146; McGill always said he liked being an Episcopalian more than a Presbyterian. See REM to Marre Dangar, 27 May 1967, Box 16 and REM to Harry Ashmore, 15 December 1959, Box 9.

35. *Linotype*, 83; "Live With the Change," *Time*, 14 December 1953, 51; *AC*, 1, 2, 4, 5, 11 December 1953.

36. Rufus Clement to REM, 4 December 1953, Box 5; James Brawley to REM, 5 December 1953, Box 5; William Holmes Borders to REM, 8 December 1953, Box 5; Monroe D. Dowling to REM, 15 December 1953, Box 5; Ernest E. Neal to REM, 11 December 1953, Box 5; Adam Clayton Powell to REM, 15 December 1953, Box 5.

37. REM to Jack Tarver, 10 December 1953 (memo), enclosing letters, Box 5; Harold Fleming interview transcript for "Dawn's Early Light," Box 110; Gershon described his frustrations in "On the Fence," 115; Arthur Raper explained dilemmas of those with family obligations in Sosna interview transcript, Box 39, Raper papers.

38. Lonnie King interview transcript for "Dawn's Early Light," Box 111; Anne C. Loveland, *Lillian Smith: A Southerner Confronting the South* (Baton Rouge: Louisiana State University Press, 1986), 145; Aubrey Williams to REM, 9 December 1953, Box 5.

39. REM to James M. Cox, 15 June 1953, Box 51; REM to Charles H. Branch, 23 June 1953, Box 26; Adlai E. Stevenson to REM, 11 May 1954, Box 5; Ralph McGill, *The Fleas Come With the Dog* (Nashville: Abingdon Press, 1954); REM to Ruby Johnson, 26 March 1954, Box 26; REM to Pat Beaird, 17 November 1953, Box 26; plans for party in Folder 3, Box 26; Merrill Moore to REM, 26 May 1954, Box 26.

40. Charles H. Branch to REM, 12 June 1953, Box 26; Dwight D. Eisenhower to REM, 4 August 1954, Box 26; Dwight D. Eisenhower to REM, 13 May 1954, Box 5.

41. *S&S*, 19-20; REM to Earl Warren and other justices, 1 June 1955, Box 6; Felix Frankfurter to REM, 6 June 1955, Box 6; *Reporter*, 208; Gene Patterson interview; Arlie Schardt, "Crisis of the *Constitution*," *Nation*, 23 December 1968, 679-684. Hereafter cited as "Crisis of the *Constitution*; "*Speak Now Against the Day*, 616 and 625.

42. REM to Garland Porter, 22 November 1955, Box 6; REM to J. C. Mathews, 4 January 1954, Box 5; C. Vann Woodward, *Thinking Back: The Perils of Writing History* (Baton Rouge: Louisiana State University Press, 1986), 16, describes how fear of making "common cause with the Yankee South-baiters" inhibited many Southern leaders.

43. Ralph McGill Jr.-Harold Martin interview audiocassette, Box 102; Jack Tarver interviews; Charles Whipple, "Ralph McGill: Conscience of the South," *Boston Globe*, 18 June 1961.

44. Dixon Preston interviews; Ralph McGill Jr. interview transcript for "Dawn's Early Light," Box 111; Dr. Joe Wilber interviews; Lucille McGill Staley interviews; FBI investigations in Box 109 addressed couple's drinking and related hers to health problems. Noted that on an occasion in 1950 she became ill after one drink.

45. Ralph McGill Jr., interview transcript for "Dawn's Early Light," Box 111; Ralph McGill Jr.-Harold Martin interview audiocassette, Box 102; Charles Whipple, "Ralph McGill: Conscience of the South," *Boston Globe*, 18 June 1961; Dixon Preston interviews.

46. FBI investigations in Box 109 noted her driving him constantly with no accidents; Ralph McGill Jr.-Harold Martin interview audiocassette, Box 102.

47. Dixon Preston interviews; Grace Lundy Tackett interviews; *Reporter*, viii; *AC*, 22 September 1954.

48. *Reporter*, 167, 149-151, 240; Lyons lynching columns in *AC*, 2 December, 11 December, 12 December 1948, 25 January 1949; Gene Patterson interview.

49. REM to Everett Walker, 9 January 1956, Box 6; Drew Pearson to REM, 8 November 1956, Box 6; *AC*, 21 January 1958.

50. *AC*, 26 December 1955; REM to Roby Robinson, 17 April 1956, Box 6; Ralph McGill, "The Angry South," *Atlantic*, April 1956, reprinted in *No Place*, 1:227; "On the Fence," 114.

CHAPTER 9:
"A LITTLE LEFT OF CENTER": 1957-1961

1. For description of Daddy King, see Ralph McGill, "Martin Luther King Jr., 1929-1968," *Boston Globe*, 14 April 1968, reprinted in *Southern Encounters*, 69-74; *AC*, 14 January 1957; "Scare McGill," 51.

2. *AC*, 6 March, 21 March, 12 September 1957; REM to Charles J. Bloch, 11 October 1957, Box 6, "I am certainly not an integrationist." "I at no time have said . . . that I am happy over the Supreme Court decision," said REM to Garland Porter, 22 November 1955, Box 6; REM to Charles L. Goodson, 22 November 1957, Box 6, "We don't advocate integration." ". . . I was not, and am not, for desegregation," said REM to Charles J. Bloch, 24 February 1958.

3. *Atlanta: Triumph*, 259; *Hartsfield*, 118-119.

4. *AC*, 8 May 1957; REM to Jack Tarver, 20 May 1957, (memo), Box 6; REM to Roy J. Beard, 10 June 1957, Box 6; *AC*, 28 May 1957, summarizes Nelson's work; Jack Nelson interview transcript for "Dawn's Early Light," Box 111.

5. Data about trip in Folder 9, Box 6 and Folder 2, Box 80; *AC*, 17 July 1957; *AC*, 5-6 August 1957.

6. Grace Lundy to REM, 19 August 1957, Box 6; see Grace Lundy to REM, 20, 21, 23, 26 August 1957 and REM to Grace Lundy, 19 August 1957, Box 6.

7. *AC*, 10 September, 5 October, 8 November 1957.

8. *AC*, 23 September, 3 October 1957.

9. *AC*, 12 September, 2 October 1957; Ralph McGill, "The Southern Moderates Are Still There," *New York Times Magazine*, 21 September 1958, reprinted in *No Place*, 1:244-253.

10. *Promised Land*, 81; Jack Tarver interviews; see also *Reporter*, 134-135, 156.

11. See REM to James M. Cox Jr., 5 November 1957, enclosing Eisenhower letter, Box 6; McGill bolstered Tarver in REM to James M. Cox Jr., 15 November 1957, Boxes 51 and 6; on NANA syndication see Jack Tarver interview transcript for "Dawn's Early Light," Box 111, Folder 4, Box 40 and REM to Paul Miller, 13 June 1958, Box 7; McGill tried unsuccessfully to place his column earlier. See Ward Greene, King Features Syndicate, to REM, 1 June 1954, Box 5.

12. REM to Dwight D. Eisenhower, 20 September 1957, Box 6; REM to Dwight D. Eisenhower, 24 September 1957 (wire), Box 6; Dwight D. Eisenhower to REM, 9 October 1957, Ann Whitman Diary Series, Presidential Papers, Eisenhower Library; REM to William J. Miller, 26 October 1957, Box 6; Dwight D. Eisenhower to REM, 4 November 1957, Box 6; in Dwight D. Eisenhower to REM, 15 February 1960, Box 9, the President stated, "I so frequently find myself wanting to say, 'Hurrah,' after reading one of your pieces that I am in danger of becoming one of your most annoying fans."

13. REM to William B. Hartsfield, 1 November 1957, Box 6; more advice in memo for Hartsfield dictated to Lundy, 23 September 1957, Box 6.

14. REM to Wilber Forrest, 20 September 1957, Box 6; efforts to get Reid fellowship for Gordon in Folder 8, Box 6; Bill Gordon to REM, 15 December 1958, Box 7 tells about fellowship experience. Grace Hamilton discussed in REM to Clarence Faust, 13 June 1958, Box 7; see also Grace Hamilton interview transcript for "Dawn's Early Light," Box 110.

15. *AC*, 11 January, 6 May 1958; see also REM to Harry Ashmore, 7 April 1958, Box 7; REM to Ann Landers, 27 March 1959, Box 7; Harry Ashmore interview transcript for "Dawn's Early Light," Box 110; on Baggs see REM to Laurence Winship, 27 March 1959, Box 7; on group see Ralph McGill Jr., interview transcript for "Dawn's Early Light," Box 111 and John Griffin interviews.

16. REM to Harry Ashmore, 3 March 1958, Box 7; REM to Chester Bowles, 13 February 1952, Box 5; *AC*, 6 May 1958.

17. REM to Owen M. Conrad, 20 September 1957, Box 6 and REM to Walker Garrott, 15 May 1958, Box 7; REM to Harry Golden, 6 January 1958, Box 7; Gene Patterson interview; Harry Ashmore to Carleton Kent, 20 March 1959, Box 7.

18. *AC*, 28 January, 17 April, 11 December 1958.

19. Jack Tarver to Robert M. Hall, 3 April 1961, Box 39; Jim Townsend, "McGill," *Atlanta Magazine*, November 1962, 43; "It's Constitutional," *Newsweek*, 13 April 1959, 103; Rufus E. Clement to REM, 5 November 1957, Box 6; J. H. Calhoon to REM, 10 October 1957, Box 6; Lucille McGill Staley interviews; Gershon interview, *Southern Encounters*, 305.

20. Ralph McGill, "The Southern Moderates Are Still There," *New York Times Magazine*, 21 September 1958, reprinted in *No Place*, 1:244-253; response to article discussed in REM to Lester Markel, 10 October 1958, Box 7; Ralph McGill, "If the Southern Negro Got the Vote," *New York Times Magazine*, 21 June 1959, reprinted in *No Place*, 1:274-281; Ralph McGill, "The Agony of the

Southern Minister," *New York Times Magazine*, 27 September 1959, reprinted in *No Place*, 1:289-297.

21. Alan Gould, Notes on Ralph McGill, Box 28, HM papers; *AC*, 28 May 1958; *AC*, 1 November 1958, 14 April 1959 and Bill Gordon to REM, 15 December 1958, Box 7.

22. On their friendship see Janice Rothschild Blumberg, *One Voice: Rabbi Jacob M. Rothschild and the Troubled South* (Macon: Mercer University Press, 1985), 133, 134, 210; *AC*, 14 October 1958; Melissa Fay Greene, *The Temple Bombing* (Reading, Mass: Addison-Wesley, 1996), 257, 279, describes how white supremacists linked McGill with Jews.

23. Grace Lundy Tackett interviews.

24. *AC*, 13 October 1958; *AC*, 14 October 1958; *AC*, 16 October 1958; Grace Lundy Tackett interviews; reader response in Folder 5, Box 7; REM to T. T. Scott, 17 October 1958, Box 7.

25. *AC*, 16 September 1957; REM to Robert W. Woodruff, 26 September 1958, Box 7; for more on closing schools see *Modern Georgia*, 191-195; great response of HOPE audience to McGill recalled in Gershon interview, *Southern Encounters*, 304-305, and in Harlee Branch III, to REM, 22 August 1963, Box 12; *AC*, 1 June 1959.

26. *AC*, 3 April 1959; "Scare McGill," 52; more on anniversary in "It's Constitutional," *Newsweek*, 13 April 1959, 102-103.

27. *AC*, 28 March 1959; *AC*, 2 January 1959; *AC*, 5 May 1959; *New York Times*, 5 May 1959, 32; feud described in *Reporter* 106-107.

28. John Griffin interview transcript for "Dawn's Early Light," Box 110.

29. *AC*, 25 July 1959; REM to James Reston, 23 June 1959, Box 9; trip consumed three weeks of columns that the Vice-President praised in Richard M. Nixon to REM, 4 September 1959, Box 9.

30. See Richard M. Nixon to REM, 9 January 1957, Box 6; Richard M. Nixon to REM, 5 June 1957, Box 6; Richard M. Nixon to REM, 27 August 1957, Box 6.

31. Stephen B. Oates, *Let The Trumpet Sound: the Life of Martin Luther King Jr.* (New York: New American Library, 1982), 145-151, explains his return. Hereafter cited as *Trumpet Sound*; for McGill on King see Ralph McGill, "Martin Luther King Jr., 1929-1968," *Boston Globe*, 14 April 1968, reprinted in *Southern Encounters*, 69-74; REM to Harry Ashmore, 15 December 1959, Box 9.

32. John Virden to Mel Ryder, 5 February 1960, Box 9; a Louisiana minister declared as had others, "There is not one drop of Southern blood in your Godless veins." H.T. Isgitt to REM, 11 January 1960, Box 9; federal advocacy in *AC*, 28 January, 9 May, 31 May, 24 August, 14 October 1958; also Ralph McGill, "If the Southern Negro Got the Vote," *New York Times Magazine*, 21 June 1959, reprinted in *No Place*, 1:274-282; *AC*, 12 February 1958.

33. Ralph McGill, "The Meaning of Lincoln Today," reprinted in *Editor & Publ*, 2:153-167 and in *Vital Speeches of the Day*, 15 March 1960, 328-332; the

President praised the speech in Dwight D. Eisenhower to REM, 15 February 1960, Box 9.

34. For more on his speaking engagements see Folders 41 and 42, Box 78; *Reporter*, 164; "Scare McGill," 52.

35. REM to Ralph de Toledano, 4 March 1960, Box 9; *AC*, 16 March 1960.

36. Dr. Joe Wilber interview explained both clinical details and how the couple handled her final illness; REM to Harold Martin, 23 February 1960, Box 9.

37. Ralph McGill Jr.-Harold Martin interview audiocassette, Box 102; REM to Mrs. J. B. Jones, 25 August 1959, Box 9; REM to Robert Bizinsky, 31 May 1960, Box 28, HM papers; REM to Robert W. Woodruff, 2 September 1960, Box 10; Grace Lundy to REM, 24 June 1960, Box 10; REM to Jack Tarver, 8 June 1961, Box 10.

38. REM to Jim Hagerty and Herb Klein, 4 May 1960 (wires), Box 9, informing Eisenhower and Nixon. Both responded. See Dwight D. Eisenhower to REM, 6 May 1960, and Richard M. Nixon to REM, 11 May 1960, Box 9; *Reporter*, 163-164, 166; REM to Brainard Cheney, 16 June 1960, Box 6, Cheney papers, Vanderbilt; Harry Ashmore to REM, 15 August 1960, Box 10; McGill constantly praised Tarver's work at ANInc. In REM to O. M. Tarver, 22 March 1960, Box 9, he said Tarver was "the outstanding young newspaper executive in the country."

39. Grace Hamilton interview transcript for "Dawn's Early Light," Box 110; Benjamin Mays, Notes on McGill, Box 24, HM papers; REM to Sam W. Drinkard, 16 January 1961, Box 10; REM to Dan Lanier, 17 January 1961, Box 10; *AC*, 14 May 1960; see also *AC*, 31 May, 5 November, 13 December 1960 and 5 January, 17 January, 26 January, 4 February, 23 February 1961.

40. *AC*, 18 May 1960; Ralph McGill, "The State of the South, 1960," *ADL Bulletin*, May 1960, reprinted in *No Place*, 2:327; Ralph McGill, "A View From A Tight Small Compartment," Harvard University Law School address, 14 June 1961, reprinted in *Editor & Publ*, 1:227. Hereafter cited as Harvard address, *Editor & Publ*.

41. REM to Miss Daisy Dean, 28 March 1960, Box 10; REM to Ken Whitaker, 31 August 1959, Box 9; REM to Mrs. Ken Whitaker, 17 May 1960, Box 9; more on NATO trip in Folder 1, Box 10 and Box 81; REM to Philip Coombs, 3 August 1960, Box 10.

42. REM to Adlai E. Stevenson, 31 May 1960, Box 9; *AC*, 18 July, 17 October, 20 October, 22 October 1960; for at least two years McGill opposed Kennedy's candidacy. See REM to Ralph Hayes, 1 August 1958, Box 7.

43. *AC*, 20 October, 28 October 1960; Lonnie King recalls in *Soul Is Rested*, 90-91; see also David J. Garrow, *Bearing the Cross: Martin Luther King Jr. and the Southern Christian Leadership Conference* (New York: William Morrow, 1986), 142-149. Hereafter cited as *Bearing the Cross*; *AC*, 5 November 1960.

44. Ralph McGill Jr., interview transcript for "Dawn's Early Light," Box 111.

45. *AC*, 12 November 1960; *Atlanta: Triumph*, 265; REM to Richard M. Nixon, 9 November 1960 (wire), Box 10; *AC*, 9 November 1960.

46. *AC*, 13 December 1960; for more on incident and McGill's reaction see "The Darkness Within," *Newsweek*, 26 December 1960, 54.

47. McGill gave his version of the crisis in unpublished article included in *No Place*, 2:347-353 and in Harvard address, *Editor & Publ*, 1:223-233; see also *AC*, 10 January, 11 January, 12 January, 13 January, 14 January, 15 January 1961; booklength version of crisis is Calvin Trillin, *An Education in Georgia: the Integration of Charlayne Hunter and Hamilton Holmes* (New York: Viking Press, 1964).

48. REM to Ralph McGill Jr., 18 January 1961; John Griffin interviews; Ralph McGill Jr.-Harold Martin interview audiocassette, Box 102; REM to Robert W. Woodruff, 2 September 1960, Box 10; REM to Walker Garrott, 15 May 1958, Box 7; REM to Clay Blair, 25 June 1959, Box 9; REM to Mrs. J. B. Jones, 25 August 1959, Box 9.

CHAPTER 10:
"BLACK WING OF A GHOSTLY BIRD": 1961-1964

1. REM to Robert M. Hall, 30 January 1961, Box 39; details of these honors in Folder 5, Box 10; David Potter to REM, 12 February 1961, Box 10, describes his impact at Yale; Jack Tarver interviews.

2. Record of appointment in Name File, White House Central Files, John F. Kennedy Papers as President, Kennedy Library and in *New York Times*, 17 February, 1; L. A. Putnam to REM, 4 April 1961, Box 10.

3. More on harrassment in FBI reports, Box 109 and in Charles Whipple, "Ralph McGill: Conscience of the South," *Boston Globe*, 18 June 1961; William Emerson interview transcript for "Dawn's Early Light," Box 110.

4. *AC*, 18 April, 21 April, 3 May, 16 June 1961; Dwight D. Eisenhower to "Bob," 3 January 1961, quoted in Stephen Ambrose, *Eisenhower*, 2 vols. (New York: Simon & Schuster, 1983), 2:606; *AC*, 24 January, 16 February, 11 March, 29 April 1961; *AC*, 25 March, 26 April, 3 May 1961.

5. Ralph McGill, "Birmingham Rotary Club Address," 17 May 1961, reprinted in *Editor & Publ*, 1:212-222; REM to Harry Ashmore, 18 May 1961, Box 10.

6. REM to Harry Ashmore, 10 April 1961, Box 10; Peter Davison to REM, 21 July 1959, Box 27; for Lundy's role see Edward Weeks to REM, 7 December 1961 and REM to Edward Weeks, 11 December 1961, both in Box 27.

7. Grace Lundy to Laurence Winship, 7 February 1961, Box 10; Charles Whipple, "Ralph McGill: Conscience of the South," *Boston Globe*, 18 June 1961; REM to Charles L. Whipple, 30 May 1961, Box 10.

8. Details of trip in Folder 4, Box 80 and in REM to Jack Tarver, 8 June 1961, Box 10; Harvard address, *Editor & Publ*, 1:225, 227.

9. Clipping in Folder 4, Box 80; *Reporter*, 181.

10. Martin, *Atlanta*, 3:326-328; *Hartsfield*, 152-154; Herbert T. Jenkins, *Keeping the Peace: A Police Chief Looks at His Job* (New York: Harper & Row, 1970), 54-59. Hereafter cited as *Keeping the Peace*; Lincoln Rockwell to REM, 24 August 1961 (wire), Box 10; REM to Walter Burket, 9 October 1961, Box 11.

11. *AC*, 12 September 1961; *AC*, 27 September 1961; *AC*, 6 September 1961.

12. REM to Harold Martin, 25 August 1961, Box 10; REM to Bill Baggs, 28 August 1961, Box 10; REM to Ralph McGill Jr., 29 August 1961, Box 2; REM to Robert M. G. Libby, 2 October 1961, Box 11.

13. REM to Mike Mahoney, 20 October 1961, Box 11; Grace Lundy to Otto Zausmer, 13 October 1961, Box 11; *AC*, 25 September, 20 September, 23 September 1961; REM to John Virden, 16 October 1961, Box 11.

14. REM to Mike Mahoney, 2 August 1961, Box 10 describes White House lunch with prime minister of Nigeria; another luncheon on 7 February 1963 noted in Name File, White House Central Files, Kennedy Library; William C. Foster to REM, 2 November 1961, Box 72; *Reporter*, 202; REM to Jack Tarver and Gene Patterson, 16 February 1961 (memo), Box 10; REM to Otto Zausmer, 6 March 1961, Box 10; REM to John Seigenthaler, 14 November 1961, Box 36, General Correspondence, Robert F. Kennedy Papers as Attorney-General, Kennedy Library.

15. Weeks correspondence in folder 1, Box 27; *AC*, 10 February, 15 November 1961.

16. Robert M. G. Libby notes, Box 28, HM papers; Grace Lundy Tackett interview transcript for "Dawn's Early Light," Box 111; REM to Laurence Winship, 28 February 1962, Box 11.

17. REM to Laurence Winship, 15 March 1962, Box 11; obituary and Gene Patterson's tribute in McGill's column space, *AC*, 22 March 1962; REM to Bill Baggs, 29 March 1962, Box 11; Ralph McGill Jr.- Harold Martin interview audiocassette, Box 102.

18. William Emerson interview transcript for "Dawn's Early Light," Box 110; condolence messages in Box 1; REM to George and Georgia Leckie, 10 May 1962, Box 11; REM to Bill Baggs, 29 March 1962, Box 11; REM to Laurence Winship, 7 June 1962, Box 11.

19. Ralph McGill Jr., interview transcript for "Dawn's Early Light," Box 111; REM to Harry Ashmore, Jack Tarver, Bill Baggs, Gene Patterson, 25 May 1962, Box 11; REM to Laurence Winship, 7 June 1962, Box 11.

20. REM to Laurence Winship, 7 June 1962, Box 11; *S&S*, 105, 100, 105; *S&S*, 107-108 has errors about the campaign and McGill's reporting. see *NB*, 17 October-6 November 1922.

21. REM to Laurence Winship, 7 June 1962, Box 11; more on trip in folders 10 and 11, Box 80.

22. *AC*, 7 August 1962; REM to Grace Lundy, 27 July 1962, Box 11; *Reporter*, 184; *AC*, 8 August 1962; more on climb in REM to Adlai E. Stevenson, 20 August

and 25 August 1962, Box 11 and in REM to Tom Chubb, 26 January 1963, Box 12.

23. *AC*, 3 August 1962; *AC*, 5 September 1962; *AC*, 14 September 1962; *AC*, 2 October 1962.

24. *AC*, 25 October 1962; *AC*, 2 November 1962; McGill praised administration's handling of crisis. see REM to John F. Kennedy, 26 October 1962 and REM to McGeorge Bundy, 12 November 1962, both Box 11.

25. Graham Jackson to REM, n.d., folder 6, Box 1; Ralph McGill, "Little Woman, Big Book: the Mysterious Margaret Mitchell," *Show*, October 1962, reprinted in *Southern Encounters*, 41-49.

26. *AC*, 7 December 1962.

27. Columns on Africa appeared in *Constitution* between 13 February and 22 March 1963; details about trip in folders 1 and 2, Box 78 and in REM to Grace Lundy, 21 February 1963, Box 12.

28. Mark B. Lewis to Edward Weeks, 4 August 1969, Box 28, HM papers; William E. Jones to Edward Weeks, 16 September 1969, Box 28, HM papers; Cozy Cole recalled in *AC*, 21 February 1964; REM to Mohamed N'Diage, 14 March 1963, Box 12.

29. Grace Lundy to REM, 1 March 1963 (wire), Box 12; William Downs to REM, 30 March 1963, Box 12; Robert Penn Warren to REM, 6 May and 7 May 1963, Box 12; Becky Warren to REM, 25 May 1963, Box 12; Mary Benson Scheib to REM, 10 July 1963, Box 12; Mary Daniel Whitney to REM, 22 July 1963, Box 12.

30. REM to Laurence Winship, 25 July 1963, Box 12; REM to Brainard Cheney, 25 October 1963, Box 6, Cheney papers, Vanderbilt.

31. Ralph McGill, "The South Looks Ahead," *Ebony*, September 1963, reprinted in *No Place*, 2:436-443; Radio "Conversation Piece," reprinted in *No Place*, 2:444-468; *Mayor*, 104-110; REM to Ivan Allen Jr., 30 July 1963, Box 12; *AC*, 10 July 1963; *AC*, 13 July 1963.

32. *AC*, 29 August 1963; *AC*, 16 October 1964.

33. *AC*, 17 September, 18 September 1963.

34. REM to Brainard Cheney, 25 October 1963, Box 6, Cheney papers, Vanderbilt; REM to John Virden, 23 July 1963, Box 12; *AC*, 17 July 1963; *AC*, 27 July 1963; John Griffin interviews; Julia James Crawford interview notes, Box 28, HM papers; Dr. Joe Wilber interview revealed McGill asked doctor to check him in July.

35. See Hatch-McGill interview transcript in *No Place*, 2:423-425, 430; REM to Randolph Claiborne, 5 August 1963, Box 12; *AC*, 2 October 1963; "Episcopal Diocese Censors McGill," *Christian Century*, 16 October 1963, 1260.

36. Malcolm Bryan to REM, 4 October 1963, Box 12; REM to Robert W. Woodruff, 6 September 1960, Box 10; REM to Mrs. J. B. Jones, 25 August 1959, Box 9; draft of new religion book sent by Grace Lundy to Edward Weeks, 12 February 1969, Box 26; "Washington H.S.," *Editor & Publ*, 2:503; *AC*, 3 November 1963 and 10 April 1964; typical reaction in Billy James Hargis to

REM, 9 September 1963, Box 12, "Your name is a curse word among the pro-American patriot Christians throughout the U.S."

37. REM to Harry Ashmore, 3 September 1963, Box 13; Jack Tarver interviews; REM to Laurence Winship, 18 October 1963, Box 13.

38. "Ralph McGill, A Memory," *Tennessee Register*, 14 February 1969, in family records; Gene Patterson interview; *AC*, 23 November 1963; Ralph McGill, "Hate Knows No Direction," *Saturday Evening Post*, 14 December 1963, reprinted in *No Place*, 2:471,470.

39. Carl Sandburg to REM, 7 December 1960, Box 23; *AC*, 22 March 1962; Jesse Outlar, "Ralph McGill's Paper," *AC*, 5 February 1969.

40. Correspondence in both McGill and Johnson papers goes back to 1955; Lyndon B. Johnson to REM, 29 November 1963, Name File, White House Central Files, Presidential Papers, Lyndon Baines Johnson Library; *AC*, 14 December 1963.

41. *AC*, 1 January 1964; *AC*, 14 February 1964.

42. REM to Brainard Cheney, 25 October 1963, Box 6, Cheney papers, Vanderbilt; REM to William Attwood, 20 May 1964, Box 13; REM to Tom Chubb, 9 July 1964, Box 14.

43. For background of Tonkin Gulf resolution see Stanley Karnow, *Vietnam: A History* (New York: Penguin Books, 1984), 365-376. Hereafter cited as *Vietnam*; *AC*, 6 August, 7 August, 21 August, 11 September, 10 November, 11 December, 12 December 1964.

44. Gershon interview, *Southern Encounters*, 313; *Reporter*, 213-214; Grace Lundy Tackett interviews; Jack Tarver interviews.

CHAPTER 11:
"NEVER GET TOO WISE TO USE YOUR LEGS": 1964-1967

1. *AC*, 25 March 1964; REM to Robert F. Kennedy, 13 March 1964, Box 13; REM to William Attwood, 20 May 1964, Box 13; *AC*, 25 April 1964; *AC*, 2 July 1964; RFK columns, *AC*, 2, 6, 8, 9 September 1964; more on RFK and REM in *Reporter*, 264 and Box 36, General Correspondence, Robert F. Kennedy papers as Attorney-General, John F. Kennedy Library.

2. *AC*, 21 July, 1 August, 1 September, 3 November 1964; REM to Lyndon B. Johnson, 5 May 1964, Box 59; REM to Lyndon B. Johnson, 21 October 1964, Name File, White House Central Files, Johnson Library; Ralph McGill, "From Atlanta: the Political Assessment 1964," *New York Herald Tribune*, 27 September 1964, reprinted in *No Place*, 2:497-502. Hereafter cited as "Political Assessment," *No Place*; *AC*, 14 January, 29 February, 3 March, 12 March, 1 August, 20 August, 7 October, 2 November, 3 November 1964; Jack Tarver interview transcript for "Dawn's Early Light," Box 111.

3. REM to John Seigenthaler, 21 November 1961, Box 36, Robert F. Kennedy Papers as Attorney-General, Kennedy Library; "Political Assessment,"

No Place, 2:502; Grace Lundy Tackett interviews emphasized how much he hoped and worked for viable Republican party in South.

4. *AC*, 17 April 1964; *AC*, 18 February 1964; *AC*, 8 February 1964; REM to Lowell McMichen, 24 March 1965, Box 14.

5. Lyndon B. Johnson to REM, 11 November 1964 and Lyndon B. Johnson to REM, 13 November 1964, Name File, White House Central Files, Johnson Library; *AC*, 2 November, 3 November, 4 November 1964.

6. REM to Jacob M. Rothschild, 13 November 1964, Box 14; REM to Granger Hansell, 6 January 1965, Box 14; Gene Patterson interview; Helen Bullard recalled problems in *Soul Is Rested*, 412; See also *New York Times*, 29 December 1964, p. 1; 30 December 1964, p. 28; 31 December 1964, p. 11; *Life Magazine*, 12 February 1965, p. 4, singled out McGill as one who fought hard for the dinner.

7. Dr. Joe Wilber interview; Grace Lundy Tackett interviews; Ralph McGill Jr.-Harold Martin interview audiocassette, Box 102.

8. For background of King in Selma see *Trumpet Sound*, 325-330, 334-339 and *Bearing the Cross*, 369-392; for voting see "Washington H.S.," *Editor & Publ*, 2:503 and Ralph McGill," A Decade of Slow, Painful Progress, 1964," *Saturday Review*, 16 May 1964, reprinted in *No Place*, 2:477-481; REM to Calvin Mayne, 4 March 1965, Box 14.

9. *Reporter*, 208-209; Gene Patterson interview.

10. REM to William Attwood, 8 January 1965, Box 14; REM to Edward Weeks, 18 January 1965, Box 14; REM to Laurence Winship, 17 May 1965, Box 14.

11. Mary Lynn Morgan interviews; Sibley, "Ralph McGill."

12. *AC*, 26 April 1965; *AC*, 28 May 1965; Name file of White House Central Files, Johnson Library includes even more letters than survive in McGill papers.

13. Jack Valenti-Lyndon B. Johnson, 20 May 1965, (memo dictated by REM), Name file, White House Central Files, Johnson Library; for more on LBJ and widening war see *Vietnam*, 411-426; *AC*, 7 June, 22 June, 29 June, 22 July, 28 August, 25 October 1965.

14. Gene Patterson interview; *AC*, 21 December 1964; REM to Laurence Winship, 17 May 1965, Box 14; Lucille McGill Staley interviews; Jack Tarver interviews.

15. REM to James H. Taylor Jr., 15 April 1965, Box 14; REM to Mrs. Herman Stotz, 3 June 1965, Box 14; *AC*, 15 November, 19 November 1965; for typical story of McGill helping a student see Carl Holman interview transcript for "Dawn's Early Light," Box 110.

16. REM to Walter Johnson, 14 June 1966, Box 15; Adlai E. Stevenson III, to REM, 10 November 1965, Box 15.

17. *Reporter*, 214-215; REM to Ann Landers, 12 April 1965, Box 14.

18. Mary Lynn Morgan interviews.

19. Lucille McGill Staley interviews; Virginia Staley Bigelow interviews; REM to James Reston, 12 July 1965, Box 14; REM to Harry Ashmore, 13 December 1965, Box 15; REM to John Martin, 5 January 1966, Box 15.

20. Mary Lynn Morgan interviews.

21. REM to Dean Rusk, 21 December 1965, Box 15; Dow Kirkpatrick to REM 16 February 1966, Box 15; REM to Dow Kirkpatrick, 18 February 1966, Box 15.

22. *AC*, 18 June, 18 August, 1 July, 5 August 1965; REM to Ivan Allen Jr., 22 September 1965, Box 15; see also Virginia H. Hein, "The Image of 'A City Too Busy to Hate': Atlanta in the 1960s," *Phylon* 33 (Fall 1972): 205-221 and Ronald H. Bayor, *Race and the Shaping of Twentieth Century Atlanta* (Chapel Hill: University of North Carolina Press, 1996), 138-143, that place these problems in the long-term context of racially biased policies.

23. *Mayor*, 158-160; *Atlanta: Triumph*, 282; *Atlanta Rising*, 131, 149-50; *AC*, 12 April 1966; *AC*, 19 July 1966.

24. For background see Stokely Carmichael & Charles V. Hamilton, *Black Power: The Politics of Liberation in America* (New York: Vintage Books, 1967); REM to Jack Valenti, 31 March 1966, Box 59; *AC*, 25 August 1966; *AC*, 7 July 1966.

25. Mary Lynn Morgan interviews; Lucille McGill Staley interviews; Virginia Staley Bigelow interviews; condolence messages in folder 4, Box 2.

26. *Keeping the Peace*, 88-90; *Mayor*, 180-190; *AC*, 8 September 1966; Hughes Spalding to REM, 8 September 1966, Box 16; see folder 10, Box 25.

27. Details of trip in folder 17, Box 82 and folders 7, 8, 9, Box 95; Earl Yates to Grace Lundy, 22 September 1966, Box 16; *AC*, 11 October 1966.

28. REM to Lyndon B. Johnson, 4 November 1966, Box 59.

29. For details see *Lester Maddox*; REM to Ellis Arnall, 25 May 1966, Box 15; REM to Lyndon B. Johnson, 4 November 1966, Box 59.

30. REM to Nancy Mason, 17 June 1966, Box 15; REM to Laurence Winship, 12 September 1966, Box 16; REM to Joe Jones, 14 September 1966, Box 2; REM to Laurence Winship, 25 November 1966, Box 16; see letters in folders 1 & 2, Box 2.

31. Harry Ashmore and William C. Baggs, *Mission to Hanoi: A Chronicle of Double-Dealing in High Places* (New York: Putnam Berkley Publishing Group, 1968); REM to Jack Tarver, 19 January 1967, Box 16; *AC*, 24 January, 11 February 1967; Hubert H. Humphrey to Lyndon B. Johnson, 11 February 1967, Name File, White House Central Files, Johnson Library; REM to Jack Tarver *et. al.*, 27 January 1967, Box 16; Jack Tarver interviews; Gene Patterson interview.

32. REM to Jack Tarver, 19 January 1967, Box 16; McGill had written to Dean Rusk and said he wished to talk while he was in Washington. see REM to Dean Rusk, 17 January 1967, Box 16; REM to W. Robert Walton, 23 February 1967, Box 39.

33. *Reporter*, 223; REM to Mary Lynn Morgan, 26 February 1967, Box 2; Mary Lynn Morgan to Louise Stevens King, 12 January 1974, Box 104; Sibley, "Ralph McGill."

34. Details about Africa trip in folders 3 & 4, Box 78; also folder 7, Box 2 and folder 7, Box 16; William L. Jones to Edward Weeks, 14 September 1969, Box 28, HM papers; *AC*, 23 March, 3 April, 17 April 1967.

35. *AC*, 24 March 1967; REM to Franklin Williams, 5 April 1967, Box 16; *AC*, 10 April 1967.

CHAPTER 12:
"ONE MORE RIVER TO CROSS": 1967-1969

1. *AC*, 19 April 1967; *Reporter*, 230-231; Dr. Joe Wilber interview.

2. REM to Lyndon B. Johnson, 7 September 1967, Box 59; John Hohenberg, *The Pulitzer Prize Story, II* (New York: Columbia University Press, 1980), 276-277; *AC*, 10 January, 11 January 1966; in Martin L. King Jr. to REM, 11 May 1967, Box 16, King appealed for "an informal, off-the-record talk" about the war.

3. Dr. Joe Wilber interview; Mary Lynn Morgan interviews.

4. *AC*, 20 June, 21 June, 22 June 1967; see also *Keeping the Peace*, 91-93; *AC*, 17 June, 7 July, 21 July 1967; McGill devoted most of his August columns to urban poverty and violence; *AC*, 31 July 1967.

5. REM to Harry Ashmore *et. al.*, 27 July 1967, Box 17, describes the service; see also *AC*, 24 July, 25 July 1967; Martin aptly described McGill's disposition, "And for all his great bulk and his seeming calm, he seethed inwardly, as restless as a captive elephant stamping and swaying in his chains." *Reporter*, 205; photo in *Southern Encounters*, 318.

6. St. John quoted in folder 12, Box 42; Dr. Joe Wilber interview; REM to George Christian, 22 August 1967 (phone dictation), Box 59 and other messages in Name File, White House Central Files, Johnson Library; Jack Tarver to Bill Baggs *et. al.*, 24 August 1967, Box 17.

7. Dr. Joe Wilber interview; REM to Lyndon B. Johnson, 7 September 1967, Box 59; Lyndon B. Johnson to REM, 13 September 1967, Box 59; *AC*, 6 November, 30 November 1967; REM to Gerald C. Lukenow, 17 November 1967, Box 17; REM to Helen and Mac Morgan, 27 October 1967, Box 2; Lyndon B. Johnson to REM, 8 December 1967, Name File, White House Central Files, Johnson Library.

8. REM to Harry Ashmore, 17 October 1967, Box 17; see also REM to James M. Cox Jr., 6 November 1967, Box 51 and REM to Harry Ashmore, 6 November 1967, Box 17; *AC*, 19 December 1967.

9. REM to Gerald C. Lukenow, 17 November 1967, Box 17; REM to Joe Cumming, 17 November 1967, Box 17, *Reporter* 237-240; Gene Patterson interview; Mary Lynn Morgan interviews.

10. *Constitution* centennial plans in folder 9, Box 44 and REM to Donald O. Rhodes, 3 January 1968, Box 18; REM to Edward Weeks, 14 September 1967,

Box 17; REM to Mike Davies, 28 September 1967 and REM to Mike Davies, 2 October 1967, Box 17; Patterson quoted in *Soul Is Rested*, 367; Gene Patterson interview.

11. Ralph McGill, "The South's Glowing Horizon—If . . . 1968," *Saturday Review*, 9 March 1968, reprinted in *No Place*, 2:593-604; Ralph McGill, US Information Agency Broadcast transcript in *No Place*, 2:589; *AC*, 22 January, 4 March, 19 May 1968.

12. *AC*, 19 December 1967; *AC*, 8 March 1968; *AC*, 29 September 1967; *AC*, 26 May 1967; REM to Donald O. Rhodes, 3 January 1968, Box 18; REM to Harry Ashmore, 6 November 1967, Box 17; REM to Bill Baggs, 15 December 1967 and REM to Bill Baggs, 28 December 1967, Box 17; REM to Bill Baggs, 12 January 1968, Box 18; Lyndon B. Johnson to REM, 8 December 1967, Name File, White House Central Files, Johnson Library; appointed to Human Rights Commission and invited to White House dinner for President of Tunisia in May 1968.

13. Dr. Joe Wilber interview; for Arms Control committee work see folder 17, Box 72 and letter to Senators urging ratification of treaty, 31 January 1968, Box 18; REM to staff, 3 April 1968, (memo), Box 18.

14. *AC*, 5 April, 6 April 1968; Richard M. Nixon to REM, 18 April 1968, Box 19; *AC*, 2 April 1968; REM to Willard Beeson, 18 April 1968, Box 19.

15. REM to Mrs. Benjamin Alsop, 9 November 1967, Box 17; letters to Ralph McGill Jr., folders 1 & 2, Box 2; REM to Jack Tarver, 23 April 1968, Box 19; *AC*, 29 April 1968; *AC*, 18 May 1968.

16. Lyndon B. Johnson to Ralph E. McGill III, 6 May 1968, Name File, White House Central Files, Johnson Library; REM to Lyndon B. Johnson, 13 April 1968, Box 59; REM to Frank Ross, 26 March 1968, Box 18; *AC*, 9 May 1968.

17. McGill-Humphrey correspondence mostly in folder 16, Box 57; REM to Roy Reed, 17 April 1968, Box 19; *AC*, 21 May 1968; REM to Harry Ashmore, 13 March 1968, Box 18; REM to Frank Ross, 26 March 1968, Box 18; *AC*, 20 March, 22 March, 11 May, 16 May 1968.

18. *AC*, 2 May, 17 April, 14 June 1968; Ralph McGill, "George Wallace: Tradition of Demagoguery," *Los Angeles Times*, 11 December 1967, reprinted in *Southern Encounters*, 277-285.

19. *AC*, 7 June, 18 June 1968; Edward M. Kennedy to REM, 26 July 1968, Box 19; RFK's papers as Attorney-General, Box 36, Kennedy Library, include many McGill messages not at Emory.

20. Ralph McGill, "The 'Constitution' Story," *Saturday Review*, 8 June 1968, 66-69, 77; Lyndon B. Johnson to REM 12 June 1968, Name File, White House Central Files, Johnson Library.

21. *AC*, 18 July, 19 July 1968; details of USSR trip in folder 22, Box 81.

22. REM to Helen Morgan, 23 July 1968, Box 2; REM to Helen Morgan, December 1967, Box 2.

23. *AC*, 16 August 1968; REM to Judy Gebre-Hiwet, 15 August 1968, Box 19; *AC*, 9 August 1968; *AC*, 6 September 1968, *AC*, 30 August 1968; McGill said more about Chicago events in interviews for *Atlanta Magazine*, February 1969, reprinted in *No Place*, 2:648-659.

24. *AC*, 26 September, 28 September 1968; interviews for *Atlanta Magazine*, *No Place* 2:648-659; for national media coverage of turmoil see *New York Times*, 26 September 1968, 21; 27 September 1968, 50; 28 September 1968, 68.

25. REM to Sissy Tarver Jason, 2 October 1968, Box 20; REM to Roy Reed, 17 April 1968, Box 19; Jack Tarver interviews; Gene Patterson interview; "Crisis of the *Constitution*," 679-684; REM to Tom Johnson, 27 September 1968, Name File, White House Central Files, Johnson Library, *AC*, 29 September 1968.

26. *Reporter*, 243; REM to Ida Pharr, 19 April 1968, Box 19.

27. *AC*, 2 May, 4 August, 1 September 1968; *AC*, 28 March, 21 June, 16 September 1968; *AC*, 6 August 1968; *AC*, 20 August 1968; *AC*, 18 November, 7 December 1968, 11 January 1969; *Reporter*, 272; McGill knew readers misunderstood his "Dixie" columns. REM to Robert Sherrill, 7 January 1969, Box 18, admitted, "Even some of my newspaper friends have attacked me."

28. *AC*, 22 October 1968; hate letter in folder 3, Box 20.

29. Don Speicker, "What's It All About, Ralphie?," *Great Speckled Bird*, 15-28 March 1968; interviews for *Atlanta Magazine*, *No Place*: 2:649.

30. Gene Patterson interview.

31. *AC*, 11 December, 1 September, 22 September, 25 November, 26 December 1968; interviews for *Atlanta Magazine*, *No Place*: 2:653; *AC*, 21 December 1968.

32. REM to Helen Morgan, 2 January 1969, Box 21.

33. *New York Times*, 27 September 1968, 50; Reg Murphy to Jack Tarver and Ralph McGill, 5 December 1968, Box 20; REM to Sam Cook, 30 January 1969, Box 21; REM to Bill Baggs, 29 October 1968, Box 20; interviews for *Atlanta Magazine*, *No Place*, 2:659.

34. Sibley, "Ralph McGill"; *AC* 9, 10, 11, 12, 13 November 1968; REM to Richard Long, 20 December 1968, Box 20.

35. Jack Tarver interview; John Griffin interviews; Harold Fleming to Harold Martin, 14 January 1970, Box 28, HM papers; REM to Craig O. Baggs, 27 January 1969, Box 21.

36. REM to Lyndon B. Johnson, 13 January 1969, and Lyndon B. Johnson to REM, 17 January 1969, Name File, White House Central Files, Johnson Library; REM to City Staff, 22 January 1969, (memo), Box 21.

37. "Washington H.S.," *Editor & Publ*, 2:499, 510, 500.

38. *AC*, 4 February 1969; *AC*, 5 February 1969; Mary Lynn Morgan interviews; Dr. Joe Wilber interview.

39. Grace Lundy Tackett interviews; Sam Hopkins, "Georgia Scene," *AC*, 5 February 1969; Mark McCrackin, "McGill," *Vanderbilt Hustler*, 7 February 1969.

40. *AC*, 5 February 1969; *Reporter*, 311; *AC*, 6 February 1969.

41. Benjamin Mays, *Born To Rebel: An Autobiography* (Athens: University of Georgia Brown Thrasher edition, 1987), 282; Edward Weeks, *Writers and Friends* (Boston: Atlantic, Little, Brown and Co., 1981), 174-175; REM to Norm Cardoza, 30 January 1969, Box 39.

SOURCES

A. WORKS BY MCGILL

Calvin M. Logue edited three collections of McGill's best speeches and articles aside from the daily columns. Only those not included in the Logue volumes are listed below.

"Atlanta As It Was." *Show*, June 1963, 9-11.

"Atlanta: the Waiting Game." *Saturday Review*, 22 May 1965, 42-43.

The Best of Ralph McGill: Selected Columns. Compiled by Michael Strickland, Harry Davis, and Jeff Strickland. Atlanta: Cherokee Publishing Co., 1980.

"Boss Crump's Town." *Atlantic*, January 1960, 63-66.

A Church, A School. Nashville: Abingdon Press, 1959.

"The *Constitution* Story." *Saturday Review*, 8 June 1968, 66-69.

The Fleas Come With the Dog. Nashville: Abingdon Press, 1954.

"Free News and Russia." *Atlantic*, April 1946, 76-79.

Israel Revisited. Atlanta: Tupper and Love, 1950.

"The Merciful Tenderizer." *Harper's*, February 1955, 79.

"My First Boss." *Atlantic*, February 1959, 68-70.

"'New Man' - Old Chains." *Saturday Review*, 28 August 1948, 7-10.

No Place To Hide: The South and Human Rights. 2 vols. Edited by Calvin M. Logue. Macon: Mercer University Press, 1984.

Ralph McGill: Editor and Publisher. 2 vols. Edited by Calvin M. Logue. Durham: Moore Publishing Co., 1969.

"Science Puts the Bite On Sharks." *Saturday Evening Post*, 14 May 1949, 17.

"She'll Talk Later." *Harper's*, October 1947, 365-368.

The South and the Southerner. Boston: Little Brown and Company, 1963.

Southern Encounters: Southerners of Note in Ralph McGill's South. Edited by Calvin M. Logue. Macon: Mercer University Press, 1983.

"Southern Exposure." *Vogue*, 1 January 1942, 44, 81, 84.
"There Is Time Yet." *Atlantic*, September 1944, 61-65.
Two Georgians Explore Scandanavia. (with David C. Thomas)
    Atlanta: State Department of Education, 1938.
"What's Wrong With Southern Cooking?" *Saturday Evening Post*,
    26 March 1949, 38-39, 102-103, 105.

B. MANUSCRIPTS

Abilene, Kansas. Dwight D. Eisenhower Library.
    Dwight D. Eisenhower Papers as President of the United
    States, 1953-1961.
        Ann Whitman Diary Series.

Atlanta, Georgia. Atlanta History Center.
    Coca Cola *Red Barrel* magazine files
    Clark Howell Foreman papers
    Franklin M. Garrett papers
    Papers of HOPE (Help Our Public Education)
    Clark Howell file
    Rosalie Howell papers
    Charlie Roberts papers.

Atlanta, Georgia. Atlanta Newspapers Incorporated, Reference
    Room.
    Clark Howell files
    Ralph E. McGill files.

Atlanta, Georgia. Woodruff Library, Emory University.
    Cullen B. Gosnell papers
    Julian L. Harris papers
    William B. Hartsfield papers
    Clark Howell papers
    Ralph E. McGill papers
    Harold H. Martin papers

Raymond R. Paty papers
Glenn Rainey papers
Richard H. Rich papers
Jacob M. Rothschild papers
Josephine Wilkins papers
Robert W. Woodruff papers.

Austin, Texas. Lyndon B. Johnson Library.
 Lyndon B. Johnson Senate papers, 1949-1961
 Lyndon B. Johnson Vice-Presidential papers, 1961-1963
 Lyndon B. Johnson archives, 1927-1967
   Lyndon B. Johnson Presidential papers, 1963-1969
     White House Central Files
     Office Files of John W. Macy, Jr.
     White House Social Files
     Diaries and Appointment Logs of Lyndon B. Johnson
 Lyndon B. Johnson Post-Presidential papers, 1969-1973.

Boston, Massachusetts. John Fitzgerald Kennedy Library.
 John Fitzgerald Kennedy Presidential Papers, 1961-1963
     White House Central Files
       Name File
   Robert Francis Kennedy Attorney-General Papers, 1961-1964
     General Correspondence.

Chapel Hill, North Carolina. Southern Historical Collection,
 University of North Carolina.
 Jesse Daniel Ames papers
 Jonathan Worth Daniels papers
 Mark Foster Ethridge papers
 Frank Porter Graham papers.

Downers Grove, Illinois. McGill family papers.

Durham, North Carolina. Perkins Library, Duke University.
 Papers of Lucy Randolph Mason.

Independence, Missouri. Harry S. Truman Library.
  Harry S. Truman Presidential Papers, 1945-1953
    White House Central Files
      General File
      Official File
      President's Personal File
    Matthew J. Connelly Files
  Harry S. Truman Post-Presidential Papers, 1953-1972.

Nashville, Tennessee. Heard Library, Vanderbilt University.
  Brainard B. Cheney papers
  James H. Kirkland papers
  files of *Vanderbilt Hustler*.

Washington, D.C. The Library of Congress.
  Papers of Joseph and Stewart Alsop.

West Branch, Iowa. Herbert Hoover Presidential Library.
  Westbrook Pegler papers.

C. NEWSPAPERS

Atlanta Constitution
Nashville Banner
Great Speckled Bird
New York Times

D. INTERVIEWS

Virginia Staley Bigelow
Franklin M. Garrett
John A. Griffin
W. Barrett Howell
Doris Lockerman
Ralph E. McGill, Jr.

Mary Lynn Morgan
Eugene C. Patterson
Dixon Preston
Celestine Sibley
Lucille McGill Staley
Grace Lundy Tackett
Jack Tarver
Dr. Joseph A. Wilber

E. THESES

Ellis, Ann Wells. "The Commission on Interracial Cooperation, 1919-1944: Its Activities and Results." Ph.D. dissertation, Georgia State University, 1975.

Kinsella, Dorothy C. "Southern Apologists: A Liberal Image." Ph.D. dissertation, University of St. Louis, 1971.

Long, Allen A. "A Study of the *Atlanta Constitution* Before and After Its Consolidation with the *Atlanta Journal*." Master's thesis, Emory University, 1952.

Marvin, Carolyn Ann. "Running On the Fence: Ralph McGill's Strategy in Five Civil Rights Crises." Master's thesis, University of Texas, 1974.

Moseley, Clement C. "Invisible Empire: A History of the Ku Klux Klan in Twentieth Century Georgia, 1915-1965." Ph.D. dissertation, University of Georgia, 1980.

Pfenning, Dennis J. "Evan and Clark Howell of the *Atlanta Constitution*: The Partnership, 1889-1897." Ph.D. dissertation, University of Georgia, 1975.

Smith, Francis Marion. "A Study of Ralph McGill's Early Life and of His Editorial Treatment of Three Southern Problems." Master's thesis, Emory University, 1953.

F. FILM

"Dawn's Early Light: Ralph McGill and the Segregated South."

After Kathleen Dowdey and Jed Dannenbaum produced this 1989 documentary, they placed valuable background material in the McGill papers at Emory. Transcripts of thirty-four videotaped interviews (Boxes 110, 111, 112) were particularly useful.

G. SECONDARY WORKS CITED IN NOTES

Allen, Frederick. *Atlanta Rising: The Invention of An International City, 1946-1996*. Atlanta: Longstreet Press, 1996.

-----. *Secret Formula*. New York: Harper Business, 1994.

Allen, Frederick Lewis. *Only Yesterday: An Informal History of the Nineteen Twenties*. New York: Bantam Books, 1946.

Allen, Ivan, Jr. with Hemphill, Paul. *Mayor: Notes on the Sixties*. New York: Simon & Schuster, 1971.

Ambrose, Stephen. *Eisenhower*. 2 vols. New York: Simon & Schuster, 1985.

Anderson, William. *The Wild Man From Sugar Creek: the Political Career of Engene Talmadge*. Baton Rouge: Louisiana State University Press, 1975.

Ashmore, Harry and Baggs, William C. *Mission to Hanoi: A Chronicle of Double-dealing in High Places*. New York: Putnam Berkley Publishing Group, 1968.

Bailes, Sue. "Eugene Talmadge and the Board of Regents Controversy." *Georgia Historical Quarterly* 53 (December 1969): 409-423.

Bardolph, Richard. *The Negro Vanguard*. New York: Rinehart & Co., 1959.

Bartley, Numan V. *The Creation of Modern Georgia*. Athens: University of Georgia Press, 1983.

-----. *The New South, 1945-1980*. Baton Rouge: Louisiana State University Press, 1995.

Bayor, Ronald H. *Race and the Shaping of Twentieth Century Atlanta*. Chapel Hill: University of North Carolina Press, 1996.

Belvin, William L. "The Georgia Gubernatorial Primary of 1946."

Georgia Historical Quarterly 50 (spring 1966): 37-53.

Blumberg, Janice Rothschild. *One Voice: Rabbi Jacob M. Rothschild and the Troubled South*. Macon: Mercer University Press, 1985.

Boylston, Elise Reid. *Atlanta: Its Lore, Legends, and Laughter*. Atlanta: Foote & Davies, 1968.

Carmichael, Stokely and Hamilton, Charles V. *Black Power: the Politics of Liberation in America*. New York: Vintage Books, 1967.

Chalmers, David M. *Hooded Americanism: the History of the Ku Klux Klan*. 2d ed. New York: New Viewpoints, 1981.

Cleghorn, Reese. "McGill." *Georgia Magazine*, January 1973, 25-30, 50, 65.

Cobb, James C. "Not Gone But Forgotten: Eugene Talmadge and the 1938 Purge Campaign." *Georgia Historical Quarterly* 59 (Summer 1975): 197-209.

Coleman, Kenneth and Gurr, Charles S., eds. *Dictionary of Georgia Biography*. 2 vols. Athens: University of Georgia Press, 1983.

Commager, Henry Steele. *The American Mind: An Interpretation of American Thought and Character Since the 1880s*. New Haven: Yale University Press, 1950.

Conkin, Paul K. *Gone With the Ivy: A Biography of Vanderbilt University*. Knoxville: University of Tennessee Press, 1985.

-----. *The Southern Agrarians*. Knoxville: University of Tennessee Press, 1988.

"*Constitution* Amended." *Time*, 5 January 1948, 48.

Cook, James F. "The Eugene Talmadge-Walter Cocking Controversy." *Phylon* 35 (June 1974): 181-192.

Cox, James M. *Journey Through My Years*. New York: Simon & Schuster, 1946.

Doyle, Don. *Nashville*. 2 vols. Knoxville: University of Tennessee Press, 1985.

Dunbar, Anthony *Against the Grain: Southern Radicals and Prophets, 1929-1959*. Charlottesville: University of Virginia Press, 1981.

Eberhard, Wallace B. "Clark Howell and the *Atlanta Constitution*." *Journalism Quarterly* 60 (spring 1983): 118-122.

Edwards, Anne. *Road to Tara*. New Haven: Ticknor and Fields, 1983.

Egerton, John. *Speak Now Against the Day: The Generation Before the Civil Rights Movement in the South*. New York: Alfred A. Knopf, 1994.

Embree, Edwin R. and Waxman, Julian. *Investment in People: the Story of the Julius Rosenwald Fund*. New York: Harper's, 1949.

English, James W. *The Prophet of Wheat Street: the Story of William Holmes Borders, A Man Who Refused to Fail*. Elgin, Ill: David C. Cook, 1973.

"Episcopal Diocese Censors McGill," *Christian Century*, 16 October 1963, 1260.

Federal Writers' Project. *Tennessee: A Guide to the State*. New York: Viking Press, 1939.

Galphin, Bruce. *The Riddle of Lester Maddox*. Atlanta: Camelot Publishing, 1968.

Garrett, Franklin M. *Atlanta and Environs: A Chronicle of Its People and Events*. 3 vols. Atlanta: Atlanta Historical Society, 1954.

Garrow, David J. *Bearing the Cross: Martin Luther King, Jr. and the Southern Christian Leadership Conference*. New York: William Morrow, 1986.

Gladney, Margaret Rose, ed. *How Am I To Be Heard? Letters of Lillian Smith*. Chapel Hill: University of North Carolina Press, 1993.

Goldfield, David R. *Promised Land: The South Since 1945*.Arlington Heights, Ill: Harlan Davidson, 1987.

Govan, Gilbert E. and Livingood, James W. *The Chattanooga Country, 1540-1962*. rev. ed. Chapel Hill: University of North Carolina Press, 1963

Greene, Melissa Fay. *The Temple Bombing*. Reading, Mass: Addison-Wesley, 1996.

Griffith, Louis T. and Talmadge, John E. *Georgia Journalism, 1763-1950*. Athens: University of Georgia Press, 1951.

Grimes, Millard B. *The Last Linotype: the Story of Georgia and Its Newspapers Since World War II*. Macon: Mercer University Press, 1985.

Hohenberg, John. *The Pulitzer Prize Story, II*. New York: Columbia University Press, 1980.

"It's Constitutional." *Newsweek*, 13 April 1959, 102-103.

Jenkins, Herbert T. *Keeping the Peace: A Police Chief Looks At His Job*. New York: Harper & Row, 1970.

Karnow, Stanley. *Vietnam: A History*. New York: Penguin Books, 1984.

Kirby, Jack Temple. *Rural Worlds Lost: the American South, 1920-1960*. Baton Rouge: Louisiana State University Press, 1987.

Kneebone, John T. *Southern Liberal Journalists and the Issue of Race, 1920-1944*. Chapel Hill: University of North Carolina Press, 1985.

Krueger, Thomas A. *And Promises To Keep: the Southern Conference for Human Welfare, 1938-1948*. Nashville: Vanderbilt University Press, 1967.

Kuhn, Clifford M., Joye, Harlan E., and West, E. Bernard. *Living Atlanta: An Oral History of the City, 1914-1948*. Athens: University of Georgia Press, 1990.

Lee, David D. *Tennessee In Turmoil: Politics in the Volunteer State: 1920-1932*. Memphis: Memphis State University Press, 1979.

"Live With the Change." *Time*, 14 December 1953, 51.

Loveland, Anne C. *Lillian Smith: A Southerner Confronting the South*. Baton Rouge: Louisiana State University Press, 1986.

Martin, Harold H. *Atlanta and Environs: A Chronicle of Its People and Events*. 3 vols. Athens: University of Georgia Press, 1987.

-----. *Ralph McGill, Reporter*. Boston: Little, Brown and Co., 1973.

-----. *William Berry Hartsfield*. Athens: University of Georgia Press, 1978.

Mays, Benjamin. *Born To Rebel: An Autobiography*. Athens: University of Georgia Brown Thrasher edition, 1987.

McKinney, Gordon B. *Southern Mountain Republicans, 1865-1900: Politics and the Appalachian Community*. Chapel Hill: University of North Carolina Press, 1978.

McWhiney, Grady. *Cracker Culture: Celtic Ways in the Old South*. Tuscaloosa: University of Alabama Press, 1988.

"Merging the Elephants." *Time*, 27 March 1950, 47-49.

Mims, Edwin. *A History of Vanderbilt University*. Nashville: Vanderbilt University Press, 1946.

Nixon, Raymond B. *Henry W. Grady: Spokesman of the New South*. New York: Alfred A. Knopf, 1943.

Nye, Russell. *The Unembarrassed Muse: the Popular Arts in America*. New York: Dial Press, 1970.

Oates, Stephen B. *Let the Trumpet Sound: the Life of Martin Luther King, Jr.* New York: New American Library, 1982.

O'Brien, Michael. *The Idea of the American South, 1920-1941*. Baltimore: The Johns Hopkins University Press, 1979.

Pomerantz, Gary M. *Where Peachtree Meets Sweet Auburn: The Saga of Two Families and the Making of Atlanta*. New York: Scribner, 1996.

Pyron, Darden A. *Southern Daughter: the Life of Margaret Mitchell*. New York: Oxford University Press, 1991.

Raines, Howell. *My Soul Is Rested: Movement Days in the Deep South Remembered*. New York: G.P. Putnam's Sons, 1977.

Raper, Arthur F. *The Tragedy of Lynching*. Chapel Hill: University of North Carolina Press, 1933.

Reed, Linda. *Simple Decency and Common Sense: the Southern Conference Movement, 1938-1963*. Bloomington: Indiana University Press, 1991.

Roosevelt, Franklin D. *FDR: His Personal Letters*. 4 vols. New York: Duell, Sloan and Pearce, 1950.

Schardt, Arlie. "Crisis of the *Constitution*." *Nation*, 23 December, 1968, 679-684.

Shavin, Norman and Galphin, Bruce. *Atlanta: Triumph of a People*. Atlanta: Capricorn, 1982.

Sibley, Celestine. "Ralph McGill, Newspaper Reporter." Ralph McGill Lecture Series, Henry W. Grady College of Journalism and Mass Communication. Athens: University of Georgia, 1991.

-----. *Peachtree Street USA*. Garden City: Doubleday, 1963.

-----. "They Don't Scare McGill." *Saturday Evening Post*, 27 December 1958, 25, 51, 52.

Spritzer, Lorraine N. *The Belle of Ashby Street*. Athens: University of Georgia Press, 1982.

Stephens, C. Ralph, ed. *The Correspondence of Flannery O'Connor and the Brainard Cheneys*. Jackson: University Press of Mississippi, 1986.

Stone, Clarence N. *Regime Politics: Governing Atlanta, 1946-1988*. Lawrence: University Press of Kansas, 1989.

"Strong Constitution." *Time*, 14 September 1942, 46.

Sullivan, Patricia. *Days of Hope: Race and Democracy in the New Deal Era*. Chapel Hill: University of North Carolina Press, 1996.

"Synthesis In Atlanta." *Newsweek*, 27 March 1950, 59.

"The Durham Conference Statement." *New South*. 19 (January 1964): 3-10.

Townsend, Jim. "McGill." *Atlanta Magazine*, November 1962, 43-46, 53.

Trillin, Calvin. *An Education In Georgia: the Integration of Charlayne Hunter and Hamilton Holmes*. New York: Viking Press, 1964.

Waldron, Ann. *Hodding Carter: the Reconstruction of a Racist*. Chapel Hill: Algonquin Books, 1993.

Weeks, Edward. *Writers and Friends*. Boston: Atlantic, Little Brown, 1981.

Wilkins, Josephine. "An Answer When Negro Southerners Spoke." *New South* 19 (January 1964): 22-26.

Woodward, C. Vann. *Thinking Back: The Perils of Writing History*. Baton Rouge: Louisiana State University Press, 1986.

INDEX

Ackerman, Carl, 122, 175, 180
Africa, 178, 202-203, 229, 230-231, 238
Agrarians, 70
agriculture, 70, 73, 75, 76, 87-88, 89. *See also* Georgia
Alexander, Will W. 87-88, 104, 139
Alexander, William A. 67, 83
All Saints Episcopal Church 206, 218, 233, 252
Allen, Ivan Jr. 204, 223, 224, 226, 268n.6
American Federation of Labor, 132
American Society of Newspaper Editors (ASNE), 121-124, 127, 152, 175
Arkansas Gazette ,128, 175
Arnall, Ellis, 113, 129, 132, 227
Ashmore, Harry, 182, 192, 207; and REM, 128, 175-76, 185, 186, 193, 199; and Vietnam War, 228-229, 236
Associated Press (AP), 132, 135, 177, 207, 208
Atlanta, Georgia, 3, 4, 23, 65, 145, 157; and REM, 118-119, 181, 183, 195; baseball in, 65, 224; black leaders in, 63, 72-73, 110, 130, 143, 157, 159, 170, 177, 181, 204, 223, 226; desegregation in, 130, 138, 143-44, 149-50, 170, 179-80, 183, 186, 187, 192, 194-95, 204; Great Depression in, 69, 72, 75, 202; Ku Klux Klan in, 98-99, 103, 131; politics in, 63-64, 72-73, 130, 143, 157, 170-171, 204; segregation in, 67, 115, 117, 134, 159, 182, 215; race riots in, 65, 225-226, 235
"Atlanta Compromise," 64
Atlanta Constitution, 71, 178, 233, 236, 237, 242; and civil rights, 145, 161, 204, 213-224, 217-218, 225; finances of, 74-75, 77, 99, 106, 114, 137; merger of, 145, 148, 151; policies of, 63-64, 68, 69, 105, 186, 207, 227, 244-245. *See also* McGill, Ralph E., career, *Atlanta Constitution*
Atlanta Daily World, 174
Atlanta Georgian, 59, 63, 72, 101
Atlanta Journal, 45, 61, 63, 65, 105, 147, 158, 163; and *Atlanta Constitution*, 77, 101, 114, 127, 137, 148, 242; merger of, 146, 151, 159
Atlanta Negro Voters League, 143

141-142, 182, 185, 204, 214-215

Civil Rights Act of 1964, 214, 216

Civil War, 16-18, 63; and REM, 159, 169-170, 182

Clement, Rufus E., 115, 157

Clift family, 11, 12-13, 17

Coca-Cola Company, 78, 79, 89, 152, 215, 264n.41

Cold War and REM, 123, 128, 135, 149, 179, 192, 230

Colescott, James, 98, 131

Collins, Floyd and REM, 50-51, 60, 180

Columbians, 134

Commission on Interracial Co-operation, 68-69, 71, 88

Communism, 91-92, 97, 98; and REM, 135, 137, 142-143, 149, 150, 153, 160, 192

Congress of Industrial Organizations (CIO), 105

Connor, Eugene "Bull," 204

Constitution, U.S., 178, 183

counterculture, 220-221, 244

county unit system (Georgia), 130, 132, 204

Cox, James M., 40, 101, 114, 137, 153, 154, 171, 181, 218, 229; and *Atlanta Constitution*, 145-146, 151-152, 242

Cox, James Jr., 173, 203, 242

Crawford, Julia James, 68, 80, 122, 127, 140, 162, 197, 198; and Ralph Jr., 125, 184; and REM, 67, 206, 216

Crump, Edward H., 44, 57

Cuba, 76, 118, 181, 192

Danforth, Ed, 58, 59-60, 63, 65, 67, 72, 95, 202

Daniels, Jonathan, 96

DeKalb County, Georgia, 150, 186

Democratic Party, 18, 44, 57, 64-65, 77, 80, 87, 102, 210, 228; and Cox, 40, 101; and REM, 24, 40, 63, 76, 108, 142, 181-182, 213, 244, 248

Dempsey, Jack, 54

desegregation, 164, 176, 246. *See also* Atlanta; McGill, Ralph E., editorial views, race relations

Dixiecrats, 142, 243

Dobbs, John Wesley, 143

Durham (NC) Conference, 115-116, 117

Ebenezer Baptist Church, 169, 181

Eisenhower, Dwight D., 123, 172, 178, 201, 243; and REM, 153, 154, 155, 160,